D0721252

Presidential Sites

L. E. SMOOT MEMORIAL LIBRARY
KING GEORGE, VA. 22485

Dedication

For William II and Michael

May the lives of the great men mentioned in this book
inspire you to work hard
and always do your best

Presidential Sites

A Directory of Places
associated with
Presidents of the United States

by

William G. Clotworthy

The McDonald & Woodward Publishing Company
Blacksburg, Virginia
1998

iii

L. E. SMOOT MEMORIAL LIBRARY
KING GEORGE, VA. 22485

The McDonald & Woodward Publishing Company
P. O. Box 10308, Blacksburg, Virginia 24060

Presidential Sites
A Directory of Places associated with Presidents of the United States

© 1998 by The McDonald & Woodward Publishing Company

All rights reserved. First printing February 1998
Printed in the United States of America by
McNaughton & Gunn, Inc., Saline, Michigan

04 03 02 01 00 99 98   10 9 8 7 6 5 4 3 2 1

Library of Congress Cataloging-in-Publication Data

Clotworthy, William G., 1926–
    Presidential sites : a directory of places associated with presidents of the United States / by William G. Clotworthy.
        p.   cm.
    Includes bibliographical references and index.
    ISBN 0–939923–64–5 (alk. paper)
    1. Presidents--United States--Homes and haunts--Directories. 2. Historic sites--United States--Directories. 3. United States--Directories. I. Title.
E176.1.C68   1998
973'.025--dc21   98-11173
                                                                        CIP

Reproduction or translation of any part of this book, except for short excerpts used in reviews, without the written permission of the copyright owner is unlawful. Requests for permission to reproduce parts of this work, or for additional information, should be addressed to the publisher.

Contents

Acknowledgments

As far as acknowledgments are concerned, I would merely like to repeat what I said in *Homes and Libraries of the Presidents*:

Most credit for any success of this book lies with the hundreds of devoted park rangers, archivists, docents, volunteers and staffers, who dedicate themselves to the preservation and maintenance of presidential homes and sites, thus perpetuating the heritage contained within their walls. It has been my privilege to meet many of these fine Americans, and I am honored to salute them.

Presidential Sites

Introduction

A few years ago the National Parks and Conservation Association sponsored a Presidential Sites Conference attended by National Park Service personnel, independent professional curators, historians, archivists and others interested in the preservation and maintenance of America's national treasures. At one seminar it was suggested that "someone" publish a cross-indexed directory of the hundreds of extant places associated with presidents — a reference volume enabling staff to learn of, and interact with, not only other sites and caretakers involved with "their" president, but with people involved with other presidents or with presidential history in general.

At that time I was researching my book *Homes and Libraries of the Presidents,* an interpretive guide devoted to eighty-eight presidential homes, libraries and museums that are open to the public, but I kept the idea of a directory in mind as I began to uncover hundreds of homes, statues, monuments, battlefields, colleges and other places associated with presidents.

Somehow I became that elusive "someone" to compile the directory of presidential sites.

I have now organized that information into a single volume, detailing each individual site with an address, telephone number and brief description — the result of my travels, consultation with presidential historians, librarians and state historical societies, and examination of The National Register of Historic Places, AAA travel booklets, the 1982 National Park Service Inventory and other sources.

Although this directory contains more than 1000 entries, it is undoubtedly still incomplete. Thus, readers are urged to amend, add to or otherwise edit the list by contacting me through the publisher. With that caveat, I believe the directory is accurate, though there are places where only legend or hearsay has placed a president in attendance. After all, who's to say definitively that "George Washington's Bathtub" in Berkeley Springs, West Virginia was really where he took the waters? Too, some information such as telephone numbers, is subject to change, and readers are strongly advised to call ahead before visiting. While I have indicated that a site may be "open," hours and seasons are flexible. Also, telephone numbers are not provided for places privately owned or otherwise not open for visitation. Respect for that privacy is encouraged.

The directory is organized chronologically, by president. In the case of sites which may have an association with more than one president, the site is annotated in the section in which it first appears, with a reference to the initial annotation in later sections. In addition, there is a "general" section devoted to museums, churches and other sites involving multiple presidents — sites such as Mount Rushmore, the American Museum of Fly Fishing, or the Museum of American Political Life. I've also given focused attention to three geographic areas considered especially important in the development of America's heritage, past and present — Colonial Williamsburg,

Philadelphia and Washington, DC. Each of these cities is filled with presidential history and treasures.

In addition to an index, I have included a listing of presidential sites by individual state for easy reference. With the exception of some birth and marriage sites, included for informational purposes, all of the places are extant, and many are open to the public. Every American is urged to visit these historic places so important to an understanding of our great national heritage. The forty-one men who have been Chief Executive came from different places and diverse backgrounds but each gave part of himself to our national character. Each added to the strength of our constitutional system. Thus these men represent the diversity of thought and political principle that has propelled our nation forward and made our form of government the envy of countries around the world. The places from whence they came must remain as they were, for to know them is to know ourselves.

A visit to any presidential birthplace, home or museum is rewarding. The host personnel, whether National Park Service rangers, professional curators, teenaged docents or senior citizen volunteers — are friendly, knowledgeable and anxious to enhance every visitor's enjoyment of the facility. More important, they want visitors to leave with a deeper awareness of the men who have led our nation through two centuries and helped achieve its preeminence in the world.

In any event, a visit to a presidential site, even a battlefield, helps to fill in a picture of the whole man, for these men, just like the rest of us, experienced disappointment and satisfaction, economic hardship and success, tragedy and joy. America's heritage is embodied in them. Calvin Coolidge once said . . .

We draw our presidents from the people. It is a wholesome thing for them to return to the people. I came from them. I wish to be one of them again.

George Washington

First President
1789–1797

Born February 22, 1732, Popes Creek Plantation, Virginia
Died December 14, 1799, Mount Vernon, Virginia
Burial Site: Mount Vernon, Virginia

George Washington Birthplace National Monument
RR #1, Box 17
Washingtons Birthplace, Virginia 22443
(804) 224-1732

George Washington was born on a plantation situated on the Potomac River east of Fredericksburg, Virginia, a property which became his brother's and eventually was passed on to Washington's nephew, William. On Christmas Day, 1779, the place known as Wakefield burned and was never rebuilt. Through the efforts of the Wakefield National Memorial Association and the Rockefeller Family, the property has been replicated and is now maintained by the National Park Service as a working farm representative of the Colonial era. Since the exact appearance of the original building is not known, a memorial house was built on the property to represent an 18th-century plantation home. Archaeological investigation determined the exact location of the birth house, the outline of which is delineated with oyster shells. Open to the public.

Washingtons Boyhood Home
Ferry Farm
240 Kings Highway
Falmouth, Virginia 22403
(540) 372-4485

When George Washington was an infant, his family moved forty miles upstream from Wakefield to a 1½-story farmhouse on Little Hunting Creek Plantation, later known as Mount Vernon. When George was six, the family moved again, this time to Ferry Farm on the eastern bank of the Rappahannock River across from Fredericksburg. According to legend, it was at Ferry Farm that George Washington chopped down his father's cherry tree and later tossed a silver dollar across the river. Ferry Farm was recently the center of controversy between preservationists and modern developers. This resulted in the purchase of the property by the Kenmore Foundation which will preserve the farm as an historically significant site helping to perpetuate the legacy of George Washington. Open to the public.

Mount Vernon
Mount Vernon, Virginia 22121
(703) 780-2000

George Washington's treasured estate on the Potomac was rescued from ignominious destruction in 1853 through the efforts of the Mount Vernon Ladies' Association who respectfully, lovingly and accurately restored it to its original grandeur. More than 150 years later the Ladies' Association remains as the caring guardian of America's most famous and popular historic home. Mount Vernon entertains more than one million visitors each year. Open to the public.

Fredericksburg Historic District
City of Fredericksburg Office of Economic Development
706 Caroline Street
Fredericksburg, Virginia 22401
(540) 373-1776

Fredericksburg, considered to be George Washington's "home

town," lies across the Rappahannock River from Ferry Farm, the plantation to which the Washington family moved when George was a toddler. A 40-square block area of Fredericksburg contains a number of buildings associated with the time of the Washington residency.

Mary Washington House
1200 Charles Street
(540) 373-1569

George Washington purchased a small house near his sister's home, Kenmore, and gave it to his mother who lived there for the last seventeen years of her life. Mrs. Washington's life-long passion was gardening, and the Garden Club of Virginia has replanted the gardens to appear as in the 1780s. The Mary Washington House is owned and operated as an historic house museum by the Association for the Preservation of Virginia Antiquities. Open to the public.

Hugh Mercer Apothecary Shop
1020 Caroline Street
(540) 373-3362

The Hugh Mercer Apothecary Shop is a restored Colonial drugstore that presents a living interpretation of Colonial-era medical techniques. The original store served as George Washington's pharmacy. The shop is owned and operated by the Association for the Preservation of Virginia Antiquities. Open to the public.

Rising Sun Tavern
1304 Caroline Street
(540) 371-1494

Rising Sun Tavern was once the home of Washington's brother, Charles, and later was operated as a tavern and meeting place for the influential men of Fredericksburg, including George Washington. This property is owned and operated by the Association for the Preservation of Virginia Antiquities. Open to the public.

Saint James House
1300 Charles Street
(540) 373-1569

A splendid example of an 18th-century gentleman's home, Saint James was built on lots that George Washington purchased from his brother-in-law, Fielding Lewis. Washington subsequently sold them to James Mercer, Mary Washington's attorney, who constructed the house in 1760. Open to the public.

Masonic Lodge No. 4 A. F. and A. M.

803 Princess Anne Street

(540) 373-5885

The Masonic Lodge has been restored near the original site on Market Street where George Washington was installed into the Masonic Order in 1752. Museum. Open to the public.

Washingtons Horse-Chestnut Tree

400 Fauquier Street

On a visit to Fredericksburg, General Washington planted a line of thirteen horse-chestnut trees, one for each of the United States. One has survived and is marked.

Kenmore

1201 Washington Avenue

(540) 373-3381

Colonel Fielding Lewis built an elegant mansion in 1770 for his bride, George Washington's sister Betty, and it is known that Washington visited often. Kenmore, famed for some of the most beautiful decorative plaster work in America, is owned and operated as a house museum by the Kenmore Foundation. Open to the public.

Chatham Manor

120 Chatham Lane

(540) 373-4461

George Washington was entertained frequently by the owner of Chatham Manor, his close friend William Fitzhugh. The house gained fame during the Civil War when it was used as a Union headquarters during the siege of Fredericksburg. Abraham Lincoln visited twice, and Clara Barton and Walt Whitman were among those who nursed the wounded when Chatham was used as a military hospital. Chatham Manor is situated on the grounds of the Fredericksburg National Military Park, a National Park Service site. Open to the public.

Mary Washington Monument and Grave

Washington Avenue

President Andrew Jackson laid the cornerstone for a marble monument to George Washington's mother in 1833, but it was never completed. During the bombardment of Fredericksburg in 1862 the unfinished monument was badly scarred by shellfire. In 1894, President Grover Cleveland dedicated the present marker.

Charles Dick House
Princess Anne Street, near Lewis Street

Charles Dick was a popular leader in Fredericksburg for four decades. His home, much enlarged, dates from around 1750 and thus is one of the oldest buildings still standing in town. He was a long-time confidante of George Washington and it is certain that Washington visited often. Closed to the public.

Saint Peters Parish Church
8400 Saint Peters Lane
New Kent , Virginia 23124
(804) 932-4846

There is dispute among historians as to whether George Washington and Martha Custis were married in her home — prophetically named "White House" — or journeyed to her parish church for the ceremony held on January 6, 1759. In any event, they lived in her home for several months following the marriage. The house no longer stands, but the church has survived.

Bel Air
US Route 1 (Minnieville Road)
Minnieville, Virginia 22192

A 2½-story country house of fourteen rooms was built circa 1740 in the traditional Colonial style, on the central-hall plan. Its owner was Major Charles Ewell, who was married to Sarah Ball, a relative of George Washington's mother. The newlywed George Washingtons were overnight guests of the Ewells on their honeymoon journey from Williamsburg to Mount Vernon. By coincidence, the house later became the home of Parson Weems who wrote the first biography of George Washington, including those famous anecdotes about chopping down the cherry tree and tossing the dollar across the Rappahannock River. Today, this privately-owned historic house is the heart of a working farm/plantation. Closed to the public.

Alexandria Historic District

"Old Town"
Alexandria Convention and Visitors Bureau
Ramsay House
221 King Street
Alexandria, Virginia 22314
(703) 838-4200

Alexandria contains the largest concentration of late 18th and early 19th-century urban architecture in Virginia as exemplified by Ramsay House, circa 1724, the residence of George Washington's close friend, William Ramsay. Ramsay House is currently utilized as Alexandria's Visitor Center. Washington was one of the early surveyors of Alexandria. He later resided at nearby Mount Vernon and became one of the area's leading citizens.

Gadsbys Tavern

134 N. Royal Street
(703) 838-4242

Gadsbys consists of two buildings, circa 1770 and 1792. The original tavern has been converted to a Colonial museum and the other is a restored, still-active restaurant featuring Colonial-era entertainment, food and drink. The museum and restaurant are operated by the City of Alexandria. It is thought that Gadsbys also hosted John Adams, Thomas Jefferson and James Madison. Open to the public.

Stabler-Leadbeater Apothecary Shop and Museum

105–107 S. Fairfax Street
(703) 836-3713

Stabler-Leadbeater, the oldest manufacturing apothecary shop in the nation, operated from 1792 to 1933. George Washington was an early patron. Open to the public.

George Washington Townhouse

508 Cameron Street

The townhouse is a replica of a house built by George Washington in 1769 and used when he surveyed in the Alexandria area. He later maintained it as an office and guest house to accommodate the overflow of visitors at Mount Vernon. The house was razed in 1855, but was rebuilt in 1960 by Virginia Governor and Mrs. Lowe, using some bricks and stones from the original building. Closed to the public.

George Washington Masonic National Memorial
King Street and Callahan Drive
(703) 683-2007

A 333-foot-high building housing an impressive Masonic museum is a memorial to George Washington, the Mason. A larger-than-life statue of Washington dominates the lobby. Open to the public.

Christ Church
118 N. Washington Street
(703) 549-1450

This handsome brick building was built in 1773 and remains in nearly its original condition. George Washington purchased Pew #60 (still marked) when the church was founded and he attended regularly. A cut-glass chandelier represents the 18th century's most advanced type of lighting fixture.

Carlyle House
121 N. Fairfax Avenue
(703) 548-2997

Alexandria's "grandest" home was built in 1752–1753 by Scottish merchant John Carlyle, probably inspired by architectural pattern books and stone manor houses in Scotland and northern England. In 1755, English General Braddock made the Carlyle house his headquarters where he and five Colonial governors planned campaign strategy and funding for the French and Indian War. George Washington was known to have been a guest and probable participant in the sessions. Museum. Open to the public.

Alexandria Canal Tidal Lock
Trans-Potomac Canal Center Plaza

George Washington was an early stockholder and corporate officer in the Potowmack Canal project. One tidal lock has been restored, representative of the locks built along the Potomac River during the latter part of the 18th century.

Old Presbyterian Meeting House
321 S. Fairfax Street
(703) 549-6670

The still-active Meeting House, dating from 1774, served as a gathering place for patriots, and was the site of Washington's funeral eulogy in 1799. Its graveyard contains the Tomb of an Unknown Soldier of the American Revolution as well as grave markers of other heroes of the Revolutionary War. The church interior is famed for its original old-fashioned gate pews.

Lee-Fendall House
614 Oronoco Street
(703) 548-1789

Philip Fendall was a cousin of George Washington's closest friend, "Light Horse Harry" Lee, and it is known that Lee and Washington visited his home often. The house is owned by the Lee-Fendall Foundation. Open to the public.

Boyhood Home of Robert E. Lee
607 Oronoco Street
(703) 548-8454

"Light Horse Harry" Lee, young cavalry hero of the Revolution, brought his family — including 5-year-old Robert — to Alexandria from Stratford Hall in 1812. The 1785 Georgian townhouse was originally the home of William Fitzhugh, another intimate of George Washington, and it is certain that Washington visited on many occasions. The house is furnished with period pieces and features a large boxwood garden. Open to the public.

Bank of Alexandria
North Fairfax at Cameron

The Bank of Alexandria was established in 1792 with George Washington as a charter stockholder. The building is original, although it currently houses a different banking institution. Open to the public.

Friendship Firehouse Museum
107 S. Alfred Street

The Friendship Fire Company was formed in 1774, the first volunteer fire company in Alexandria. Although unsubstantiated, it is believed by some historians that George Washington was a founding member, that he donated the company's first engine and that he was an active firefighter. In 1855, the original firehouse burned, and was replaced by the existing structure, a brick building in the then-popular Italianate style. In 1993, the building was opened as a museum, the first floor engine room featuring hand-drawn fire engines, buckets, hoses and other historic equipment. Additional exhibits in the second floor meeting room consist of early uniforms, banners and other regalia. Open to the public.

River Farm
7391 E. Boulevard Drive
Alexandria, Virginia 22308
(703) 768-5700; (800) 777-7931

George Washington bought the River Farm property in 1760, making it one of the five farms to make up the Mount Vernon estate, and he may have planted the walnut trees still on the grounds. The American Horticultural Society owns River Farm and maintains the house, floral displays and colorful gardens as they were in the Washington era. Open to the public.

Woodlawn Plantation
9000 Richmond Highway, Box 37
Alexandria, Virginia 22309
(703) 780-4000

In 1799, George Washington presented a wedding gift of 2000 acres of his Mount Vernon estate to Nelly Custis, his wife's granddaughter, and her husband, Major Lawrence Lewis, Washington's nephew. The Georgian mansion was designed by William Thornton, first architect of the US Capitol building. Spacious rooms and landscaped grounds reflect Virginia plantation life in the early 1800s. Woodlawn is an historic house museum owned and operated by the National Trust for Historic Preservation. Open to the public.

George Washingtons Grist Mill Historical State Park.
5514 Mount Vernon Highway
Alexandria, Virginia 22308
(703) 780-3383

George Washingtons Grist Mill Historical State Park contains a reconstruction of a mill built by George Washington when he ran the nearby Mount Vernon plantation. Open to the public.

Washington Historic District
US Route 211
Washington, Virginia 22747

Washington, Virginia, is the oldest of twenty-five American towns and cities named for George Washington. Named in 1796, this is a well-preserved example of a 19th-century county seat — built on a grid plan laid out by Washington himself in 1749. It is now a residential area of seven hundred structures with streets named for early residents.

Mrs. Coxes Tavern
411 Main Street
(540) 675-1900

One of the few remaining buildings in Washington dating to its founding is Mrs. Coxes Tavern, circa 1740. The name of the original owner has been lost, but the establishment was purchased by the Coxe family in 1798 and served as an ordinary/tavern for more than 150 years. The two-story clapboard structure with a double front porch was recently purchased and lovingly restored to its pre-Colonial charm, the architecture, original flooring and furnishings reflecting the ambiance of a bygone era. Mrs. Coxes Tavern is open to the public as a modern restaurant.

Thornton Hill
off Route 522
Sperryville, Virginia 22740

Thornton Hill was constructed circa 1740–1750 by wealthy landowner Francis Thornton as the centerpiece of his thirty thousand acre farm-holdings. George Washington stayed at Thornton Hill when he was a young surveyor and, later, several times again when it was the residence of his aunt. Thornton Hill is a lovely mansion of 2½ stories with sixteen rooms, including a formal dining room. Still a working farm, Thornton Hill is privately owned. Closed to the public.

Montpelier
off Virginia State Route 231
Sperryville, Virginia 22740

Montpelier, also built by Francis Thornton as a manor house for another farm, is similar to Thornton Hill in its architecture and history. Montpelier later served as a residence for a relative of Washington's mother, Mary Ball. It is known that Washington visited this home many times. Montpelier is privately owned. Closed to the public.

Weems-Botts Museum
Duke and Cameron Streets, Box 26
Dumfries, Virginia 22026
(703) 221-3346

Parson Weems was a famous biographer of Washington, best-known for his apocryphal stories about cherry-tree chopping and dollar-tossing across the Rappahannock. Weems used his home as a bookstore which has been converted to a museum devoted to the history of the Dumfries area. The town of Dumfries was once a thriving river port, and George Washington was known to have visited friends in the area. Open to the public.

Smallwoods Retreat
Smallwood State Park
Route 1, Box 54
Marbury, Maryland 20653
(301) 743-7613

George Washington, George Mason and other patriots met at the home of Washington's friend, General William Smallwood, to discuss launching a new republic. The restored two-story brick building, now a museum, is operated by the Maryland Park Service. Open to the public.

Rising Sun Inn
1090 Generals Highway
Crownsville, Maryland 21032

The Rising Sun, circa 1753, served as a way-station for Washington and other travelers on the busy road between Annapolis and Baltimore. Restored by the Anne Arundel Chapter of the Daughters of the American Revolution, it is presently utilized as a private residence. Closed to the public.

Hampton National Historic Site
535 Hampton Lane
Towson, Maryland 21286
(410) 823-1309

Hampton, a glorious Georgian mansion with sixty acres of formal gardens and manicured lawns dating from 1783, is representative of the opulence of the post-Revolutionary period. Hampton was owned by Charles Ridgely, confidante of George Washington and other leaders, so it is probable that Washington visited Hampton on many occasions. Open to the public.

La Grange
Maryland State Route 6, west of US Route 301
La Plata, Maryland 20646

La Grange, a 2½-story Georgian formal mansion built circa 1760, was the home of Doctor James Craik, intimate friend and personal physician to George Washington. Craik, who served as Physician General of the Revolutionary Army, accompanied Washington on his post-war trip to the west and was in attendance at his death in 1799. Washington visited Craik's

17

home on numerous occasions. La Grange is privately owned. Closed to the public.

Gunston Hall
Mason Neck
Lorton, Virginia 22079
(703) 550-9220

Gunston Hall is the centerpiece of a plantation begun in 1755 by George Mason, author of the 1776 Virginia Declaration of Rights and a framer of the United States Constitution. The plantation house, restored to its original state, is situated on 550 acres of formal boxwood gardens, pastures and woodlands reaching to the Potomac — an outstanding example of Virginia plantation architecture, decorated with 18th-century furnishings and splendid woodcarving by William Buckland. Mason's many visitors included George Washington, Thomas Jefferson, James Madison, James Monroe and Patrick Henry. Open to the public.

Upper Valley Regional Park
Grand Caverns, Box 478
Grottoes, Virginia 24441
(540) 249-5705

Upper Valley Park contains three separate caverns. The largest, Grand Caverns, is known for its size, rare formations and military history — at different times both Confederate and Union troops used it as a barracks! Adjacent caverns are believed to have been visited by George Washington, Thomas Jefferson and James Madison. Grand Cavern is open to the public.

Rodgers Tavern
Old Post Road
Perryville, Maryland 21903
(410) 642-6066

This inn, also known as Stevensons Tavern, was conveniently located on the Washington-Philadelphia Road, thus becoming a favorite stopping-place for George Washington, Thomas Jefferson, James Madison and other Colonial-era travelers. Closed to the public.

Sun Inn
564 Main Street
Bethlehem, Pennsylvania 18018
(610) 866-1758

Sun Inn was built about 1758 and used as a way-station for Colonial travelers including George Washington. Fully-restored, it is a working restaurant operated by the Sun Inn Preservation Association. Museum. Open to the public.

Yew Hill
Rectortown, Virginia 22140

Washington's diary entries for March, 1769, include the following: *Set out for Robt. Ashby's, and after dining by the way, reached it a little after dark.* Yew Hill is a wooden frame farmhouse typical of the period; it is situated in Rectortown, about five miles east of Delaplane near the intersection of State routes 55 and 17. Closed to the public.

Great Dismal Swamp National Wildlife Refuge
Box 349
Suffolk, Virginia 23434
(757) 986-3705

George Washington was an early investor in a company interested in draining the swamp and developing the Great Dismal area for farmland, an effort doomed to practical and financial failure. However, Washington made several trips to observe the abortive work, the first being in 1763. Open to the public.

Natural Bridge Village
Box 57
Natural Bridge, Virginia 24578
(540) 291-2121

Thomas Jefferson, who bought the property from the English Crown, called Natural Bridge "the most beautiful place on Earth." The natural limestone arch still has George Washington's initials visible twenty-three feet up on the side of the bridge, carved when he was surveying in the area for Lord Fairfax. (The story of the initials is disputed by some historians, but it is charming nonetheless.) Open to the public.

Loudoun Museum
16 Loudoun Street, SW
Leesburg, Virginia 22075
(703) 777-7427

George Washington spent much time in the Leesburg area and it is probable that he surveyed some of the houses that are still standing. The Loudoun Museum conducts a walking tour that includes one of Washington's military headquarters buildings. Open to the public.

Stratford Hall Plantation

Stratford, Virginia 22558
(804) 493-8038

Stratford Hall is a colonial architectural masterpiece, the manor house and its dependencies built on a promontory above the Potomac River in the late 1730s by prominent planter Thomas Lee. Lee's nephew, "Light Horse Harry" Lee, was a Revolutionary War hero and close personal friend of George Washington. It is more than likely that Washington visited Stratford Hall on occasion when visiting his family at nearby Popes Creek. Stratford Hall was built from thousands of bricks formed and fired on site. Craftsmen using local timber constructed a thirteen-room, H-shaped manor house formed around eight chimneys. A large bedroom on the second floor was the birth room of "Light Horse Harry's" son, Robert E. Lee, in 1807. Stratford Hall reflects opulence of the Colonial period, an uncommon tribute to the success of its owner and the dedication of his descendants. Open to the public.

Great Falls Park

Georgetown Pike
Fairfax County, Virginia 22066
(703) 285-2966

To increase and facilitate trade with the interior of the expanding nation, the Potowmack Canal Company was formed with George Washington as its first president. The company built a canal and five locks considered even now to be the most significant engineering achievement of the 18th century in Colonial America. The Potomac River at Great Falls Park falls seventy-six feet into a deep gorge and the ruins of the lock system are still visible. Open to the public.

Belle Air

11800 John Tyler Memorial Highway (Virginia State Route 5)
Charles City, Virginia 23030
(804) 829-2431

One of America's oldest frame dwellings, circa 1700, Belle Air is a unique architectural monument and probably the oldest of the great James River plantation homes, albeit more modest in design and size than most. As social life in the Colonial period was insular, it is probable that George Washington, John Tyler and William Henry Harrison were guests. The mansion includes the finest Jacobean staircase in America and is furnished with antiques. Open to the public by appointment.

Wilton House Museum
South Wilton Road, PO Box 8225
Richmond, Virginia 23226
(804) 282-5936

Wilton, a stately Georgian house, was built in 1753 by William Randolph III on a two-thousand-acre James River plantation. This is an impressive example of an elegant 18th-century plantation home, and all the walls — those in every room, hall and closet — are paneled from floor to ceiling. The Randolph's family friend George Washington stayed at Wilton on March 25 and 26, 1775, when attending a meeting of the second Virginia Convention at nearby Saint Johns Church. In 1933, threatened by industrial encroachment, the house was purchased by the Colonial Dames of America, dismantled and moved to its present location. Thomas Jefferson visited Lafayette at Wilton in May, 1781. Owned and operated by the Colonial Dames of America. Open to the public.

Mount Airy
Rosaryville, Maryland

Washington's stepson, Jackie Custis, was married at the home of his bride's parents in 1774. George and Martha Washington were part of the gala festivities. The house, much changed since the 18th century, has been allowed to deteriorate. It is owned by the Maryland Department of Natural Resources which has no plans to refurbish the historic house. Closed to the public.

The Brice House
42 East Street
Annapolis, Maryland 21401
(410) 267-8249

James Brice was an ardent patriot who entertained many early political leaders including George Washington, John Adams and James Madison. The estate home is now owned by the National Masonry Institute. Closed to the public.

Berkeley Springs
Travel Berkeley Springs, Inc.
304 Fairfax Street
Berkeley Springs, West Virginia 25411
(304) 258-9147; (800) 447-8797

Nestled along the Potomac River in the foothills of the Appalachians, Berkeley Springs prospers as a spa resort. These warm mineral springs have been used as healing, relaxing baths ever since George Washington founded the spa that he named Bath, after the famous spa area in England. "George Washington's Bathtub," a natural indentation in the rock face of the spring, is purported to be Washington's favorite spot for relaxation, although proof of that has not been ascertained. Other presidential visitors have included James Madison, Martin Van Buren, James K. Polk, Millard Fillmore and Franklin D. Roosevelt. Open to the public.

Mansion House
Tu-Endie-Wei State Park
Point Pleasant, West Virginia 25550
(304) 675-3330

It is claimed that George Washington named this area Point Pleasant when he surveyed it in the late 1740s. Mansion House, built of hewn logs, is the oldest structure in the Kanawha Valley. The house is furnished with Colonial artifacts and relics from the Battle of Point Pleasant, fought on October 10, 1774, between Virginia frontiersmen and Indians of the federated western tribes goaded by Royal Governor Dunmore. The day-long battle, won by the settlers, is said by some historians to be the opening engagement of the American Revolution. The park, also known as Point Pleasant Monument State Park, is operated by the State of West Virginia in cooperation with the Daughters of the American Revolution. Open to the public.

Belvoir
Fort Belvoir, Virginia 22060

Belvoir was the mansion home of the Fairfax family, George Washington's benefactors and neighbors. It is thought that Mrs. Sally Fairfax was the true love of Washington's life. The house has been lost, but its outline is visible on the grounds of the army base, Fort Belvoir. Closed to the public.

Ampthill
211 Ampthill Road
Richmond, Virginia 23233

Archibald Cary was a close friend of George Washington who stayed with the Carys when visiting Richmond. Cary's 1732 Georgian house, after some modifications, was moved from its original location to the west side of Richmond near the James River in 1929. Ampthill is privately owned and closed to the public.

Point State Park
101 Commonwealth Place
Pittsburgh, Pennsylvania 15222
(412) 281-9284

Recently reclaimed from more than a century of industrial use, an imposing thirty-six-acre park preserves the foundations of the fortress upon which the city of Pittsburgh was built. Fort Prince George, the first to be built here, was a small British garrison begun in 1754. Its location, on the point where the Allegheny and Monongahela rivers join to form the Ohio River, had been selected by Major George Washington who called the place *extremely well-situated . . . as it has the absolute command of both rivers.* Along with restored earthworks and a museum of regional history, the blockhouse is one of the attractions of present-day Point State Park.

George Washington Office Museum
Adam Kurtz House
Braddock and Cork
Winchester, Virginia 22601
(540) 662-4412

A small log home owned by Adam Kurtz was used by Virginia Militia Colonel George Washington while assigned to protect the colony's three-hundred-mile western frontier during the French and Indian War. The office museum displays colonial artifacts, rare surveying instruments and a model of Fort Loudoun to which Washington moved in 1756. The museum is owned and operated by the Winchester/Frederick County Historical Society. Open to the public.

Washingtons Headquarters
Fort Cumberland
Riverside Park
Cumberland, Maryland 21501
(301) 777-8214

A simple log building was headquarters for English General Edward Braddock and twenty-one-year-old Lieutenant George Washington during the French and Indian War. The room where Washington assumed his first command has been preserved in the building which is owned by the City of Cumberland. Visitors may look at the room through a picture window while listening to a recorded lecture. Open on a limited schedule.

Fort Necessity National Battlefield
1 Washington Parkway
Farmington, Pennsylvania 15437
(412) 329-5512

In 1754, Colonel George Washington led Virginia militiamen and South Carolina regulars against the French and Indians, his first military campaign — and a losing one. The climactic battle of the campaign took place on July 3. The fort he built and defended has been rebuilt, together with entrenchments and earthworks. National Park Service Site. Open to the public.

Fort Ashby
Box 97
SR 46 at intersection with SR 28
Fort Ashby, West Virginia 26719-0097
(304) 298-3318

Fort Ashby, built in 1755, is the sole surviving fort of sixty-nine constructed by Colonel George Washington to protect western Virginia. The fort, rebuilt by the WPA in the early 1930s, is owned and operated by the Daughters of the American Revolution. Open by appointment.

Michael Cresap Museum
Main Street and Shawnee Indian Trail
19009 Oldtown Road, SE
Oldtown, Maryland 21555-9702
(301) 478-5154

A stone house, circa 1760, was the home of an 18th-century frontiersman and Revolutionary War hero, scion of the famous Cresap family which pioneered in the area. George Washington was a long-time acquaintance of the family and he visited the Cresap house when he was stationed at nearby forts. The museum contains nine rooms of historical treasures. Open to the public by appointment.

Fort Bedford Museum
Fort Bedford Drive, Box 1758
Bedford, Pennsylvania 15522
(814) 623-8891, (800) 259-4284

Old Fort Bedford was a British outpost constructed in 1758 during the French and Indian War, another in a series of staging and supply areas created to support General John Forbes' assault on Fort Duquesne. Colonel George Washington accompanied Forbes on this campaign. The conquest of Fort Duquesne determined, with finality, that English-speaking people would control the Ohio Valley. The fort itself has long been gone, but a large scale model located close to the site of the original is the core of the Fort Bedford Museum. The museum displays Native American artifacts and thousands of household items, all aiding in dramatically recreating the atmosphere of pioneer days in western Pennsylvania.

Fort Ligonier
216 South Market Street
Ligonier, Pennsylvania 15658–1206
(412) 238-9701

The final staging area for the British assault on Fort Duquesne was a "Post at Loyalhanna," fifty miles from the fort. The "post" was named Fort Ligonier in honor of Sir John Ligonier, Forbes' superior in London. In the 18th century, Fort Ligonier helped open the west, but by the 19th century is had been abandoned and was deteriorating. In the 20th century, a foundation was formed to recreate the fort and build a modern museum, an effort that has been magnificently completed. The impressive recreated fort has been built to scale on the hilltop site of the original.

Sun Inn
Town Green
Fairfield, Connecticut

Originally called Penfield's after its builder/owner, this Colonial "ordinary" hosted George Washington on at least two occasions. The first was on April 11, 1776; the other during his presidential tour of New England on October 16, 1789. The house, currently owned by the Town of Fairfield, is used as a private residence for a town employee. Closed to the public.

George Washington's Revolutionary War Career

Wadsworth House
Harvard Square
Harvard University
Cambridge, Massachusetts 02138

In June, 1775, General George Washington arrived in Cambridge unexpectedly, in the middle of a rainstorm, his new command not ready to greet him properly. Lodging and headquarters had been prepared at the home of Harvard University President Samuel Langdon, a 1726 home named for Benjamin Wadsworth, a former president of Harvard. Washington utilized the house for a few weeks before moving to a larger and more suitable home a few blocks away. The Wadsworth House is currently in use as University offices and is not open to the public.

Longfellow National Historic Site
105 Brattle Street
Cambridge, Massachusetts 02138
(617) 876-4491

A Georgian-style dwelling built in 1759 for Major John Vassall, a wealthy Tory who fled Cambridge on the eve of the Revolutionary War, served as General Washington's headquarters in 1775–1776. It was here that Washington planned the Siege of Boston and where he and Mrs. Washington celebrated their seventeenth wedding anniversary in January, 1776. In 1843, the poet Henry Wadsworth Longfellow became the owner of this house and lived there until his death in 1882. National Park Service Site. Open to the public.

Warren Tavern
2 Pleasant Street
Charlestown, Massachusetts 02129
(617) 241-8142

The oldest working inn in the Boston area, built around 1780, Warren Tavern hosted George Washington and Paul Revere. Open to the public.

Soldiers Monument
Dorchester Heights
Boston National Historical Park
Thomas Park
Boston, Massachusetts 02127

A 115-foot-tall monument marks the site where General George Washington and his troops fortified Dorchester Heights in 1776. This action forced the British to evacuate the city because, from the heights, the patriots could bombard the enemy with impunity.

City Hall Park
Chambers Street and Broadway
New York, New York 10007
(212) 788-4636

In the presence of George Washington, the Declaration of Independence was read to the Revolutionary Army on July 9, 1776.

Morris-Jumel Mansion
Jumel Terrace at 165th Street
New York, New York 10032
(212) 923-8008

The Morris-Jumel Mansion, circa 1765, is a Georgian masterpiece designed by Roger Morris. This is one of New York City's oldest houses and the most important surviving landmark of the Battle of Harlem Heights fought on September 15, 1776. General Washington had appropriated it for headquarters following the retreat from Long Island the previous month. The 2½-story house is noted for its front facade featuring four slim pillars. The house museum, filled with Colonial, Revolutionary, Federal and American Empire furniture and artifacts, is maintained by the Historic House Trust of New York. Open to the public.

Washingtons Headquarters Museum
140 Virginia Road
North White Plains, New York 10603
(914) 949-1236

Washingtons Headquarters is an 18th-century farmhouse, the home of Elijah and Anne Miller, which George Washington used as his headquarters for a day when directing the final engagements of the Battle of White Plains, October 28 to November 1, 1776. The artillery of the Revolutionary Army was located on the hill just above the house. The tiny one-story house is maintained by Westchester County as a base for educational activities. Open to the public.

The Purdy House
60 Park Avenue
White Plains, New York 10603
(914) 328-1776

The location of Washington's headquarters during the Battle of White Plains is controversial. Some claim the Miller Farmhouse as the location of Washington's headquarters, whereas the White Plains Historical Society claims and manages the 1721 Purdy House on the crest of Purdy Hill facing Chatterton Hill across the Bronx River.

White Plains National Battlefield Site
White Plains, New York 10603

Three monuments mark the positions of General Washington's forces during the Battle of White Plains — one is on Chatterton Hill and the others are on Battle Avenue.

Fort Lee Historic Site
Palisades Interstate Park
Hudson Terrace
Fort Lee, New Jersey 07024
(201) 461-1776

Fort Lee was built by Washington's troops in 1776 as a major link in the fortifications defending New York City and the Hudson River. Fort Lee, with its dramatic view overlooking the modern George Washington Bridge and New York City, has been replicated with earthworks and redans. The park is operated by the Palisades Interstate Park Commission. Museum. Open to the public.

Van Cortlandt House Museum
Broadway at 246th Street
Bronx, New York 10471
(718) 543-3344

Since 1748, Van Cortlandt House has stood as a symbol of New York's Colonial past. The estate was a prosperous plantation with fields, livestock, grist mill and a resident community of craftsmen and farm workers. During the Revolutionary War the house sat near or behind enemy lines and was twice used as headquarters by George Washington. Van Cortlandt is owned by the City of New York and operated as a house museum by the Society of Colonial Dames. Open to the public.

Richard Holcombe House
Lambertville, New Jersey 08530

General Washington was a guest here prior to the Continental Army's retreat into Pennsylvania in November of 1776. Closed to the public.

Historic Summerseat
Hillcrest and Legion Avenues
Morrisville, Pennsylvania 19067
(215) 295-7339

Summerseat is a sturdy eight-room Colonial house that dates from the 1760s. George Washington stayed at Summerseat from December 8–14, 1776, preceding the dramatic crossing of the Delaware River and the subsequent Battle of Trenton. It had been built as a summer house for wealthy Philadelphians. Historic Summerseat is owned and operated as a house museum by the Historic Morrisville Society. Open to the public.

Washington Crossing Historic Park
1112 River Road, Box 103
Washington Crossing, Pennsylvania 18977
(215) 493-4076

Washington Crossing is the place where the Continental Army embarked for New Jersey on Christmas night, 1776. It is connected by a bridge with New Jersey's Washington Crossing State Park (see next entry).The park contains an observation tower; wildflower preserve; a Revolutionary War-era graveyard and historic buildings which include the McKonkey Ferry Inn where Washington was believed to have dined before the crossing; and the Thompson-Neely House, circa 1702, the scene of many military conferences. Museum. Tours. Open to the public.

Washington Crossing State Park
Route 546
Titusville, New Jersey 08560
(609) 737-0623

When the Americans landed in New Jersey after crossing the Delaware they marched to Trenton over what is now called Continental Lane, an extant road extending the length of the park. The Nelson House, near the river bank, is a small museum with historical exhibits and Colonial crafts demonstrations. Open to the public.

Ferry House State Historic Site
Route 546
Titusville, New Jersey 08560
(609) 737-2515

Located at the south end of Continental Lane within the Washington Crossing State Park, a small building sheltered General Washington after the cold and dangerous crossing of the Delaware. The house has been restored as a Colonial inn with a taproom, kitchen and bedroom containing period furnishings. Open to the public.

Old Barracks Museum
Barrack Street
Trenton, New Jersey 08608
(609) 396-1776

The barracks was filled with Hessian mercenaries when General Washington led a surprise attack on Christmas Day, 1776 — a daring raid that was a tremendous military and psychological victory for the patriots. It is the only surviving British barracks from the war. A cultural history museum on the premises contains a restored soldiers' squad room, a period

29

L. E. SMOOT MEMORIAL LIBRARY
KING GEORGE, VA. 22485

room with 18th-century furnishings and permanent and changing exhibits. Costumed interpreters and guides portray New Jerseyans of the Revolutionary period. Open to the public.

Princeton Battlefield State Park
Thomas Clarke House
Princeton, New Jersey 08542
(609) 921-0074

A memorial arch and the 18th-century Thomas Clarke House are situated on the site of the battle where General Washington and the Revolutionary Army defeated the British on January 3, 1777. The house is furnished in the Revolutionary style and is currently being developed as a working Colonial farm. Open to the public.

Washington Rock State Park
Plainfield, New Jersey 07060
(908) 754-7940

A picturesque 45-acre park was once the sight of a vantage point in the Watchung Mountains from which Washington's army observed British troop movements.

Morristown National Historical Park
Washington Place
Morristown, New Jersey 07960
(973) 539-2085

Morristown was the main encampment for the Continental Army from January through May, 1777, and again during the bitter winter of 1779–1780. The surrounding mountains afforded natural protection. The park contains Washington's headquarters in the Ford House; Jockey Hollow with reconstructed soldiers' huts and earthworks; Fort Nonsense, site of an earthen fort; and a Historical Museum and Library displaying material relating to the 1779–1780 encampment plus thousands of manuscripts and printed works pertaining to the Colonial and Revolutionary periods. National Park Service Site. Open to the public.

Governor Jonathan Trumbull House/ Wadsworth Stable/ The War Office
169 Town Street
Lebanon, Connecticut 06249
(860) 642-7558

Jonathan Trumbull, Governor of Connecticut during the

Revolutionary War, was said to be the only Colonial governor to support the war. Trumbull served as a counselor to George Washington, who used Trumbull's house as headquarters for strategy sessions. A small house nearby was called The War Office. Wadsworth Stable, which stabled Washington's horse, Nelson, was moved to Lebanon from Hartford. The 1735 Trumbull House has a number of unusual design features and is furnished in period style. The complex is owned and operated by the Daughters of the American Revolution and the Sons of the American Revolution. Open to the public.

John MacCurdy House
1 Lyme Street
Old Lyme, Connecticut 06371

John MacCurdy was a prosperous merchant who, in 1754, bought a small four-room house that had been built around 1700, and added to it until it was a ninety-foot mansion with eight gables. Subsequent owners made Gothic Revival alterations, including medieval chimneys and point-arch windows. The MacCurdy family entertained General Washington on April 10, 1776, during the Continental Army's march from Boston to New York. The John MacCurdy House is privately owned. Closed to the public.

General Jedidiah Huntington House
223 East Town Street
Norwich, Connecticut 06360

General Huntington served the American Revolution with great distinction. His 1765 house was utilized to entertain Washington on April 8, 1776, during the march from Boston to New York. Across the street from the Jedidiah Huntington House is the home of Governor Samuel Huntington, signer of the Declaration of Independence and president of the Continental Congress from 1779 to 1781. Both homes are privately owned today. Closed to the public.

Leffingwell Inn
348 Washington Street
Norwich, Connecticut 06365
(860) 889-9440

Leffingwell Inn, built in 1665, was opened by Thomas Leffingwell in 1701. Officers in the Continental Army, including George Washington, often stopped here for food, drink and rest. The inn has been restored and furnished with period pieces. Open to the public.

31

Drake House Museum
602 West Front Street
Plainfield, New Jersey 07060
(908) 755-5831

The Drake House was George Washington's headquarters during the Battle of Short Hills, June 26, 1777. Open to the public.

Holcombe-Jimison Farmstead Museum
Lambertville, New Jersey 08530
(609) 782-1091

General Washington used a Colonial farmhouse as his headquarters from July 18 to July 31, 1777, and June 21 to 22, 1778. Holcombe-Jimison is owned and operated by the Hunterdon County Historical Society. Open to the public.

Van Allen House
Franklin Avenue
Oakland, New Jersey 07436
(201) 337-0924

The Van Allen Home became George Washington's headquarters following British General Burgoyne's capture of Fort Ticonderoga in northern New York in August, 1777. Owned by the Town of Oakland. Open to the public.

Moland House
1641 Old York Road
Hartsville, Pennsylvania 18974
(215) 343-8485

In the summer of 1777, George Washington led his troops southward from Morristown, New Jersey, unsure of the intentions of his opponent, British General Howe, whose army had left New York by ship, destination unknown. Washington set up temporary headquarters at the Moland farmhouse north of Philadelphia, where he stayed from August 10 to 23. When news arrived that Howe had been spotted on Chesapeake Bay, Washington left for Philadelphia. The Moland House, which had been neglected, was purchased in 1966 by the Hartsville Historical Society which has initiated an ambitious four-year project to refurbish the house. Due to the reconstruction process, the Moland House is not open to the public.

Hale-Byrnes House
606 Stanton-Christina Road
Stanton, Delaware 19808
(302) 998-3792

George Washington held a council of war in the Hale-Byrnes House with generals Lafayette, Wayne and Greene preceding the Battle of Brandywine in September, 1777. Operated by the Delaware Department of State. Open by appointment.

Brandywine Springs Park
3300 Faulkland Road
Wilmington, Delaware 19808
(302) 577-3534

The park is the site of a once-popular hotel where, under a council oak, Washington and Lafayette met once again to discuss the impending Battle of Brandywine. Open to the public.

Brandywine Battlefield Park
Chadds Ford, Pennsylvania 19317
(215) 459-3342

The Battle of Brandywine, fought September 11, 1777, was a defeat for the Americans as it left Philadelphia open to the British. The park has a Visitor Center and restored farmhouses used by Washington and Lafayette as headquarters buildings. Open to the public.

Pottsgrove Mansion
Route 100 and King Street
Pottstown, Pennsylvania 19464
(610) 326-4014

Pottsgrove, built by ironmaster John Potts in 1752, is only a few miles from Camp Pottsgrove where the Continental Army rested and waited for reinforcements following their defeat at Brandywine. The strategic position, however, enabled the Americans to control roads to supply depots in Reading, Pennsylvania. Open to the public.

General Wayne Inn
625 Montgomery Avenue
Merion, Pennsylvania 19066
(610) 667-3330

This house hosted Washington, Lafayette and General Wayne in September, 1777, following the Americans' defeat at Brandywine. The building has been converted to an operating public restaurant. Open to the public.

Malin Hall
Conestoga and Swedesford Road
Malvern, Pennsylvania 19355

General Washington's expense account for September 16, 1777, shows an entry for *Cash paid Mr. Malin for sundrys used+his house and trouble+ 7&10f.* The Malin House is a typical stone farmhouse of the period, now privately owned and closed to the public.

Fatlands aka James Vaux House
Pawling Road
Valley Forge, Pennsylvania 19482

This stone farmhouse, located across the Schuylkill River from Valley Forge, was visited by General Washington on September 21, 1777, during an inspection trip. Fatlands is privately owned and is closed to the public.

Castleberry House
Level Road
Evansburg, Pennsylvania 19426

General Washington reportedly used the stone Castleberry farmhouse as headquarters from 19 to 22 September, 1777. The house was enlarged in the 19th century as attested by a line of demarcation visible on the walls. A mansard roof was added, somewhat blemishing the original Colonial lines. The house is privately owned and is closed to the public.

Historic Antes House
318 Colonial Road
Upper Frederick Township
Perkiomenville, Pennsylvania 18074
(215) 234-8953

Following the disaster at Brandywine, Washington headquartered at the farmhouse of Frederick Antes in September, 1777, before moving on to Pottsgrove. The Antes house had been built by Frederick's father, Henry, one of the great master builders of the Colonial period and responsible for many of the early Moravian structures in Pennsylvania. The stone 2½-story house, built about 1736, was considered a mansion with a medieval quality — a steeply-sloping roof, central chimney and traditional three-room floor plan. The Goschenhopper Historians, a group of dedicated private volunteers, purchased the house in 1988 and initiated an extensive restoration project to return the home to its appearance at the time of Washington's visit. The Antes House is currently closed, but is scheduled to open to the public in 1998.

Pennypacker Mills and Mansion
5 Haldeman Road
Schwenksville, Pennsylvania 19473
(610) 287-9349

Pennypacker, mostly rebuilt, was General Washington's headquarters during the Continental Army's encampment of 1777 preceding the Battle of Germantown. It is currently an historic house museum that features a portion of the original stone work from the 18th century. Open to the public.

Cliveden
6401 Germantown Road
Philadelphia, Pennsylvania 19106
(215) 848-1777

The country home of Pennsylvania Chief Justice Benjamin Chew was the scene of pivotal action between General Washington's troops and British forces occupying the house during the Battle of Germantown on October 4, 1777. Fog and poor timing led to an American defeat. Furnishings, including 18th- and 19th-century pieces, span two centuries of Chew family history. Open to the public.

Stenton
4601 N. 18th Street
Philadelphia, Pennsylvania 19140
(215) 329-7312

James Logan, secretary to William Penn, built Stenton in 1730. The three-story Georgian served as Revolutionary War headquarters for both George Washington and British General Richard Howe. Open to the public.

Peter Wentz Farmstead
Box 240
Center Point, Pennsylvania 19490
(215) 584-5104

The Peter Wentz farmhouse was used by General Washington as a headquarters both before and after the Battle of Germantown. The farm has been restored. Tours. Open to the public.

Fort Washington State Park
50 Bethlehem Pike
Pennsylvania Turnpike, Exit 26
Montgomery County, Pennsylvania 19034
(215) 646-2942

Following their defeat at Germantown, Washington and 12,000 soldiers retreated to Whitemarsh, Pennsylvania, where a fort was built to defend the encampment. The area is now a park containing historic buildings, a library and museum. Open to the public.

Hope Lodge
553 Bethlehem Pike
Fort Washington, Pennsylvania 19034
(215) 646-1595

Hope Lodge, circa 1750, was built by Samuel Morris, a prosperous Quaker farmer-entrepreneur. It is a fine example of early Georgian architecture. During the Whitemarsh encampment of the Continental Army, the time between the Battle of Germantown and Valley Forge, Hope Lodge was used as headquarters by George Washington's Surgeon General, John Cochran, and it is likely that Washington was a visitor at this lodge on many occasions. Open to the public.

Red Lion Inn
Whitfield Road and South Village Avenue
Lionville, Pennsylvania 19353

To handle the overflow of sick and injured soldiers at Yellow Springs, the Continental Army took over the Quaker Meeting House in Lionville, a short distance away. During visits to the patients confined there, General Washington stayed at the Red Lion Tavern, a drover's inn across the street. A small stone building of 2½ stories, it has been converted to a private home, although part of the original remains. The Quaker Meeting House, which dates from 1711, is now called the Uwchlan Meeting House and serves as the headquarters of the Uwchlan Conservation Trust. Both structures are privately owned. Closed to the public.

Dawesfield
565 Lewis Lane
Whitpain Township
Ambler, Pennsylvania 19002

The stone farmhouse of James Morris was visited on October 21,

1777, during the Whitemarsh encampment. This house is privately owned. Closed to the public.

Emlen House
Pennsylvania Avenue
Fort Washington, Pennsylvania 19034

Following their defeat at Germantown, Washington's troops retreated to Whitemarsh where Fort Washington was built to defend the encampment. General Washington moved his headquarters into the home of George Emlen where he remained from November 2 to December 11, 1777. The magnificent three-story Colonial house is the centerpiece of a 100-acre estate. Emlen House is privately owned and not open to the public.

Valley Forge National Historical Park
Box 953
Valley Forge, Pennsylvania 19481
(610) 783-1000

Valley Forge, west of Philadelphia, was the location of the Continental Army's winter encampment, 1777–1778. The park encompasses over 3,000 acres and contains Washington's headquarters, earthworks, barracks, monuments and historical markers. Valley Forge National Historical Park is among the best known of all Revolutionary War sites. National Park Service Site. Open to the public.

Historic Yellow Springs
Chester Springs, Pennsylvania 19425
(610) 827-7414

Yellow Springs is a 145-acre complex of hotels and residences; all based on a bathhouse opened in 1722 as a Colonial-era health spa. During the War for Independence, the bathhouse was requisitioned for use as the hospital for the Continental Army camped nearby at Valley Forge. General and Mrs. Washington visited the troops hospitalized at Yellow Springs many times. Yellow Springs is now an historic village operated by a private, non-profit historical organization. Open to the public.

Redding Furnace Farm
South Branch of French Creek
East Nantmeal, Pennsylvania 19421

As early as 1736, iron furnaces and foundries had been established in the area west of Valley Forge. One of the surviving remnants of the business that supplied cannons to the Revolutionary Army is Redding

Furnace Farm, a stone farmhouse built by William Branson, iron master and owner. General Washington inspected the forges and foundries during the Valley Forge encampment. Redding Furnace Farm is privately owned and closed to the public.

Fell House
Doylestown, Pennsylvania 12940

On June 19, 1778, the Continental Army broke camp at Valley Forge and marched north in search of the British who had abandoned Philadelphia and were heading to New York. On the second day they reached Doylestown where General Washington camped on the property of Jonathan Fell, taking his meals inside the small home. His diary entry for that day reads: *to cash paid: Jn Fell for breakfast, dinner for general and suite ... 6 pounds.* The Fell House, which has been expanded over the years, is privately owned and not open to the public.

Village Inn
2 Water Street
Englishtown, New Jersey 07726
(732) 462-4947

The Village Inn is where Washington drew up plans for the Battle of Monmouth and, unhappily, where he later drafted charges against General Charles Lee for his inept and unprofessional behavior during the battle. Owned by the Battleground Historical Society. Open by appointment.

Joseph Stout House
Province Line Road
Hopewell, New Jersey 08525

This 2½-story Georgian farmhouse, circa 1752, served as headquarters for George Washington in June, 1778, when he was in Hopewell preceding the Battle of Monmouth. This stone house has been slightly altered but it retains the architectural integrity and symmetry of its original construction. This property is known today as Hunt House Farm and is privately owned. Closed to the public.

Monmouth Battlefield State Park.
Route 33
Manalapan, New Jersey 07726
(908) 462-9616

Monmouth was the scene of one of the longest battles of the Revolutionary War, fought on June 28, 1778, between the forces of George

Washington and Sir Henry Clinton. Washington's victory was particularly important at the time as it convinced the British that the revolutionaries were a viable military force. Monmouth is also famed as the battle which made Mrs. Mary Hays famous as "Molly Pitcher" — the soldier's wife who braved enemy fire to bring water to the American troops fighting on a hot and dry day. Open to the public.

The Hermitage
335 Franklin Turnpike
Ho-Ho-Kus, New Jersey 07423
(201) 445-8311

The Hermitage was erected circa 1750 as a modest two-story brownstone by Lieutenant Colonel James Prevost whose wife, Theodosia, invited George Washington and his officers, including future President James Monroe, to partake of her hospitality following the Battle of Monmouth. The invitation was accepted and the guests stayed for four days! An associated story is that another of Washington's staff officers, Aaron Burr, smitten by Mrs. Prevost, stayed in contact, then courted and won her hand following Colonel Prevost's death. In 1847, the Hermitage was almost totally razed, then remodeled into a romantic Gothic Revival mansion of great beauty. Open to the public.

Wallace House State Historic Site
38 Washington Place
Somerville, New Jersey 08876
(908) 725-1015

The Wallace House in Somerville was the residence for George and Martha Washington from December, 1778, to June, 1779, while the army camped at nearby Middlebrook. Operated by the State of New Jersey as a house museum. Open to the public.

Old Dutch Parsonage State Historic Site
65 Washington Place
Somerville, New Jersey 08876
(908) 725-1015

A Colonial house, across the street from the Wallace House, was built for Reverend Hardenbaugh of the First Reformed Church, a distinguished educator who founded Queens College, now Rutgers University. It is known that neighbor George Washington visited often. Open to the public.

Stony Point Battlefield State Historic Site
Box 182
Stony Point, New York 10980
(914) 786-2521

In May, 1779, the British had captured the peninsula at Stony Point and begun fortifications that endangered the American defenses at West Point and the Hudson Valley. General Washington marched his troops north from New Jersey in an effort to combat the provocation, observing the enemy works from nearby Buckberg Mountain. He devised a bold plan that was carried out successfully by "Mad Anthony" Wayne who produced a needed victory that boosted flagging American morale. The battlefield has been restored as an important relic of our military heritage. Open to the public.

Dey Mansion/Washingtons Headquarters Museum
199 Totowa Road
Wayne, New Jersey 07470
(973) 696-1776

An interesting brick and brownstone Georgian house with eleven furnished rooms was General Washington's headquarters in July, 1780, and again in October and November following the discovery of Benedict Arnold's treachery at West Point. Dey Mansion is operated by the Passaic County Department of Parks. Open to the public.

The Square House
Purchase Street and Boston Post Road
Rye, New York 10580
(914) 967-7588

A two-story house with hand-split shingles and wooden beams was built in 1700 and was operated as an inn between 1760 and 1830. George Washington and John Adams were guests when they traveled to and from New England. The house has been restored and is operated by the Rye Historical Society. Open to the public.

The Great Oak
Gaylord Road
New Milford, Connecticut

General Washington and his war council met under the oak's spreading branches sometime in 1780. There is a marker.

40

Oliver Wolcott House
South Street
Litchfield, Connecticut 06759

Oliver Wolcott was a member of the Continental Congress, signer of the Declaration of Independence, and Governor of Connecticut. His large frame and clapboard house, circa 1753, was the site of a visit by General George Washington on September 23, 1780, as he made his way to a fateful meeting with Rochambeau in Newport. The Wolcott House is privately owned. Closed to the public.

Old Colony House
Washington Square
Newport, Rhode Island 02840
(401) 846-2980; (800) 326-6030

The Declaration of Independence was read to the citizens of Rhode Island from the balcony of the Old Colony House, French General Count de Rochambeau was greeted in it by George Washington, and the United States Constitution was ratified in 1790 in its great hall when Old Colony House served as the state capitol, the second oldest in the nation. Thomas Jefferson, Andrew Jackson and Dwight D. Eisenhower have been entertained in the house that dates from 1739. Open to the public by appointment.

Governor Stephen Hopkins House
Benefit and Hopkins Streets
Providence, Rhode Island 02903
(401) 751-7067

An early red clapboard house with an 18th-century *parterre* garden was the home of Stephen Hopkins, ten-time governor of Rhode Island and signer of the Declaration of Independence. He entertained George Washington in his home twice, once following the march from Boston to New York in 1776, and in 1781 when Washington was in Rhode Island to confer with French General Rochambeau. Open to the public.

Vernon House
Mary and Clarke Streets
Newport, Rhode Island 02840

A simple, two-story clapboard home served as headquarters for General Rochambeau and it is known that he used it when conferring with George Washington. Closed to the public.

41

Webb-Deane-Stevens Museum

211 Main Street
Wethersfield, Connecticut 06109
(860) 529-0612

The Deane House was built in 1766 by Silas Deane, a member of the Continental Congress who undertook many important diplomatic assignments. In 1774, his friend John Adams wrote of being entertained at Deane's . . . *most genteely with punch, wine and coffee.* In 1781, General George Washington met General Rochambeau to discuss plans for the Battle of Yorktown, and the room in which Washington slept has been preserved. Open to the public as a three-house museum complex.

Fowler House

Root Avenue (Old Simpson Road)
Carmel, New York 10512

Enroute to an encampment in Pawling, General Washington stayed one night in the Fowler House, a 1½-story vernacular frame farmhouse. It has been enlarged through the years. The Fowler House is privately owned. Closed to the public.

John Kane House

South Main Street, Box 99
Pawling, New York 12564
(914) 855-9316

During the autumn of 1778, following the British evacuation of Philadelphia and the Battle of Monmouth, a large part of the Continental Army was moved to the Pawling area. Commanding General George Washington headquartered in the home of John Kane, a Tory who had been stripped of his property and forced to flee to British protection. The kitchen wing remains from the original home; the rest has been replaced by a Federal-style structure. The house is currently owned by the Historical Society of Pawling which operates it as a house museum. Open to the public.

Van Wyck Homestead Museum

Routes 9 and I-84
Fishkill, New York 12524
(914) 896-9560

A wood-frame house was requisitioned by the Continental Army as a headquarters building, visited and utilized on occasion by Washington, Lafayette and Von Steuben. Open to the public.

Griffins Tavern
231 New York State Route 82
Fishkill, New York 12524

On January 9, 1994, an historic home known as Griffins Tavern was heavily damaged by fire. Its residents escaped injury and moved to temporary quarters, but vowed to reconstruct the landmark house as it appeared in the 18th century when it was frequented by George Washington, the Marquis de Lafayette, Baron Von Steuben and other prominent figures of the Revolutionary era. It was known to these visitors as The Rendezvous, as it was a favorite meeting place for continentals and French soldiers. It was also the site, on August 15, 1775, for signing the Articles of Association, oaths of allegiance designed to ferret out Tories and spies. The list of those who signed — and those who refused to sign — was forwarded to the New York Provincial Congress for action. Today (1998) only the stone walls are visible, although foundation work has begun for the reconstruction.

John Brinckerhoff House
Lomala Road
Fishkill, New York 12524

Black bricks inlaid among the red bricks in the west gable indicate that the John Brinckerhoff House was built in 1738. Originally built of stone and 1½-stories high with large attic space, the front wall is now covered with cement and the east gable is clapboard. In the autumn of 1778, General Washington made this house his headquarters from time to time; when here, he occupied a parlor-bedroom at the rear of the west side. An apocryphal anecdote of Washington's stay in this house is that, when questioned by his host about military affairs, Washington asked him if he could keep a secret. When assured he could, Washington replied, *So can I.*

Hendrick Kip House
Old Glenham Road
Fishkill, New York 12524

The Kip House is associated with Baron Von Steuben, the Prussian volunteer who joined Washington at Valley Forge and became the essential army drillmaster. During the war, the Kip House served for a period as Von Steuben's headquarters, and it is likely that Washington visited the house on occasion. The privately-owned Kip House has been described as one of the best surviving Dutch stone farmhouses in the Hudson Valley. Closed to the public.

Madam Brett Homestead

50 Van Nydeck Avenue
Beacon, New York 12508
(914) 831-6533

The Madam Brett Homestead is considered Dutchess County's oldest home, an architectural gem with scalloped red cedar shingles. Most of the furnishings are family-owned and the original formal garden graces the rear yard. The first part of the house was built in 1709 by Catheryna and Roger Brett. Widowed at an early age, Mrs. Brett remained in what was then the wilderness to raise three sons, operate a mill and form a trading cooperative. During the Revolutionary War, the home was occupied by Madam Brett's granddaughter, whose husband, Major Henry Schenck, was the purchasing agent for the Commissary Department of the Continental Army. Supplies were stored in the cellar. Since this was a prominent home in the area during the war, there is little doubt that Washington, Lafayette, and Von Steuben were entertained there.

Mandeville House

Route 9D, Box 214
Garrison-on-Hudson, New York 10524
(914) 424-3626

The main portion of the Mandeville House was built by tenant farmer Jacob Mandeville in 1737 with a kitchen wing, parlor and bedroom added before the Revolutionary War. During the conflict, the Dutch-English house served as headquarters for General Israel Putnam, and George Washington is known to have visited. His expense account contains an entry for July 26, 1779, *to cash paid at Mandeville's for house, rooms, etc. £2.5.* The Mandeville House is owned and maintained by the Perry-Gething Foundation which opens the house on a limited basis for group tours, by appointment.

New Windsor Cantonment State Historic Site

Box 207
Temple Hill Road
Vails Gate, New York 12584
(914) 561-1765

New Windsor was the site of the last winter encampment of the Continental Army, 1780–1781. The Cantonment includes exhibit buildings and features periodic demonstrations of 18th-century army life and procedures. Museum. Open to the public.

Beekman Arms Hotel
4 Mill Street (Route 9)
Rhinebeck, New York 12572
(914) 876-7077

The Beekman Arms, recognized as "America's oldest inn," has long been a resting place for travelers along the Old Albany Post Road. The first two-story stone tavern was built in 1700 as a combination hotel and shelter for local residents against Indian attacks. Later General Washington utilized the Beekman Arms as a headquarters and watched his troops drill on the town square. The hotel has evolved over the years into a splendid modern facility of fifty-five rooms, retaining to this day the welcoming spirit and authentic atmosphere of its early Colonial days. Martin Van Buren and Franklin D. Roosevelt, both residents of the Hudson Valley, have also been welcomed at the Beekman Arms. Open to the public.

Washingtons Headquarters State Historic Site
84 Liberty Street
Newburgh, New York 12550
(914) 562-1195

The 1750 Hasbrouck House was utilized by Washington as headquarters in 1782–1783. It was from here that he declared a successful end to the Revolutionary War on April 18, 1783. The building is extant, furnished as a military headquarters and museum, operated by the New York State Department of Parks and Recreation. Open to the public.

Knoxs Headquarters State Historic Site
Box 207
Vails Gate, New York 12584
(914) 561-5498

Colonel Thomas Ellison was a veteran of the French and Indian War who built a sturdy stone farmhouse in Orange County, New York, in 1754. In 1779, war came to the Ellison family once again when Major General Henry Knox, Washington's commander of artillery, occupied the house when military campaigns were ongoing in the Hudson Highlands. In 1779, Knox shared the house with General Nathanael Greene, and in 1782, General Horatio Gates, hero of Saratoga, was installed when commanding the garrison at nearby New Windsor Cantonment. General Washington found his own quarters at Newburgh *dreary and confined,* and he visited the Ellison house on numerous occasions as it became the social center for his officers. Open to the public.

Denning House
Orrs Mill Road
Salisbury Mills, New York 12577
(914) 496-6771

This 1½-story farmhouse of shingle and stone construction was built circa 1770 by Tory James Peters who sold it to William Denning, possibly to prevent its being confiscated. There is a story that Peters hid in a secret recess to escape arrest, then fled to Canada. Denning was an important Revolutionary-era figure whose competence in financial affairs led to work as a Commissioner on the Board of the Treasury and service with the Quartermaster Department. He was close to General Washington during the latter's residence in Newburgh, and Washington visited the Denning home on occasion. The Denning House is privately owned. Closed to the public.

Mount Gulian Historic Site aka The Verplanck Homestead
145 Sterling Street
Beacon, New York 12508
(914) 831-8172

On May 13, 1783, a group of Continental Army officers gathered in the headquarters of General Baron Von Steuben and formed the Society of Cincinnati, the nation's first fraternal organization, named to honor the famous Roman farmer-general who led an army to victory, then returned to the farm rather than assume the mantle of dictator. The society's first president was, appropriately, George Washington, who emulated the Roman hero by returning to Mount Vernon after final victory over the British was achieved. Mount Gulian, built around 1730, was the home of the Verplanck family; it is a significant example of early Dutch architecture in the Hudson Valley. Open to the public.

Derick Brinckerhoff House
Routes 52 and 82
Fishkill, New York 12524

Derick Brinckerhoff, a third-generation family farmer, was active in governmental affairs as early as 1768 when he was a representative in the legislature of the New York Colony. During the Revolutionary War, he served as a Colonel of Militia and a member of the State Assembly. Some time before the conflict, Brinckerhoff added a frame half to the stone house that had been built by his father in 1719; this raised the structure by one-half its previous height. The house served as headquarters for the commander of Highland troops, General Alexander McDougall, and his many guests included generals Washington, Lafayette, Knox, Arnold, and Gates, and

New York Governor Clinton. From its front porch, General Washington reviewed thousands of British and Hessian prisoners being marched between Boston and Virginia. To commemorate that event, the present owner of the house has instituted an unusual tradition: each year, the 4th-graders from a nearby school stand on the front porch and "take the salute" from prisoners and guards as they march past. Otherwise, the Brinckerhoff House, still owned by the Brinckerhoff family, is closed to the public.

Storm-Adriance-Brinckerhoff House
Sylvan Lake Road and County Route 9
East Fishkill, New York 12524

Named for three early residents, the original 1½-story frame structure was built in 1759, with additions being made in 1771. Thomas Storm, who lived in the home during the Revolutionary War, was a captain in the militia, and it is thought that Tory and British prisoners were confined in the cellar. Since the house was located on a major east-west route, Storm extended hospitality to travelers, including George Washington and John Adams. The house is privately owned and closed to the public.

Old Fort House Museum
27 Broadway, Box 106
Fort Edward, New York 12828
(518) 747-9600

Headquarters at various times for American Generals Schuyler, Washington, Arnold, Stark and English General Burgoyne, Old Fort House is currently operated as a house museum, home to the Fort Edward Historical Association. Open to the public.

Steuben House
1209 Main Street
River Edge, New Jersey 07661
(201) 487-1739

Baron Von Steuben was an ex-Prussian army officer who joined George Washington at Valley Forge as a training officer — credited with bringing military discipline and European training methods to the Continental Army. After the war a grateful nation presented him with a 1713 Bergen Dutch mansion as partial payment for his services. During the conflict it had been used as headquarters by both Washington and his rival, Lord Cornwallis. It is now the home of the Bergen County Historical Society, which maintains it as a house museum and displays its collection of artifacts dating from 1650. Open to the public.

Ringwood State Park

1304 Sloatsburg Road
Ringwood, New Jersey 07456
(973) 962-7031

A 785-acre park has been built on the site of important Revolutionary-era ironworks, visited and inspected by General Washington on several occasions. Ringwood Manor, on the park grounds, is on the site of the former grand home of General Robert Erskine, an ironmaster who became the Surveyor General of the Continental Armies. Many of the manor's 78 rooms have been restored and a third floor museum contains exhibits depicting the history of the iron industry from 1740 to the 1920s. Open to the public.

Shaw Mansion

305 Bank Street
New London, Connecticut 06320
(860) 443-1209

An impressive three-story granite building of Georgian design was built by sea captain Nathaniel Shaw in 1756. During the Revolutionary War, his son was New London's Marine Agent and the house became Connecticut's Naval Office. George Washington, Lafayette and Nathan Hale met here for strategy sessions. It is presently the home of the New London Historical Society. Open to the public.

Rockingham State Historic Site

Route 518
Rocky Hill, New Jersey 08553
(609) 921-8835

George Washington resided in "Berrien House" for several months in 1783 when he attended the Continental Congress session in Princeton. It was here that he wrote his "Farewell to the Armies" speech. The restored house contains period furnishings. Open to the public.

General Philip Schuyler House

US Route 4
Schuylerville, New York 12871
(518) 664-9821

The federal government rebuilt the Schuyler house to replace one destroyed by the British during their retreat from Saratoga, New York, in

1777. The home is part of Saratoga National Historical Park, a 2,800-acre site commemorating the two Battles of Saratoga, fought on September 19 and October 7, 1777. General Horatio Gates' American forces defeated General John Burgoyne's British forces, a victory some historians consider to be the turning point of the Revolution. Washington honored the battles and his friend Schuyler with a visit after the war. Open to the public.

George Washington Masonic Shrine
DeWint House
Livingston Avenue and Oak Tree Road
Tappan, New York 10983
(914) 359-1359

The DeWint House hosted Washington at least four times during the war, serving as his headquarters at the time of Benedict Arnold's betrayal and the capture of British Major Andre in September, 1780 . Several rooms are furnished in the period. The DeWint House is operated by the Grand Lodge of Free and Accepted Masons of the State of New York. Open to the public.

West Point
West Point, New York 10966
(914) 938-2638

West Point is, of course, the location of the United States Military Academy, founded in the early 1800s. During the Revolutionary War, however, it was an important strategic defense facility of the Americans, overlooking as it does a ninety-degree turn in the Hudson River where ships must slow down. A battery of cannon and a chain stretched across the channel below the bluffs at West Point controlled all Hudson Valley commerce where the Hudson River cut the United States in two. George Washington visited West Point several times, most dramatically in 1780 when he learned with horror of General Benedict Arnold's treason, and then to order the execution of the British spy, Major John Andre. The modern-day Academy contains a number of tourist-oriented features − a Visitor Center, chapels, Trophy Point and the West Point Museum. Open to the public.

Colonial National Historical Park
Box 210
Yorktown, Virginia 23690
(757) 898-3400

Colonial National Park, lying on a peninsula between the York and James rivers, commemorates the final and victorious stage of the

Revolutionary War. The park covers 9,000 acres encompassing the Yorktown Battlefield, Jamestown Island and the Colonial Parkway. National Park Service Site. Open to the public.

Yorktown Battlefield

The last major battle of the Revolutionary War was fought in the autumn of 1781. A Celebration of Victory is held every October 19th to commemorate the final American victory and the surrender of the British forces.

Grace Episcopal Church

Grace Church, circa 1697, is built of native marl. During the siege of Yorktown the building was used by the British as an ammunition magazine. Communion silver dating from 1649 is still in use during services.

Moore House

Commissioners from the combined French and American armies met in the Moore House with British representatives on October 18, 1781, to draft the terms of Lord Cornwallis' surrender to General Washington.

Nelson House

The home of General Thomas Nelson, Jr., is a fine example of Georgian architecture. Nelson was Yorktown's most famous son and one of the signers of the Declaration of Independence. It is purported that, during the siege of Yorktown, Nelson directed artillery fire at his own home, thinking that British Commanding General Lord Cornwallis was using the house as headquarters.

Visitor Center

The events of the siege of Yorktown are set forth in an entertaining and educational theater program at a modern Visitor Center. A museum displays American military tents and part of a reconstructed British frigate, plus other treasures from the ultimate American victory.

Yorktown Victory Center
Box 1976
Yorktown, Virginia 23690
(757) 887-1776

The Yorktown Victory Center is independently owned and operated by the Jamestown-Yorktown Foundation, an educational agency of the

Commonwealth of Virginia, although it lies within the boundaries of Colonial National Historical Park. The Victory Center is part of Virginia's famous Historic Triangle, which also includes Colonial Williamsburg and the Jamestown Colony. The Center contains a museum and a re-created Continental Army encampment. Open to the public.

Fraunces Tavern
54 Pearl Street
New York, New York 10004
(212) 269-0144

At the end of the Revolutionary War, General Washington led his triumphant troops back to New York and bid an emotional farewell to his officers at a private dinner at Fraunces Tavern on December 4, 1783. Fraunces was built in 1719 as a residence, then turned into a highly-popular eating establishment in 1763 by Samuel Fraunces, a West Indian *émigré* who went on to become Washington's steward. Fraunces is still an active restaurant with a small museum on the premises. Open to the public.

George Washington's Post-War Career

Maryland State House
State Circle
Annapolis, Maryland 21401
(410) 974-3400

The Maryland State House, oldest in use in the nation, was capitol of the fledgling United States from November 11, 1783, until August 13, 1784. George Washington resigned his commission as Commander-in-Chief of the Continental Army here on January 14, 1784. Open to the public.

Annapolis City Hall
150 Duke of Gloucester Street
Annapolis, Maryland 21401
(410) 263-7942

George Washington was a regular social visitor to Annapolis where he attended the races and visited friends, and he made frequent rest stops in the city on his innumerable trips between Mount Vernon and the north. In 1783, he was guest of honor at a ball in a building built as a social hall/meeting room for the elite citizens of Annapolis. Greatly expanded, the building currently serves as the Annapolis City Hall with the original ballroom used as the City Council Chamber. Open to the public.

Buccleuch Mansion and Park
College Road
New Brunswick, New Jersey 08901
(908) 745-5094

Known as White House Farm when constructed for a British officer in the mid-18th century, George Washington visited this farm after the war. It is operated by the Daughters of the American Revolution as an historic house museum. Open to the public.

Amstel House
2 East 4th Street
New Castle, Delaware 19720
(302) 322-2794

George Washington attended a wedding at Amstel House in 1784. Open to the public.

Robinson House
Namans Road and Philadelphia Pike
Claymont, Delaware 19703
(302) 792-0285

From time to time, both George Washington and Lafayette lodged at the Robinson House during journeys between Baltimore and Philadelphia. Furnished in period style, it is now a museum owned and operated by the State of Delaware. Open to the public by appointment.

Rippon Lodge
Blackburn Road
Woodbridge, Virginia 22194

and

Williams Ordinary
Stagecoach Inn
US Route 1
Dumfries, Virginia 22026

The Potomac Path, or Kings Highway, was a major transportation route linking the northern and southern colonies. Lafayette, Washington and Rochambeau were travelers along this route, stopping at Gunston Hall, the Woodbridge plantation of George Mason; Rippon Lodge, home of Colonel Richard Blackburn; and the Stagecoach Inn, also known as Williams Ordinary. Today, US Route 1 closely follows the Potomac Path. Rippon Lodge and Stagecoach Inn are closed to the public.

Middletons Tavern
2 Market Space
Annapolis, Maryland 21401
(410) 263-3323

George Washington spent a great deal of time in Annapolis, but few places he is known with certainty to have visited remain from that time, although many claim to have hosted him. One of the few who did entertain Washington was Middletons Tavern, circa 1750, an "ordinary" then and still popular today as a restaurant. Open to the public.

The Rectory of Saint Annes Parish
215 Hanover Street
Annapolis, Maryland 21404

Jonathan Boucher, Rector of Saint Annes, conducted a boys' academy in his home. George Washington sent his stepson as a boarding student. Washington and Boucher became friendly and they spent many hours in lively political discussions that finally terminated as a result of Boucher's Tory views. A 19th-century mansard roof and gallery porch disguise the Colonial brick residence. The Rectory is privately owned. Closed to the public.

Saint Johns College
60 College Avenue
Annapolis, Maryland 21404
(410) 263-2371

President Washington began a visit to Annapolis at a new seminary, Saint Johns. Responding to a letter from the faculty, he wrote *The satisfaction which I have derived from my visit to your infant seminary, is expressed with real pleasure, and my wishes for its progress to perfection are preferred with sincere regard.* Washington demonstrated his sincerity by enrolling his ward and two nephews as students. McDowell Hall remains from the time of Washington's visit; it is still used for classrooms. Closed to the public, but the campus is a part of the Annapolis Historical Tour.

Montpelier Mansion
Route 197 and Muirkirk Road
Laurel, Maryland 20707
(301) 953-1376

Montpelier Mansion, one of the finest examples of 18th-century Georgian architecture in Maryland, was built by Thomas Snowden. His close friend George Washington visited the plantation on numerous occasions when traveling between Mount Vernon and Philadelphia. Montpelier is owned and operated by the Maryland Capital Park and Planning Commission. Open to the public.

Kings Chapel
58 Tremont Street
Boston, Massachusetts 02109

The first Anglican church, circa 1754, in Boston became America's first Unitarian church after the Revolutionary War. Its fortress-like exterior was designed by Peter Harrison, its light and airy interior considered one of the most beautiful in the United States. On October 27, 1789, President Washington attended an oratorio at Kings Chapel during his New England tour.

Old State House
206 Washington Street
Boston, Massachusetts 02109
(617) 720-3290

The Old State House, Boston's oldest public building, was the site of the Boston Massacre on March 4, 1770, when five Americans were killed at the front steps by a squad of British regulars clashing with an unruly mob of citizens. One of the proudest moments of the State House was in 1789 when President George Washington reviewed a parade from the steps where a commemorative plaque states *In celebration of America's independence, President George Washington's triumphal visit to the Old State House marked the transition of Massachusetts from 'Colony to Commonwealth' and the emergence of a new nation. Despite the many changes it has since witnessed, the Old State House survives today as a revered symbol of American independence and freedom.* In 1881, the Bostonian Society meticulously restored the building and has operated it ever since as Boston's History Museum. Open to the public.

Fort Ticonderoga
Box 390B
Ticonderoga, New York 12883
(518) 585-2821

On his northern "vacation" trip in 1783, General Washington stopped at Fort Ticonderoga to honor its importance in the War for Independence — the daunting raid of Ethan Allen and Benedict Arnold that was America's first victory, then Colonel Henry Knox's remarkable transfer of Ticonderoga's ordnance to Boston. The fort was restored to its original glory in 1908, and stands as one of the most prominent military reconstructions in the nation. The Fort Ticonderoga Museum houses a valuable collection of 18th-century military memorabilia. Open to the public.

Lee House National Historic Landmark
161 Washington Street
Marblehead, Massachusetts 01945
(617) 631-1069

This is a magnificent Georgian townhouse that was owned by Colonel Jeremiah Lee, whose widow entertained generals Washington and Lafayette in his home after the war. This house is presently the home of the Marblehead Historical Society. Open to the public.

Kingston Free Library
2605 Kingstown Road
Kingston, Rhode Island 02881
(401) 783-8254

During the Revolutionary War, the Rhode Island General Assembly met in Kingston when Newport was occupied by the British. Following the war, the building in which they met was visited by George Washington and Benjamin Franklin. The building has been refurbished and converted to a public library. Open to the public.

Boxwood Hall State Historic Site
1073 East Jersey Street
Elizabeth, New Jersey 07201
(908) 648-4540

Elias Boudinot was a president of the Continental Congress and signer of the Treaty of Peace with Great Britain. George Washington was entertained in Boxwood Hall, Boudinot's red clapboard home, on April 23, 1789, while enroute to his presidential inauguration in New York City. Museum. Open to the public.

Oliver Ellsworth Homestead
778 Palisado Avenue
Windsor, Connecticut 06095
(860) 688-8717

Oliver Ellsworth was one of the five men who drafted the Constitution of the United States and who later served as a United States Senator and Chief Justice of the United States Supreme Court. George Washington and John Adams visited Ellsworth's home which has been restored to its Colonial condition. Open to the public.

John Brown House

52 Power Street
Providence, Rhode Island 02906
(401) 331-8575

George Washington was entertained at the John Brown House, referred to by John Quincy Adams as "The most magnificent and elegant private mansion that I have ever seen on this continent." The 1786 Georgian masterpiece houses a museum of china, glass, pewter and 18th-century furniture. Open to the public.

Governor John Langdon House

143 Pleasant Street
Portsmouth, New Hampshire 03081
(603) 436-3205

Governor Langdon's mid-Georgian-style house was host to President George Washington in 1789. It is now operated by the Society for the Preservation of New England Antiquities as part of the Portsmouth Historical Trail. Open to the public.

Munroe Tavern

1332 Massachusetts Avenue
Lexington, Massachusetts 02173
(617) 862-1703

President Washington dined here in 1789 during his tour of New England. On April 19, 1775, this building served as headquarters for British General Earl Percy. The Tavern, built in 1695, has been transformed to a museum containing period furnishings and artifacts. It is operated by the Lexington Historical Society as part of a three-house complex close to Lexington Green. Open to the public.

Youngs House

Cove Beach Road
Oyster Bay, New York 11771

George Washington stayed in this house during his Long Island tour in 1790. Closed to the public.

David Conklin Farmhouse

2 High Street
Huntington, New York 11743
(516) 427-7045

The Huntington Historical Society owns and operates the David

Conklin Farmhouse as a museum furnished to reflect its architectural history – pre-Revolutionary, Federal and Victorian – and includes furniture used by George Washington on his tour of Long Island in 1790. Open to the public.

President Washington's Southern Tour, April 7–June 12, 1791

In 1789, George Washington announced plans to visit each of the new states *to become better acquainted with their principal characters and internal circumstances, as well as to be more accessible to numbers of well-informed persons who might give useful information and advice on political subjects.* In the spring of 1791, he embarked on an almost-two-thousand-mile journey that began at the capital city of Philadelphia, then extended south as far as Savannah, Georgia, before ending at his sister's home in Fredericksburg, Virginia. The trip was a tremendous success, although from today's perspective it is hard to visualize such an arduous journey – by carriage or on horseback over poorly-maintained and sometimes non-existent roads, across rushing rivers, and through sometimes inclement weather. Some of the places where the President stayed or visited still exist.

Tryon Palace Restorations and Gardens
John Wright Stanly House
Route 17
New Bern, North Carolina 28560
(919) 638-1560

Acclaimed in its day as the finest government building in the colonies, the magnificent Tryon Palace mansion was completed in 1770 as the home of Royal Governor William Tryon, and it served two succeeding governors before the Revolution. One wing escaped a disastrous fire in 1798 but the remainder has been reconstructed on its original foundation. The grounds are landscaped in the manner of 18th-century English gardens, and Colonial crafts are demonstrated by costumed artisans. George Washington was entertained here in 1791 at a public dinner and dance. The President's two nights in New Bern were spent in the nearby home of wealthy shipowner, John Wright Stanly, which he described as *exceeding good lodgings.* Distinctive American furniture of the period complements the elegant interior woodwork. The home is part of the Tryon Palace complex. Open to the public.

Benjamin Allston House

now The Parker Stewart House
1019 Front Street
Georgetown, South Carolina 29442
(803) 546-4163

An Adam-style, 2-story brick house with a hipped roof standing on a raised basement was owned by Benjamin Allston who hosted President Washington on April 30. The house is presently owned by Carolina First Bank which uses it as a corporate conference facility, available for rental. The grounds, overlooking the Sampit River, are open to the public.

Hampton Plantation State Park

1950 Rutledge Road
McClellanville, South Carolina 29458
(803) 546-9361

Hampton Plantation is one of the most impressive homes in the South Carolina Lowcountry, its mansion the centerpiece of a state park and a monument to South Carolina's glorious age of rice. A colossal Adam-style portico at the entrance is one of the finest examples of its kind in America, and the extensive grounds offer unique opportunities to examine the wildlife of the Lowcountry. President Washington visited Hampton during his southern tour. Open to the public.

Snee Farm

Charles Pinckney National Historic Site
1254 Long Point Road
Mt. Pleasant, South Carolina
(803) 881-5516

Snee Farm was the country seat of patriot and South Carolina governor Charles Pinckney. Tradition holds that President Washington dined under the trees in the yard of Snee Farm on his way to Charleston, May 2, 1791. Twenty-eight of the original 715 acres of the plantation remain, together with an 1827 house museum featuring panels describing Pinckney and his family's major contribution to American political life. National Park Service Site. Open to the public.

Heyward-Washington House

87 Church Street
Charleston, South Carolina 29401
(803) 722-0354

The Heyward-Washington House takes its name from the wealthy rice planter who built it and its most famous occupant, President George Washington, who leased it for eight days on his southern tour in 1791. The Heyward-Washington, owned and operated as a house museum by the Charleston Museum, contains a valuable collection of 18th-century Charleston-made furniture. Open to the public.

The Old Exchange Building and Provost Dungeon
122 East Bay Boulevard
Charleston, South Carolina 29401
(803) 727-2165

In the 1760s, Charles Town was a thriving shipping town, part of the royal colony of South Carolina. An important exchange and custom house was completed in 1771 on the site of a former council hall and dungeon. The Exchange Building, now owned by the Daughters of the American Revolution, has been refurbished to its former glory as "The Independence Hall of South Carolina." It was in the Exchange Building that South Carolina declared its independence from England, where the Constitution of the United States was ratified in 1788, and where President George Washington was entertained several times during his southern tour. Open to the public.

Saint Michaels Episcopal Church
80 Meeting Street
Charleston, South Carolina 29401
(803) 723-0603

Designed after Saint Martins in-the-Fields in London, Saint Michaels church is considered a notable architectural achievement, with a Palladian Doric portico, a steeple rising 186 feet above the street and a tower clock that has marked time since 1764. The richly ornamented interior includes old-fashioned pew boxes and the original pulpit. President Washington not only worshipped at Saint Michaels during his southern tour in 1791 (Pew #43 is marked) but he climbed the steeple to enjoy an unparalleled view of the city of Charleston. He also worshipped at Saint Philips Episcopal Church but that building has been replaced with a more modern structure.

John Rutledge House Inn
116 Broad Street
Charleston, South Carolina 29401
(803) 723-7999; (800) 476-9741

John Rutledge was one of the fifty-five men who signed the Constitution of the United States. His home, circa 1763, is one of only fifteen belonging to those signers that has survived the years. A caring rejuvenation has restored the beautiful details of the home's architecture — elaborately carved Italian marble fireplaces, the original plaster moldings, inlaid floors and graceful ironwork. His diary tells us that President Washington breakfasted with Mrs. Rutledge during his southern tour while her husband, by then Chief Justice of the South Carolina Supreme Court, was "on the circuit". Currently operated as a Bed and Breakfast. Open to the public.

Edward McCradys Tavern
2 Unity Alley
Charleston, South Carolina 29401
(803) 577-7472

Edward McCradys Tavern was the scene of a dinner held in honor of George Washington by the Society of Cincinnati on May 4, 1791, in the "Long Room" on the second floor. Many historians thought the tavern had been razed, but in 1992 preservationists found it behind a warehouse, still intact. Restored to its original condition, the tavern is housed on the ground floor, with a modern bistro, Restaurant Million, replacing the Long Room on the second floor. Open to the public.

Fort Johnson
Fort Moultrie
Fort Sumter National Monument
1214 Middle Street
Sullivans Island, South Carolina 29482
(803) 883-3123

On May 5, 1791, President Washington visited forts Johnson and Moultrie, both part of the Charleston harbor defenses during the Revolutionary War. Fort Johnson, on James Island, was occupied by the British by 1780 as they encircled the city. The site of Fort Johnson is visible today only from tourist boats. Fort Moultrie, across the harbor to the north, was the scene on June 28, 1776, of the first bloodshed of the war in South Carolina, when it repulsed the attack of a British fleet of nine warships commanded by British Admiral Sir Peter Parker. After a nine-hour battle, the ships were forced to retire and Charleston was saved from occupation, if only temporarily, and the fort was named in honor of its commander, William Moultrie. Fort Moultrie defended the countryside for four years before falling in 1780. Very little of the original fort remains, although it has been rebuilt several times as national defense required. Fort Moultrie is administered by the National Park Service. Open to the public.

Lachlan McIntosh House
110 E. Oglethorpe Avenue
Savannah, Georgia

President Washington spent two days in Savannah, then a struggling municipality of perhaps 1500 citizens. He was entertained lavishly with dinners, balls and other entertainment. Unfortunately only one landmark of the President's visit remains, that being the home of his patriot-in-arms, General Lachlan McIntosh, which the President used as his Savannah headquarters. The three-story plaster and brick house was saved from destruction by Historic Savannah, Inc., and is still in use as a private law office. Closed to the public.

Washington House
Chesnut House
1413 Mill Street
Camden, South Carolina 29020
(803) 432-2525 (Cof C)

Washington's last day in South Carolina was spent in Camden, an important shipping center — and scene of two pitched battles during the Revolutionary War. The President's lodgings were burned long ago but the imposing frame residence of merchant and patriot James Chesnut, where he was entertained with a festive reception and formal dinner, remains. Moved from its original location, it is privately owned, open to the public only during seasonal historical tours

Salem Tavern
Old Salem, Inc.
Box F, Salem Station
Winston-Salem, North Carolina 27108
(910) 721-7300

In the 18th century, the Moravians created towns which were refuges for mission work and havens from despair — meticulously planned and organized communities where church members led secure and productive lives while seeking personal salvation. Old Salem is a restoration of an original 1766 Moravian village with many buildings restored or reconstructed on their original sites. Costumed interpreters recreate late 18th- and early 19th century life in a small German-speaking town. President George Washington stayed at the Salem Tavern near the end of this southern tour and was reportedly delighted with the subdued welcome, consistent with the pacific nature of the Moravians. Open to the public.

Guilford Courthouse National Military Park
Box 9806
Greensboro, North Carolina 27249
(919) 288-1776

A closing engagement of the Revolutionary War, the Battle of Guilford Courthouse pitted General Nathanael Greene's mixed continental and militia army against Lord Cornwallis' smaller but veteran forces on March 15, 1781. Cornwallis won the battle but suffered heavy losses; he failed to destroy the Americans and was forced into Virginia where he surrendered at Yorktown. In 1791, President Washington honored the heroes of Guilford Courthouse by visiting the battle site. Open to the public.

Forrest-Marbury House
3350 M Street, NW
Washington, DC 20007

George Washington and other commissioners met at Forrest-Marbury in 1791 to determine the boundaries of a proposed District of Columbia. The house is now part of an office complex. Closed to the public.

The Espy House
123 E. Pitt Street, Box 1794
Bedford, Pennsylvania 15522

A small brick house was headquarters for President Washington during the Whiskey Rebellion in 1794. Closed to the public.

Red Fox Inn
Box 385
Middleburg, Virginia 22117
(703) 687-6301

George Washington made innumerable trips to Winchester throughout his life and it is probable that he stopped at the Red Fox Inn, circa 1728, on many of those occasions. Open to the public.

Cocks Residence
21 South Loudoun Street
Winchester, Virginia 22606

The home of Captain William Cocks was George Washington's

residence when he stayed in Winchester following the Revolutionary War. The house is now utilized as a law office. Closed to the public.

Harpers Ferry National Historic Park
Box 65
Harpers Ferry, West Virginia 25425
(304) 535-6223

George Washington surveyed in this area in the 1750s. Later, as President, he was instrumental in establishing the Federal Armory here. Thomas Jefferson visited here in 1783 and declared the view of the cascading Potomac and Shenandoah rivers to be *one of the most stupendous scenes in nature.* National Park Service site. Open to the public.

Blue Bell Inn
7303 Woodland Avenue
Philadelphia, Pennsylvania 19153
(215) 365-5927

The Blue Bell Inn, built in 1766, was a popular way-station on Kings Highway, the southernmost stagecoach route from the southern colonies to Philadelphia. George Washington visited this inn more than once, including a visit shortly after his election as President. The Blue Bell is being refurbished by the Friends of the Blue Bell; the inn is opened to visitation on a limited basis from May through October.

Bartrams Garden
54th Street and Lindbergh Boulevard
Philadelphia, Pennsylvania 19142
(215) 685-2681

John Bartram, America's first native-born botanist, started a garden in 1748 on a prosperous farm overlooking the Schuylkill River. Eventually his reputation spread to Europe where he was respected by scientists, philosophers and politicians. Benjamin Franklin and George Washington frequently visited Bartram's farm. Today, the twenty-seven-acre garden features descendants of Bartram's original cuttings and the stone house the great botanist remodeled over the years. Open to the public.

Toliver House Restaurant
209 N. Main Street
Gordonsville, Virginia 22942
(804) 832-3485

In 1787, Nathaniel Gordon founded the Gordon Tavern in the historic crossroads town of Gordonsville. The Tavern was, in the words of

Thomas Jefferson, *a good house* that played host to many travelers including George Washington, James Madison and James Monroe. The present restaurant is on the site of the original Gordon holdings. Open to the public.

Churches Associated with George Washington

Saint Johns Church
2401 East Broad Street
Richmond, Virginia 23223
(804) 648-5015

Saint Johns was the site of Patrick Henry's impassioned *Give me Liberty or Give me Death!* speech at the second Virginia Convention on March 23, 1775. Listening with great interest were two future Presidents of the United States – George Washington and Thomas Jefferson.

Saint Pauls Episcopal Church
Box 134
King George, Virginia 22485
(540) 663-3085

Saint Pauls, originally Choatank Parish, dates from the late 17th century, the present building from 1766 – a fine example of Colonial architecture. It is in the form of a Greek cross, the walls laid in Flemish bond with brick thought to have been produced locally. It is documented that George Washington worshipped at Saint Pauls when visiting his relatives in the Choatank area of the Northern Neck.

Historic Old Saint Augustines Catholic Church
4th and New Streets
Philadelphia, Pennsylvania 19106

George Washington, though not a Catholic, was an early (1796) contributor to the building fund of Saint Augustines.

Falls Church
115 E. Fairfax Street
Falls Church, Virginia 22046
(703) 532-7600

George Washington was a vestryman of Truro Parish at the time Falls Church was in disrepair – declared unsafe – so he advertised for financial help for restoration efforts which were completed in 1769. The church building was used as a recruiting station during the Revolution.

During the Civil War the church was used as a federal hospital. Falls Church has been restored to its 18th-century appearance.

Pohick Episcopal Church
9301 Richmond Highway
Lorton, Virginia 22079
(703) 339-6572

Pohick was the Colonial parish church for Mount Vernon, Gunston Hall and Belvoir. George Washington chose the site for the church building and served as a vestryman for twenty-three years. During the Civil War the original 1774 interior was torn out by Union troops who used the building for stables, but the church was restored in the early part of the 20th century. The original stone baptismal font was found many years later being used as a trough on a nearby farm.

Saint Pauls Chapel
Fulton and Broadway
New York, New York 10035
(212) 732-5564

The oldest public church building in Manhattan was dedicated in 1766. Washington worshipped here and participated in a special service following his inauguration as President in 1789. His pew is marked.

Touro Synagogue National Historic Site
85 Touro Street
Newport, Rhode Island 02840
(401) 847-4794

Touro, the oldest active synagogue in the United States, was built around 1763 by Spanish Jews escaping religious persecution in Europe. The synagogue was visited by President Washington in 1790. The interior is considered an architectural masterpiece, and the synagogue proudly displays a copy of President Washington's letter to the congregation guaranteeing religious freedom in the new nation.

Christ Church, Durham Parish
8685 Ironsides Road (Maryland Route 425)
Nanjemoy, Maryland 20662
(301) 743-7099

Durham was the parish of Washington's friend, Revolutionary War commander and Governor of Maryland, General William Smallwood. Washington was a visitor to the church, commonly referred to as Old Durham Church, in 1771.

Christ Church

0 Garden Street
Cambridge, Massachusetts 02138
(617) 876-0200

The oldest church building in Cambridge was designed by Peter Harrison. During the siege of Boston in 1776, Connecticut troops used the church as a barracks and melted the organ pipes to make bullets. On New Year's Eve of that year the church reopened for services, an event attended by George and Martha Washington.

Trinity Church

Queen Anne Square.
Newport, Rhode Island 02840
(401) 846-0660

Trinity was the first Anglican church in Rhode Island and has continued in service since 1726. The slim church spire is tipped with the golden bishop's mitre of the Church of England. A three-tiered wineglass pulpit, Tiffany windows and an organ tested by George Frederick Handel grace the interior where original chandeliers hang from ropes extending to ceiling medallions in the same style as the original. When visiting Newport, George Washington was a communicant and his pew is marked.

Monuments, Museums and Memorials to George Washington

George Washington Memorial Parkway

Turkey Run Park
McLean, Virginia 22101

The George Washington Memorial Parkway is a landscaped riverfront parkway that links many landmarks associated with George Washington and provides easy access to a number of other sites commemorating American Presidents. The Parkway begins at Mount Vernon and continues northwest for forty miles through northern Virginia, providing easy access to nearby Maryland and the District of Columbia.

Washington Monument State Park

Boonsboro, Maryland 21713
(301) 432-8065

Washington Monument State Park houses a rough-stone thirty-four-foot shaft dedicated on July 4, 1827, the first substantial monument in the nation to honor George Washington.

Baltimore Washington Monument
Mount Vernon Place Historic District
Mount Vernon Place and Washington Place
Baltimore, Maryland 21201
(301) 396-7939

This slim, handsome 164-foot column topped by a sixteen-foot statue of the first President is considered an architectural masterpiece. Designed by Robert Mills, it was one of the first memorials erected in honor of George Washington. Construction began in 1815, but it was not until 1829 that the figure of Washington, holding his scroll of resignation, was put into place.

George Washington Statue
Washington Circle
Washington, DC 20037

A bronze equestrian statue by sculptor Clark Mills was dedicated in 1860 by President James Buchanan.

Washington Monument
The National Mall
Washington, DC
(202) 619-PARK

The most distinctive landmark in the nation's capital is a 555-foot obelisk designed by Robert Mills. The Washington Monument was dedicated in 1850. Visitors ascend to an observation level near the top of the obelisk by elevator. National Park Service Site. Open to the public.

George Washington Statue
The State House
Columbia, South Carolina 29201
(803) 734-2430

This replica of French sculptor Jean Antoine Houdon's statue of Washington executed for the Virginia State House stands proudly on the front steps of the South Carolina Capitol.

George Washington Statue
Union Square
New York City, New York 10003

Union Square features an equestrian statue of George Washington in bronze, sculpted by Henry Kirke Brown.

George Washington Statue
Manhattan Avenue and 114th Street
New York City, New York 10025

A statue of George Washington standing with the Marquis de Lafayette, as sculpted by Frederick Bartholdi, dominates a New York street corner.

George Washington Statue
Masonic Hall
71 West 23rd Street
New York, New York 10010
(212) 741-1323

A massive statue of a standing Washington dominates the Hollender Room of the recently renovated Masonic Hall in downtown New York. A duplicate statue, from the same casting, is in the George Washington Masonic National Memorial in Alexandria, Virginia. Open to the public.

George Washington Statuary
Virginia State Capitol and Capitol Square
Richmond, Virginia 23219
(804) 786-4344

The rotunda of the Virginia Capitol building features a life-sized statue of George Washington surrounded by busts of the other presidents born in Virginia. The Washington figure, sculpted by Jean Antoine Houdon, is the only statue for which the President posed. Just outside the main entrance of the Capitol building is a park area featuring the noted Crawford equestrian statue of Washington encircled by the figures of Thomas Jefferson, Patrick Henry, John Marshall and other distinguished Virginians. Open to the public.

George Washington Statue
Boston Public Gardens
Boston, Massachusetts 02111

The Arlington Avenue entrance of the Boston Public Gardens is enhanced by a larger-than-life bronze equestrian statue of George Washington, sculpted in 1869 by Thomas Ball.

Washington College
Chestertown, Maryland 21620

President Washington was presented an honorary degree by

68

Washington College in 1794, and was further honored as the college took his name.

Washington and Lee University
Lexington, Virginia 24450

Washington and Lee is a distinguished university housed in white colonnaded buildings within a tree-filled campus of rare beauty. The school was founded in 1749 as Augusta Academy and was renamed Liberty Hall in 1776. In 1796, Liberty Hall was endowed by George Washington and, in honor of that contribution, it took his name. Confederate General Robert E. Lee became president of the school following the Civil War and his name was added to that of the college when he passed away in 1870.

Lancaster Historic District
Lancaster, Virginia 22503
(804) 529-5031

The town of Lancaster boasts of several buildings of historical interest. The Mary Ball Washington Museum and Library, a four-building complex, honors George Washington's mother who was born in Lancaster County. Lancaster House, circa 1798, is a museum building containing Washington family memorabilia and other items pertaining to Lancaster and Colonial life on Virginia's Northern Neck. The Lancaster County Courthouse contains county records complete from 1652. Open to the public.

See also: **Mount Rushmore** (p. 285).

John Adams

Second President
1797–1801

Born October 30, 1735, Braintree (now Quincy), Massachusetts
Died July 4, 1826, Braintree (now Quincy), Massachusetts
Burial Site: United First Parish Church, Quincy, Massachusetts

Adams National Historic Site
1250 Hancock Street
Quincy, Massachusetts 02669
(617) 773-1177

The Adams National Historic Site comprises four separate units relating to John Adams and his son, John Quincy Adams. National Park Service Site. Open to the public.

133 Franklin Street.

The house in which John Adams was born is a modest wooden frame house built in what later generations would refer to as the New England "saltbox" style — a house with sloping roof and multiple fireplaces around a central chimney. It consisted of two upper and two lower rooms, although other rooms were added later. The house dates to around 1670; it is the oldest surviving presidential birthplace.

141 Franklin Street.

Upon his father's death, John Adams inherited a house similar and next door to 133 Franklin Street, that he used as a combination home and law office and where, in 1779, Adams and others framed the Massachusetts State Constitution, the document that became the model for the Constitution of the United States. John Adams' son, John Quincy Adams, was born in an upstairs bedroom of this house.

135 Adams Street

Peacefield, or The Old House, was purchased by John and Abigail Adams in 1787 when he was serving on a diplomatic assignment in Europe. Through the years it has evolved from a rough farmhouse to a gracious mansion, home to generations of the Adams family and filled with exquisite furniture and antiques. Peacefield is located about a mile from the Franklin Street homes.

United First Parish Church.

The family church of the Adamses, and final resting place for the father and son presidents and their wives.

Abigail Adams House
Norton Street
East Weymouth, Massachusetts 02189
(617) 740-4427

Abigail Adams, nee Smith, was destined to be one of the most influential First Ladies in American history. She and John Adams were married in her home on October 25, 1764. The house was moved from its original site on Bridge Street in 1956. Museum. Open to the public.

Pownalborough Courthouse
Route 128
Dresden, Maine 04342
(207) 737-2504

Pownalborough, owned and operated by the Lincoln City Historical Association, is the only pre-Revolutionary courthouse remaining in Maine. John Adams once tried a case here. Museum. Open to the public.

Stafford Springs, Connecticut 06076
(860) 763-2578

In 1771, John Adams traveled to Stafford Springs to bathe in its therapeutic waters. Open to the public.

Conference House
7455 Hylan Boulevard
Staten Island, New York 10307
(718) 984-2086

The Billopp House, built by Royal Navy Captain Christopher Billopp circa 1680, was the location of an abortive Revolutionary War peace conference on September 11, 1776, between British Lord Howe and Americans Benjamin Franklin, Edward Rutledge and John Adams. Known as Conference House, it is the only pre-Revolutionary manor house still surviving in New York City, maintained by the Tottenville, Staten Island, Department of Parks. Museum. Open to the public.

Old Pine Street Presbyterian Church
412 Pine Street
Philadelphia, Pennsylvania 19106
(215) 925-8051

The only Colonial Presbyterian church remaining in Philadelphia, designed by Robert Smith, was the church home for John Adams and other Revolutionary figures. Old Pine sent 75 parishioners to the Revolutionary army.

Quincy Historical Society Museum
Adams Academy Building
8 Adams Street
Quincy, Massachusetts 02669
(617) 773-1144

The Quincy Historical Society maintains a museum featuring artifacts of the Revolutionary period in New England. Open to the public.

Abigail Adams Smith Museum
421 E. 61st Street
New York, New York 10021
(201) 838-6878

Abigail Smith was the daughter of John and Abigail Adams, and they visited her often. The house was originally a 1799 carriage house converted to a country hotel. Museum. Open to the public.

Christopher Gores Country Home
52 Gore Street (SR 20)
Waltham, Massachusetts 02154
(617) 894-2798

Christopher Gore was a Boston attorney, American envoy to Europe, Governor of Massachusetts and a United States Senator. Presidents John Adams and James Monroe were among the distinguished guests entertained by Gore in his twenty-two-room mansion patterned after an English country estate. The home is maintained by the Gore Place Society. Open to the public.

See also: **Gadsbys Tavern** (p. 12); **The Brice House** (p. 21); **The Square House** (p. 40); **Webb-Deane-Stevens Museum** (p. 42); **Oliver Ellsworth Homestead** (p. 55); **Library of Congress** (p. 292).

Thomas Jefferson

Third President
1801–1809

Born April 13, 1743, Shadwell, Virginia
Died July 4, 1826, Monticello, Charlottesville, Virginia
Burial Site: Monticello, Charlottesville, Virginia

Shadwell
US Route 250
3 miles east of Charlottesville, Virginia

     Shadwell, the house in which Thomas Jefferson was born, was destroyed by fire. Archeological excavations of the site have been carried out by the Thomas Jefferson Memorial Foundation since 1941; the latest activity was begun in 1991 in an attempt to understand the Shadwell landscape of Jefferson's time. The work-in-progress is not open to the public although there is a marker indicating the probable site of the birth house.

Tuckahoe Plantation
12601 River Road
Richmond, Virginia 23233
(804) 784-6736

Thomas Jefferson's father was the resident farm manager of Tuckahoe Plantation, and his family lived on the premises from 1745 to 1752 when young Tom was seven to fourteen years of age. He was fortunate to be tutored along with the son of the plantation owner, Thomas Randolph. The original two-boy schoolhouse and the gracious Georgian mansion remain as centerpieces of the still-active plantation. Tuckahoe is owned by Mr. and Mrs. Addison Thompson who graciously open it to visitors by appointment.

Monticello
Box 316
Charlottesville, Virginia 22902
(804) 984-9800

Monticello, located at the top of a mountain that affords a sweeping view of the rolling Virginia Piedmont and Blue Ridge, is Jefferson's architectural masterpiece. Monticello also is considered by many to be America's most beautiful home, a living testimony to Jefferson's ingenuity and range of interests. Monticello was Jefferson's life-long passion and he constantly built, rebuilt and improved the house and grounds. Over a twenty-year period the house was enlarged from eight rooms to twenty-one, and became more-or-less finished in 1809 when Jefferson retired from the presidency. Monticello is owned and operated by the Thomas Jefferson Memorial Foundation, Inc. Open to the public.

The Forest
near Williamsburg, Virginia

Thomas Jefferson married Martha Skelton at her home, The Forest, on January 1, 1772. The house has been demolished.

Poplar Forest
Box 419
Forest, Virginia 24551-0419
(804) 525-1806

Poplar Forest, with an unusual and comfortable octagonal shape, was built by Jefferson in 1806 as a retreat and refuge from visitors to Monticello. It is currently an architectural work-in-progress undertaken by the Corporation for Jefferson's Poplar Forest. Open to the public.

Jacob Graff, Jr. House aka **Declaration House**
Seventh and Market
Philadelphia, Pennsylvania 19106
(215) 597-8974

Jacob Graff, Jr., a builder, rented two second-floor rooms to Thomas Jefferson, who, working alone, prepared the first draft of the Declaration of Independence. The Graff House, part of Independence National Historical Park, is a reconstruction with a first-floor display delineating the history of the Declaration and Jefferson's contribution. The upstairs parlor where he wrote has been conscientiously recreated with quill pens and candlesticks lying on a green baize-topped table. It is not hard for modern visitors to visualize the young man working feverishly into the night to complete this most important document. Open to the public.

Governors Mansion
Capitol Square
Richmond, Virginia 22066
(804) 358-5511

Four presidents have lived in the Virginia Governors Mansion, three as governor — Thomas Jefferson, James Monroe and John Tyler — while William Henry Harrison resided in the house when his father was governor. The mansion has been the official residence of Virginia's governor since 1799, and has been refurbished many times. It was heavily damaged by fire in 1926, so that little of the original structure remains. Closed to the public.

Weston Manor Plantation
Box 851
Hopewell, Virginia 23860
(804) 458-4682

Weston is proudly described as *a classic example of Virginia Georgian architecture . . . . An elegant, formal five-bay dwelling with hipped roof — the very essence of a Tidewater plantation manor.* Weston's thirteen rooms feature carved paneling and a twenty-eight-foot entrance hall. The Eppes family owned the estate property as early as 1668, and a portrait of an 18th-century resident, John Wayles Eppes, hangs in the dining room. John Wayles Eppes' first wife, Maria, was the daughter of Thomas Jefferson, and it is likely, though unproved, that Jefferson visited Weston, a hint of this being that the dumbwaiter in the dining room is similar to the one at Monticello. Weston is owned by the Historic Hopewell Foundation. Open to the public.

Eppington
Appamattox River and Winterpock Creek
Petersburg, Virginia

Francis Eppes VI, scion of one of the oldest families in the Virginia Colony, began construction of Eppington shortly before the Revolutionary War. It began as a simple two-story box, but was improved and added to through the years until it became an "evocative example of a big frame Virginia gentry house." Thomas Jefferson married Eppes' cousin/sister-in-law, Martha. Eppes and Jefferson became friends and shared many common interests, especially horticulture. The families visited each other frequently. Eppington was recently acquired by Chesterfield County which is planning to refurbish the house and eventually open it to visitation. Closed to the public.

Jefferson Rock
Harpers Ferry National Historic Park
Harpers Ferry, West Virginia 25425
(304) 725-3444

Legend has it that Thomas Jefferson sat at this place, observing in wonder the beautiful river valley, and wrote in his book *Notes on the State of Virginia* that it was *one of the most stupendous scenes in nature!* Open to the public.

Peaks of Otter
Milepost 86, Blue Ridge Parkway
Bedford, Virginia 24523
(800) 933-9535

The Peaks of Otter are twin mountain peaks with similar elevations located in the Blue Ridge Mountains. The view at sunrise is spectacular, and Thomas Jefferson, when residing at nearby Poplar Forest, is reported to have visited frequently to enjoy the symmetry and view. Open to the public.

The Homestead
Hot Springs, Virginia 24445
(540) 839-5500, (800) 468-7747

One of America's premier hotels is situated on the site of famous therapeutic springs visited by Thomas Jefferson. The hotel was also the site for the honeymoon of Woodrow Wilson and Edith Galt. Open to the public.

Woodbourne
Bedford County, Virginia

Woodbourne was built on land purchased from Thomas Jefferson, although he never lived there The house still stands. Closed to the public.

Federal Hill
Forest Vicinity
Campbell County, Virginia

Federal Hill was the home of Jefferson's close friend, James Steptoe. Jefferson's architectural influence may have persuaded Steptoe to employ a Palladian-derived plan. Closed to the public.

Albemarle County Courthouse
Court Square
Charlottesville, Virginia 22902

The north wing of the courthouse was utilized in the 1820s as a "common temple" shared by Episcopalians, Methodists, Baptists and Presbyterians — each having the temple one Sunday a month, with all who so wished attending each Sunday. Thomas Jefferson, James Madison and James Monroe worshipped at Albemarle. Open to the public.

Thomas Jefferson, Architect

In addition to Monticello and Poplar Forest, Jefferson was involved with, or influenced, the design of many other public and private buildings in Virginia.

University of Virginia
Box 9018
Charlottesville, Virginia 22906-9018
(804) 924-7969

The University of Virginia was founded by Thomas Jefferson who designed not only the early buildings but the curriculum as well. The campus is considered one of the most beautiful in the country. The Rotunda stands as the signature landmark of the University — a half-scale interpretation of the Pantheon in Rome. James Madison was a co-founder of the University and acted as its second rector. James Monroe served on the state-appointed board that began planning the University and he attended the laying of the cornerstone on October 6, 1817, along with Madison and Jefferson. Open to the public.

Rosewell Ruins
Gloucester, Virginia 23061

Rosewell was once the largest mansion in Virginia, one of the finest in the colonies. The country seat of the Page family, it was begun in 1720 by Mann Page, whose grandson was a close friend of Thomas Jefferson. Jefferson visited often and architectural historians believe that much of Jefferson's architectural inspiration was the result of his study of Rosewell. The house burned in 1916 with only a few walls surviving. The ruins are maintained as a site of historic interest by the Rosewell Foundation Inc. Open to the public.

Brandon Plantation
Spring Grove, Virginia 23881
(757) 866-8416

A magnificent James River estate cultivated since 1614, Brandon may be the longest continuous farming enterprise in the United States. The main house on the property was built in 1765 by Nathaniel Harrison for his son, Benjamin. Family tradition holds that Thomas Jefferson designed the house as a favor for his friend, Benjamin, but that authorship cannot be documented. Brandon remained in the Harrison family until 1926. The grounds are open to the public; the house by appointment.

Barboursville Ruins
Routes 33 and 20
Orange City, Virginia 22960
(540) 832-3824

Barboursville Mansion, designed by Jefferson, was the home of his close friend, James Barbour. The house burned to the ground at Christmas, 1884, but the property has been preserved as an historical ruin on the grounds of the Barboursville Vineyards. Open to the public.

The Residence
Madison County, Virginia 22727

A mansion designed by Thomas Jefferson for the brother of James Madison is now part of Woodberry Forest School. Closed to the public.

Edgemont
South of Charlottesville, Virginia on US Route 29
Albemarle County, Virginia

Edgemont, a frame house, shows some Jefferson influences, although direct attribution to him is not confirmed. Closed to the public.

Farmington
Off US Route 250W
Charlottesville, Virginia 22902

Currently the clubhouse of the Farmington Country Club, the building is visible from the road. Closed to the public.

Botetourt County Courthouse
Fincastle Historic District
PO Box 219
Fincastle, Virginia 24090
(540) 473-8274

Thomas Jefferson designed the Botetourt County courthouse early in the 19th century. The building was replaced in the middle 1800s generally following Jefferson's original plans, but was gutted by fire in 1970. Plans to rebuild the interior within the remaining shell were deemed un-safe. The present building is a copy of its predecessor. Open to the public.

Carr-Brooks House
Ruckersville, Virginia 22968

Thomas Jefferson's ward and nephew, Peter Carr, was schooled in Charlottesville from 1795 to 1815, and lived in a house that shows Jefferson's influence in the design, although there is no confirmation of his direct involvement. Closed to the public.

Buckingham Courthouse Historic District
Buckingham , Virginia 23921
(804) 969-4755

The Buckingham building committee asked Thomas Jefferson to draw plans for a new courthouse, and he submitted a design for a temple-form structure with a Roman Doric portico. The building burned in 1869, but was rebuilt with only minor modifications to Jefferson's original concept. Open to the public.

Mount Athos
Kelly
Campbell County, Virginia

Mount Athos, now a stone ruin atop a steep ridge overlooking the James River, was once the plantation home of William J. Lewis. Its elevated site, one-story plan and classical portico have led to speculation that its design was influenced by Lewis' good friend, Thomas Jefferson. Closed to the public.

Belle Grove
Route 11, Box 137
Middletown, Virginia 22645
(540) 869-2028

The plantation home of the Hite family was built in 1794 using architectural advice tendered by brother-in-law James Madison who conscripted his friend, Thomas Jefferson, for assistance. The historic homestead is still used to display regional arts and crafts. Belle Grove is owned and operated by the National Trust for Historic Preservation. Open to the public.

Corner of Celebrities
100 Capital Avenue
Frankfort, Kentucky 40601
(502) 875-8687

The neighborhood around Capital Avenue in Frankfort, Kentucky, spawned two Supreme Court Justices, two Cabinet Officers, nine United State Senators, one Governor, four Congressmen and five Ambassadors. The area was visited by Thomas Jefferson, James Madison, James Monroe, Andrew Jackson and Theodore Roosevelt.

Memorials to Thomas Jefferson

Jefferson National Expansion Memorial
11 North 4th Street
Saint Louis, Missouri 63102
(314) 425-4465

A two-hundred-acre park on the Mississippi waterfront memorializes Jefferson and others who directed America's westward expansion. The park is dominated by The Gateway Arch, Eero Saarinen's graceful 630-foot-high masterpiece. National Park Service Site. Open to the public.

Jefferson Memorial
South Bank of the Tidal Basin
The National Mall
Washington, DC
(202) 619-PARK

The Jefferson Memorial is a circular, colonnaded structure in the Classic style that was introduced into this country by Jefferson himself. The interior walls contain inscribed excerpts from his speeches and writings, all encircling Rudolph Evans' heroic statue of the great statesman. National Park Service Site. Open to the public.

Thomas Jefferson Statue
Jefferson County Courthouse
Jefferson Street
Louisville, Kentucky 40202
(502) 625-5761

The courthouse is complemented by a rendering of the great statesman and thinker by Moses Ezekial.

Thomas Jefferson Statue
College of William and Mary
Williamsburg, Virginia 23187

In 1992, a life-size bronze statue of Thomas Jefferson was placed on the lawn between Washington Hall and Tercentary Hall, dedicated to William and Mary's most famous alumnus. The statue was a gift from the University of Virginia, signifying the link between the two institutions that played such important roles in Jefferson's life.

Thomas Jefferson Religious Freedom Monument
Washington Avenue
Fredericksburg, Virginia 22401

Thomas Jefferson wrote his own epitaph listing his proudest accomplishments, one of which was "Author of the Statute of Virginia of Religious Freedom" which he prepared while visiting Fredericksburg. A dignified granite memorial commemorates that distinguished act.

See also: **Gadsbys Tavern** (p. 12); **Gunston Hall** (p. 18); **Rodgers Tavern** (p. 18); **Upper Valley Regional Park** (p. 18); **Natural Bridge Village** (p. 19); **Belle Air** (p. 20); **Wilton** (p. 21); **Harper House** (p. 63); **Toliver House Restaurant** (p. 63); **Saint Johns Church** (p. 64); **Virginia State Capitol** (p. 68); **Belle Grove** (p. 81); **Mount Rushmore** (p. 285); **Forest Lawn Memorial Park** (p. 288); **Library of Congress** (p. 292).

James Madison

Fourth President
1809–1817

Born March 16, 1751, Port Conway, Virginia
Died June 28, 1836, Montpelier, Virginia
Burial Site: Montpelier, Virginia

Conway House
4 miles north of Port Royal, Virginia, on US Route 301
Port Conway, Virginia

James Madison was born in a small house on the estate of his maternal grandmother. In the 1930s, the house eroded and fell into the Rappahannock River in the area now spanned by the James Madison Memorial Bridge. There is a birth site marker on the south side of the river.

Montpelier
Box 67
Montpelier Station, Virginia 22957
(540) 672-2728

James Madison's magnificent Georgian mansion is situated four miles south of Orange, Virginia, high on a hill affording a sweeping view of the Blue Ridge Mountains. The exterior of the house is beautiful and impressive, while the interior is presently undergoing extensive investigation and renovation. The house has undergone substantial additions and other changes since the Madison occupancy. The woods and gardens, however, remain much as they were two centuries ago. Montpelier is owned and operated as a house museum by the National Trust for Historic Preservation. Open to the public.

The James Madison Museum
129 Caroline Street
Orange, Virginia 22960
(540) 672-1776

A small but very complete museum with artifacts and displays pertinent to Madison's public career and personal life is a useful adjunct to a visit to nearby Montpelier. Open to the public.

Harewood
Route 51
Charles Town, West Virginia 25414

James Madison and Dolley Payne Todd were married in the home of her sister on September 15, 1794. Closed to the public.

Octagon House
1799 New York Avenue, NW
Washington, DC 20006
(202) 638-3105

An unusual six-sided (not eight-sided at all) house was the French Embassy, lent to President Madison for use as the Executive Mansion in 1814 after the President's House had been torched by British invaders during the War of 1812. Octagon House is owned by the American Institute of Architects which has done a marvelous job of reconstruction and refurbishing, now operating it as a house museum. Open to the public.

Nassau Hall
Princeton University
Princeton, New Jersey 08542

James Madison roomed at Nassau Hall when attending Princeton, known at the time as The College of New Jersey. Nassau Hall was also used by the Continental Congress when meeting in 1783. It remains in use by the University. Closed to the public.

Stride-Madison Residence
429 Spruce Street
Philadelphia, Pennsylvania 19106

A gable-roofed house was utilized by James and Dolley Madison during congressional sessions from 1794 to 1797. The present house is a restoration. Closed to the public.

Salona
1214 Buchanan Street
McLean, Virginia 22101

President Madison fled Washington on the afternoon of August 24, 1814, as British invaders approached the capitol during the War of 1812. He remained overnight in a Federal-style house in McLean before proceeding into Maryland the next day. Closed to the public.

Caleb Bentley House
Georgia Avenue and Brookeville Road
Brookeville, Maryland 20833

President Madison's hideout after escaping the British. Closed to the public.

Historic Sully
3601 Sully Road
Chantilly, Virginia 22003
(703) 437-1794

Sully is a lovely nine-room frame and clapboard plantation home built in 1794 by Congressman Richard Bland Lee, brother of "Light Horse Harry" Lee and friend and confidante of many early patriots and political leaders, including James Madison. Lee and his wife Elizabeth furnished Sully with fine items from Philadelphia. The reconstructed Sully, featuring most of its original interior woodwork, is owned and operated by the Fairfax County Park Authority. Open to the public.

Saint Thomas Episcopal Church
119 Caroline Street
Orange, Virginia 22960
(540) 672-3761

James Madison's parish church, located near Montpelier, was constructed shortly before his death. It has not been proven that he attended

Saint Thomas, although wife Dolley is recorded as being a contributor to the building fund. It is likely, however, that he attended services at Saint Thomas previous building, the "Brick" or "Middle" Church, since destroyed, which was located at Meadowfarm on the Taylor property outside of the town of Orange. Madison may also have attended the Blue Run Baptist Church located on Route 20 between Somerset and Barboursville.

See also: **Gadsbys Tavern** (p. 12); **Gunston Hall** (p. 18); **Upper Valley Regional Park** (p. 18); **Berkeley Springs** (p. 21); **Toliver House Restaurant** (p. 63); **Albemarle County Courthouse** (p. 78); **University of Virginia** (p. 78); **Belle Grove** (p. 81); **Corner of Celebrities** (p. 81); **Library of Congress** (p. 292).

James Monroe

Fifth President
1817–1825

Born April 28, 1758, Monroe Hall, Colonial Beach, Virginia
Died July 4, 1831, New York, New York
Burial Site: Hollywood Cemetery, Richmond, Virginia

James Monroe Family Home Site
Monroe Hall
Virginia SR 209
near Colonial Beach, Virginia 22443

A 70-acre county park encompasses the site of the birthplace of James Monroe — a 1½-story frame house that was dismantled before 1850. The outline of the house site is marked. Open to the public.

Ash Lawn-Highland
Route 6, Box 37
Charlottesville, Virginia 22909-8722
(804) 294-9539

James Monroe moved to the Charlottesville area at the behest of

Thomas Jefferson, who dreamed of instituting a colony of intellectuals and other leaders. Monroe built a modest farmhouse with Jefferson's assistance, and the property remains a working plantation. The house is filled with Monroe memorabilia and the exterior is graced with a formal boxwood garden and strolling peacocks. Ash Lawn-Highland is owned and operated by The College of William and Mary. Open to the public.

Kortright House
Lower Broadway
New York, New York

James Monroe and Elizabeth Kortright were married in her family's home on March 2, 1786. The location is speculative as the house has long since been demolished.

The Jones House
Monroe Home
301 Caroline Street
Fredericksburg, Virginia 22401

James Monroe's uncle, Judge Joseph Jones, invited the newlywed Monroes to live in a house he owned, which they did from 1786 to 1790. Closed to the public.

James Monroe Museum
908 Charles Street
Fredericksburg, Virginia 22401
(540) 654-1043

The James Monroe Museum stands on property that Monroe owned from 1786 to 1792. This tract is identified in town records as "Town Lot #127." The museum contains many artifacts and displays pertinent to Monroe's life and career and is the largest repository of Monroe papers, souvenirs, artifacts, furniture and clothing in the United States. Open to the public.

Saint Georges Episcopal Church
Princess Anne and George Streets
Fredericksburg, Virginia 22401
(540) 373-4133

James Monroe served as a vestryman at Saint Georges when residing and working in Fredericksburg. The congregation was formed in 1732 — the present building dating from 1849 when it was built on the site of the original church.

Lafayette House
5 Hale Street
Dover, New Hampshire 03820
(603) 742-3155

The three-story Federal-style Lafayette House, circa 1750, was built by William Hale who entertained the Marquis de Lafayette and President James Monroe at a reception in 1825. The building is now the parish hall of Saint Thomas Episcopal Church. Open to the public.

Monroe Hall
Box 9018
University of Virginia
Charlottesville, Virginia 22906-9018

James Monroe owned land in this area around 1789. He resided and maintained a law office in a building that is still part of the University. Open by appointment.

Monroe-Adams-Abbe House
2017 I Street, NW
Washington, DC 20001
(202) 331-7282

The Monroe-Adams-Abbe House on I Street was James Monroe's home during part of his presidency when waiting for the completion of repairs to the President's House. Also known as the Timothy Caldwell House, it is presently the headquarters of the Arts Club of Washington. Open by appointment.

Moses Myers House
323 Freemason Street
Norfolk, Virginia 23510
(804) 622-1211

The pre-Revolutionary Myers House contains collections of silver and dishes used by President Monroe on a visit. Open to the public.

Oak Hill
Aldie, Virginia 22001

Oak Hill, designed by James Hoban, architect of the White House, was James Monroe's retirement estate. A splendid forest grove contains oak trees planted by Monroe to represent every state of the Union. Severe financial problems in retirement bedeviled Monroe who was forced to sell Oak Hill. Privately owned. Closed to the public.

Liberty Hall
218 Wilkinson Street
Frankfort, Kentucky 40601
(502) 227-2560

Kentucky lawyer and United States Senator John Brown entertained presidents James Monroe, Andrew Jackson and John Tyler at various times in his home, named for his grammar school in Virginia . The L-shaped Georgian features a Palladian window and period furniture. Liberty Hall is operated by the Colonial Dames of America as a house museum. Open to the public.

Locust Grove
561 Blankenbaker Lane
Louisville, Kentucky 40207
(502) 897-9845

Locust Grove was the retirement home of patriot and explorer George Rogers Clark who entertained many prominent people including James Monroe, Andrew Jackson and Zachary Taylor. The house museum is operated by the Historic Homes Foundation. Open to the public.

The Wren Building
College of William and Mary
Williamsburg, Virginia 23185

The Wren Building is the dormitory in which James Monroe lived when a student at William and Mary. Open to the public.

James Monroe's Military Career

James Monroe was a young officer in the 3rd Virginia Regiment, Virginia Militia, during the Revolutionary War in which he served with great distinction.

Washington Crossing State Park (p. 29)

James Monroe was an advance scout preceding Washington's crossing of the Delaware River on Christmas Day, 1776. Monroe was badly wounded at the subsequent Battle of Trenton.

Valley Forge National Military Park (p. 37)

Major James Monroe served at Valley Forge as an aide to Lord Stirling during the Continental Army's bitter winter encampment, 1777–1778.

See also: **Gunston Hall** (p. 18); **Belle Air** (p. 20); **Old Barracks Museum** (p. 29); **Washington Crossing Historic Park** (p. 29); **Morristown National Historical Park** (p. 30); **The Hermitage** (p. 39); **Toliver House Restaurant** (p. 63); **Saint Johns Church** (p. 64); **Christopher Gores Country Home** (p. 73); **Virginia Governors Mansion** (p. 76); **Albemarle County Courthouse** (p. 78); **University of Virginia** (p. 78); **Corner of Celebrities** (p. 81).

John Quincy Adams

Sixth President
1825–1829

Born July 11, 1767, Braintree (Now Quincy), Massachusetts
Died February 23, 1848, Washington, DC
Burial Site: United First Parish Church, Quincy, Massachusetts

Adams National Historic Site
1250 Hancock Street
Quincy, Massachusetts 02269
(617) 773-1290

  The Adams National Historic Site is the only site dedicated to two presidents, the only father-and-son – John Adams and John Quincy Adams – to become the nation's chief executive. Historians often remark on the coincidence of John Adams and Thomas Jefferson dying on July 4, 1826, the fiftieth anniversary of the signing of the Declaration of Independence. Yet one may think that John Adams willed his life to linger until he could witness his son's inauguration as President. The birthplace and homes of the Adams National Historic Site are described in the section of this book devoted to John Adams (pp. 70–73).

Abigail Adams Cairn
Franklin Street at Viden Road
Boston, Massachusetts 02110

A marker identifies the place where Abigail Adams and her young son, John Quincy Adams, witnessed the Battle of Bunker Hill.

Church of All-Hallows by the Towers
London, England

John Quincy Adams and Louisa Johnson were married on July 26, 1797, while he was on a diplomatic mission to Europe. The church was destroyed in World War II.

Chesapeake and Ohio Canal National Historic Park
Visitor Center
11710 MacArthur Boulevard
Potomac, Maryland 20854
(301) 299-3613
    and
Superintendent
Box 4
Sharpsburg, Maryland 21782
(301) 739-4200

On July 4, 1828, President John Quincy Adams turned the first spadeful of earth near Georgetown to inaugurate construction of a canal up the Potomac Valley to Cumberland, Maryland. The present park follows the Maryland shore of the 184-mile canal which operated from 1850 to 1924. The canal features seventy-four lift locks, eleven aqueducts and a number of historic lock houses. About fifteen miles northwest of Washington, the Great Falls make a thundering descent in a series of picturesque falls and rapids. Open to the public.

William H. Seward House
33 South Street
Auburn, New York 13608
(315) 252-1283

William H. Seward was Secretary of State in the cabinets of presidents Lincoln and Andrew Johnson. His home contains original family furnishings, clothing, antique toys and mementos of Seward's career, the highlight of which was the purchase of Alaska ("Seward's Folly"). Visitors to Seward's home included General Ulysses S. Grant and presidents John Quincy Adams and Martin Van Buren. Open to the public.

All Souls Church
16th and Harvard Streets, NW
Washington, DC 20009
(202) 332-5266

All Souls Church was the Washington church home for presidents John Quincy Adams, Millard Fillmore and William Howard Taft.

See also: **Great Falls Park** (p. 20); **John Brown House** (p. 56); **Adams National Historic Site** (p. 70).

Andrew Jackson

Seventh President
1829–1837

Born March 15, 1767, The Waxhaws, South Carolina
Died June 8, 1845, The Hermitage, Hermitage, Tennessee
Burial Site: The Hermitage, Hermitage, Tennessee

Andrew Jacksons Birthplace
The Waxhaws
14 miles south of Rock Hill on South Carolina State Route 5

There is controversy about the exact place where Andrew Jackson was born, except that it was somewhere near the border between North and South Carolina. South Carolina believes it was on the farm of Jackson's uncle, James Crawford, in the Waxhaws area. The house has been lost, but there is a marker.

Andrew Jacksons Birthplace
McKamie Farmhouse
Union County, North Carolina

The other candidate site for Andrew Jackson's birthplace,

considered by the State of North Carolina to be the true birth site, is only a few miles away from The Waxhaws at the farm home location of Jackson's uncle. There is a marker.

Andrew Jackson State Park
Route 1
Lancaster, South Carolina 29720
(803) 285-3344

A 360-acre park located near The Waxhaws features a museum emphasizing life in the Carolina back-country with an accent on Andrew Jackson's life. Open to the public.

The Hermitage
4580 Rachels Lane
Hermitage, Tennessee 37076-1331
(615) 889-2941

Andrew Jackson's magnificent mansion, situated in a pine forest near Nashville, is one of America's treasures. The property contains plantation buildings, "Rachel's Garden" and Tulip Grove, a large Greek Revival mansion built for Mrs. Jackson's nephew, who served as the President's secretary. The Hermitage, which is owned and operated by the Ladies' Hermitage Association, sponsors self-guided tours of The Hermitage property. Open to the public.

The Old Hermitage Church
At The Hermitage

Many times Andrew Jackson said that he was brought up as a Presbyterian, the church of his mother, although he did not join until after his wife's death, fulfilling a deathbed promise to her. The President, however, had donated three acres of the Hermitage property to the neighboring community as the site for a new church in 1823 and even headed the building fund when a second structure was erected in 1838. The tiny Presbyterian church is part of The Hermitage self-guided walking tour.

Springfield Plantation
Natchez Trace Parkway, Route 1
Fayette, Mississippi 39069
(601) 786-3802

The first mansion built in Mississippi, circa 1786, was believed to be the location of Andrew Jackson's marriage to Rachel Robards, possibly in August of 1791. Due to embarrassing questions as to the validity of the marriage, the Jacksons remarried in Nashville, Tennessee, in January, 1794, although there is no conclusive information as to where that ceremony took place. The Springfield Plantation house has been restored. Open to the public.

Francis McNairy House
1130 Summit Avenue
Greensboro, North Carolina 27405
(910) 373-2043

A log house with a separate frame kitchen served as Andrew Jackson's residence for a short time when he was a young lawyer practicing in Greensboro. The house has been restored to the period 1762–1862 and is maintained by the Greensboro Historical Society. Open to the public.

Cragfront
Route 1, Box 73
Castalian Springs, Tennessee 37031
(615) 452-7070

Completed in 1802 by owner General James Winchester, Cragfront was the finest mansion on the Tennessee frontier, standing tall on a rocky bluff — a two-story rectangular structure with twelve fully-furnished rooms. Noted guests included Andrew Jackson and Sam Houston. Open to the public.

Wynnewood
SR 25
Castalian Springs, Tennessee 37031
(615) 452-5463

Built in 1828, Wynnewood served as a stagecoach inn and mineral springs resort. In the 1840s, the facility included a racecourse which attracted Andrew Jackson, who raced his horses at the track frequently. The 142-foot-long log structure has been restored and furnished in period. Open to the public.

Rowan House Hotel
116 S. Jackson Street
Salisbury, North Carolina 28145-4044
(704) 633-5946

The present-day Rowan House Hotel was a boarding house where Andrew Jackson stayed when studying law in Salisbury from 1784 to 1787. Open to the public.

Dickson-Williams Mansion
115 Academy Street
Greeneville, Tennessee 37743
(423) 636-4111

One of the prime examples of Federal architecture anywhere, the Dickson-Williams Mansion was built by Greeneville's postmaster in 1821. Two craftsmen brought from Ireland designed it after a lovely Irish country seat, with double chimneys, massive brick walls and large rooms with high ceilings. The mansion was recently acquired by the Dickson-Williams Historical Association which has lovingly restored it to its original grandeur as "The Showplace of East Tennessee" when it hosted such personages as Presidents Andrew Jackson and James K. Polk. Open by appointment.

Shepards Inn
136 East Main Street
Dandridge, Tennessee 37725

Shepards Inn was a way station hostelry that hosted Andrew Jackson, James K. Polk and Andrew Johnson on their travels between Washington and their homes in Tennessee. Shepards Inn is now a private residence. Closed to the public.

Carnton Mansion
Franklin, Tennessee 37064
(615) 794-0903

Andrew Jackson and James K. Polk were both entertained at Carnton, one of the most elegant estates in Tennessee. During the Civil War, wounded and dying confederate troops were brought to the mansion from the Battle of Franklin. Carnton is the site of an important Confederate cemetery. Open to the public.

Chester Inn
Jonesborough, Tennessee 37659
(423) 753-5961

Jonesborough, the oldest town in Tennessee, was a prosperous transportation center in stagecoach days. The modern Jonesborough Historic District consists of 50 Victorian, Greek Revival and Federal-style buildings which have been restored, refurbished or replicated. Andrew Jackson, James K. Polk and Andrew Johnson were among the guests of the Chester Inn, currently the headquarters building for the National Storytelling Association. Open to the public.

Christopher Taylor House
117 Boone Street
Jonesborough, Tennessee 37659
(423) 753-5961

Andrew Jackson boarded in a two-story log house when he practiced law in Jonesborough from April to September, 1788. The house has been moved to a downtown location — restored and utilized as a Visitor Center for the Jonesborough Historic District. Open to the public.

Rocky Mount
200 Hyder Hill Road
Piney Flats, Tennessee 37686
(423) 538-7396

Rocky Mount, built by William Cobb in 1770, has been reconstructed by the State of Tennessee to appear as it was in 1791 when it served as the territorial capitol. Andrew Jackson visited the building often. First-person interpretation of living history is offered daily. Open to the public.

Travellers Rest
636 Farrell Parkway
Nashville, Tennessee 37219
(615) 832-2962

Travellers Rest, a home owned by John Overton, Andrew Jackson's campaign manager, was the scene of many social and political gatherings involving Jackson. Open to the public.

The Tavern
222 East Main Street
Abingdon, Virginia 24210

The Tavern, built about 1779, was a well-known "ordinary" serving travelers on the Great Valley Road between Philadelphia and the southern end of the Appalachian Mountains. Guests at the Tavern included luminaries such as Louis Philippe, King of France, and President Andrew Jackson. The Tavern was restored in 1984 as a building of historic significance and currently serves the Abingdon area as a dining spot of culinary excellence in a Colonial atmosphere of quiet charm.

Treber Inn
Ohio SR 41
NE of West Union, Ohio

Treber Inn was an early log house, built about 1798 along Zanes Trace, Ohio's first road. It was operated as an inn by John Treber and his son until 1850. One notable guest was Andrew Jackson. Closed to the public.

Netherland Inn
2144 Netherland Inn Road
Kingsport, Tennessee
(423) 247-3211

Guests at the Netherland Inn included Andrew Jackson, James K. Polk and Andrew Johnson. It is now a gem of a restoration, filled with authentic period furniture. Open to the public.

Hale Springs Inn
Rogersville, Tennessee 37857
(423) 272-5171

Tennessee's oldest continuously operating inn, dating from 1824, hosted Andrew Jackson, James K. Polk and Andrew Johnson. It has been restored to its former condition. Open to the public.

The Pillars
Washington Street
Bolivar, Tennessee 38008
(615) 658-3600

The oldest building in Bolivar was home to John Houston Bills, a businessman who purchased it in 1823. Andrew Jackson, Sam Houston, James K. Polk and Jefferson Davis were all entertained in the Federal-style house which has significant Greek Revival additions. Open to the public.

Old Talbott Tavern
107 Stephen Foster Avenue
Bardstown, Kentucky 40004
(502) 348-3494

Among the distinguished guests at the Old Talbott Inn were Andrew Jackson, William Henry Harrison and Abraham Lincoln. Open to the public.

In 1802, by now a prominent political and judicial figure, Andrew Jackson was elected a major general in the Tennessee militia. During the War of 1812, he led his militia to victory over the Creek Indians at Horseshoe Bend which led to a commission as a major general in the Regular Army.

Fort Strother Site
Ohatchee, Alabama 36271

There are no visible remains of the most important of several forts built by General Jackson during action against the Creek Indians. The Daughters of the American Revolution erected a small monument in 1913 to mark the location. The site is privately owned. Closed to the public.

Battle of Talledega and Fort Lashley
Talledega, Alabama 35160

General Jackson constructed Fort Lashley following his victory over the Indians on November 19, 1813. There are no visible remains. There is a marker.

Horseshoe Bend National Military Park
Route 1, Box 103
Daviston, Alabama 36256
(205) 234-7111

On March 27, 1814, at a horseshoe bend of the Tallapoosa River, General Jackson's forces defeated the Creek Indians at Horseshoe Bend and broke the power of the Upper Creek Indian Confederacy, thus opening up part of Georgia and Alabama for expansion. An earlier battle at the same site on January 21, 1814, had been inconclusive. National Park Service Site. Open to the public.

Fort Toulouse/Jackson Park National Historic Landmark
3 miles west of US Route 231
Wetumpka, Alabama 36092
(205) 567-3002

A lovely wildlife sanctuary features an active archaeological dig searching for information about Forts Toulouse and Jackson, part of the defense system built by Andrew Jackson following his victory over the Creek Indians. Open to the public.

Popes Tavern
203 Hermitage Drive
Florence, Alabama 36530
(520) 760-6439

Florence's oldest surviving structure was built as a tavern, then served as a field hospital during the Civil War. Andrew Jackson stopped at the tavern in 1814. Museum. Open to the public.

Fort San Carlos de Barrancas
US Naval Air Station Property
Pensacola, Florida 32508
(800) 874-1234

This site features the remains of fortifications built by the Spaniards dating from 1787. The fort was important as one of the northernmost outposts of New Spain until captured by Andrew Jackson on November 6, 1814. Open to the public.

Old Natchez Trace Parkway
Visitor Center
Milepost 266
Tupelo, Mississippi 38801
(601) 842-1572

The Parkway, open from Natchez, Mississippi, to Leipers Fork, Tennessee, fifteen miles south of Nashville, was once a rough trail connecting the Choctaw and Natchez Indian tribes and later a commercial route between Nashville and Natchez. The road was used by General Jackson in 1815 to reach New Orleans. The National Park Service is developing the parkway to commemorate the old road. Open to the public.

The Old Absinthe House Restaurant
Bienville and Bourbon Street
New Orleans, Louisiana 70130
(504) 523-3181

History (or mythology, perhaps) relates that the Old Absinthe House is where General Andrew Jackson and the pirate Jean Lafitte met to plan the defense of New Orleans in 1815. It is known that a once-secret room on the second floor was used by Lafitte to store contraband and that the barroom reached its pinnacle of fame in 1870 with the invention of the Absinthe Frappe. The Absinthe House, dating to 1798–1806, remains one of New Orleans' most popular restaurants and tourist attractions. Open to the public.

Chalmette National Historic Park
419 Decatur Street
Chalmette, Louisiana 70043
(504) 589-4428

Chalmette was the site of the Battle of New Orleans in 1815, the final struggle of the War of 1812. The American victory was overwhelming and the leader, General Andrew Jackson, became an instant national hero. National Park Service Site. Open to the public.

Jackson Square National Historic Landmark
New Orleans, Louisiana

The City of New Orleans greeted Andrew Jackson in a central square following the Battle of New Orleans, and the American flag was raised in victory. A statue of Andrew Jackson executed by Clark Mills dominates the square.

Jackson House
619 Saint Peter Street
New Orleans, Louisiana 70116
(504) 568-6968

A house in the French Quarter was General Jackson's residence following the Battle of New Orleans. It is now utilized as office space for the Louisiana State Museum. Closed to the public.

The Cottage
US Route 61
Saint Francisville, Louisiana 70775
(504) 635-3674

Following the Battle of New Orleans and the reception in the city, Andrew Jackson stayed for a short while in a "raised cottage, " built in 1795. The house and fifteen plantation buildings are extant, featuring furnishings dating from 1795–1815. The Cottage is owned and operated by Mr. and Mrs. J. E. Brown as a hotel. Open to the public.

San Marcos de Apalachee State Museum
Saint Marks, Florida 32305
(904) 925-6216

General Andrew Jackson seized a fort from Spain on this site in 1818, an action in which he exceeded instructions, but it did lead to diplomatic negotiations that resulted in America's acquisition of Florida by treaty in 1821. Open to the public.

Plaza Ferdinand VII
Pensacola, Florida 32501
(800) 875-1234

West Florida was formally transferred to the United States on this site in 1821, and Andrew Jackson served as the American government's official observer and first Territorial Governor. There is a marker.

Memorials to Andrew Jackson

Fort Jackson Museum
Jackson Boulevard
Columbia, South Carolina 29201
(803) 751-7511

Fort Jackson Museum traces the history of the modern army and displays memorabilia from the career of General Jackson, although he never visited Columbia. Open to the public.

Presidential Memorial
Capitol Square
Raleigh, North Carolina 27603

North Carolina is proud to claim Andrew Jackson as one of its three native-born Presidents. He is commemorated, along with James K. Polk and Andrew Johnson, with a monument on the grounds of the State Capitol building.

Andrew Jackson Statue
Lafayette Square
Washington, DC 20005

The most famous equestrian statue of Andrew Jackson is located in Lafayette Square facing the White House across Pennsylvania Avenue in Washington, DC. The statue was sculpted by Clark Mills in 1853.

Andrew Jackson Statue
State Capitol
Charlotte Avenue
Nashville, Tennessee 37219
(615) 741-2692

The Tennessee capitol building is a fine example of Greek Revival architecture, designed by William Strickland in 1859. The grounds are enhanced by a Clark Mills equestrian statue of General Andrew Jackson, made from the same casting as the statues in Washington, DC, and New Orleans, Louisiana.

See also: **Corner of Celebrities** (p. 81); **Liberty Hall** (p. 90); **Locust Grove** (p. 90).

Martin Van Buren

Eighth President
1837–1841

Born December 5, 1782, Kinderhook, New York
Died July 24, 1862, Kinderhook, New York
Burial Site: Kinderhook Cemetery, Kinderhook, New York

Martin Van Buren Birthplace
46 Hudson Street
Kinderhook, New York 12106

The tiny cabin in which President Van Buren was born has been razed. There is a marker.

Martin Van Buren National Historic Site
Box 545, Route 9H
Kinderhook, New York 12106
(518) 758-9689

Following his presidency, Van Buren bought a decrepit farm and transformed it into an opulent "Italian villa," complete with a tower and mural wallpaper in the entry hall. He named the estate Lindenwald after the lovely grove of linden trees surrounding the property. National Park Service Site. Open to the public.

Decatur House
748 Jackson Place, NW
Washington, DC 20006
(202) 842-0920

Decatur House was built by Commodore Stephen Decatur, early American naval hero, and is the cornerstone of Lafayette Square, the capital's most famous historic district, located across Pennsylvania Avenue from the White House. The home has hosted innumerable politicians and world leaders and was Martin Van Buren's residence when he served as Secretary of State in the cabinet of Andrew Jackson. Decatur House is owned and operated by the National Trust for Historic Preservation as a house museum. Open to the public.

Moses and Christina Cantine House
251 West Main Street
Catskill, New York 12414

The wedding of Martin Van Buren and Hannah Hoes on February 21, 1807, may have taken place in the Cantine House which still stands, although much altered. Closed to the public.

Greenbrier River Inn
Caldwell, West Virginia 24925
(304) 647-5632

The Greenbrier River Inn, still active, hosted a reception for Martin Van Buren in 1837. Open to the public.

Jed Prouty Tavern
52–54 Main Street
Bucksport, Maine 04416
(207) 468-3113

A hostelry built in 1798 was once a rest stop on a stagecoach route. Its famous guests have included presidents Martin Van Buren, William Henry Harrison and John Tyler. Open to the public.

See also: **Berkeley Springs** (p. 21); **Beekman Arms Hotel** (p. 45); **William H. Seward House** (p. 93).

William Henry Harrison

Ninth President
March, 1841–April, 1841

Born February 9, 1773, Charles City, Virginia
Died April 4, 1841, Washington, DC
Burial Site: Harrison Tomb State Memorial, North Bend, Ohio

Berkeley Plantation
12602 Harrison Landing Road
Charles City, Virginia 23030
(804) 829-6018

William Henry Harrison was born in a splendid ancestral house on the James River, a remarkable example of pre-Revolutionary (1726) architecture. Berkeley has been called Virginia's most historic plantation as it was ancestral home to generations of Harrisons, the birthplace of a signer of the Declaration of Independence (Benjamin Harrison V) and a United States President. Early English settlers came ashore at Berkeley as early as 1619 and observed the first official Thanksgiving on its grounds. Berkeley has been restored to its original grandeur by its owners, Mr. and Mrs. Malcolm Jamison. Open to the public.

Westover Church

6401 John Tyler Memorial Highway
Charles City, Virginia 23030
(804) 829-2488

The church building dates from 1730, although the congregation can trace its lineage to the Jamestown Colony. Presidents William Henry Harrison and John Tyler were communicants when they resided on nearby plantations.

Grouseland

3 West Scott Street
Vincennes, Indiana 47591
(812) 882-2096

Grouseland was built by William Henry Harrison when he was serving as governor of the Northwest Territory which included what is now Indiana. Grouseland, architecturally patterned after Harrison's ancestral home at Berkeley, is set high on a bluff overlooking the Wabash River, reinforced with eighteen-inch thick walls as protection against hostile Indians. In addition, the walls and ceilings were reinforced against stress to the structure caused by Harrison's many guests. The house's seventeen rooms were always full as the Harrisons had eight children and entertained frequently. Grouseland is owned and maintained by the Francis Sligo Chapter, Daughters of the American Revolution. Open to the public.

North Bend Plantation

12200 Weyanoke Road
Charles City, Virginia 23030
(804) 829-5176

North Bend is a Greek Revival Federal-period manor built in 1819 for Sarah Harrison, sister of William Henry Harrison, and a place he frequently visited when in Virginia. It has been refurbished and opened as a Bed and Breakfast. Group tours by appointment.

Vincennes University

1002 N. 1st. Street
Vincennes, Indiana 47591

Vincennes University was founded by Governor William Henry Harrison in 1801, named Jefferson Academy in honor of President Thomas Jefferson. Harrison served as the first chairman of the board. The campus is open to the public.

Indiana Territory Capitol State Historic Site
Vincennes University Campus
1 West Harrison Street
Vincennes, Indiana 47591
(812) 882-7472

The Territory Capitol Site, part of the Indiana State Museum System, includes the two-room frame building which was the home of the Territorial Assembly in 1811 when William Henry Harrison was governor. The nearby Western Sun Print Shop is a replication of the building where the Indiana Territory's first newspaper was printed on July 4, 1804. Open to the public.

John Cleves Symmes House
North Bend, Ohio 45052

John Cleve Symmes was a major land speculator whose daughter, Anna, married William Henry Harrison in the Symmes home on November 22 or 25, 1795. The house no longer stands.

Corydon Historic District
Corydon, Indiana 47112
(812) 738-4890

The town of Corydon was founded by Governor William Henry Harrison in 1800 and it served as the Indiana Territorial Capital in 1813. Harrison had many commercial interests in the town, including ownership of a mill and an orchard. Corydon's historic district preserves Harrison's original grid plan although the sole remaining vestige of his residency is the Harrison House-Branham Tavern, built on property he owned and thought to be his hangout when in the area on business.

Jeffersonville, Indiana

Jeffersonville was plotted by Governor Harrison in 1802.

William Henry Harrison's Military Career

Fort Knox II
Vincennes, Indiana 47591
(812) 882-1776

Fort Knox was the second of three outposts on the Wabash River built to protect western settlers from Indian attacks. General Harrison left from Fort Knox to fight the Battle of Tippecanoe. The archeological site of Fort Knox II is two miles north of town. Interpretive markers tell its history, although only the outline of the fort is visible. Self-guided tours are permitted, in season. Open to the public.

Tippecanoe Battlefield
Lafayette, Indiana 47901
(317) 567-2147

The battle of Tippecanoe was fought near the Tippecanoe River on November 7, 1811. This battle was indecisive in quelling the Indian threat to westward expansion, but it served to make William Henry Harrison a national hero and led to his nomination and subsequent election as President. The property is owned by the State of Indiana which has developed a ninety-acre park that includes a commemorative monument, picnic area and scenic trails. Museum. Open to the public.

Fort Meigs State Memorial
Route 655
Perrysburg, Ohio 43551
(419) 874-4121

Fort Meigs was built by General Harrison in 1813. It successfully repulsed British attackers in the War of 1812, action that made Harrison's subsequent invasion of Canada possible. A reconstruction was undertaken by the State of Ohio, and the fort is now part of a fifty-seven-acre park. Open to the public.

Fort Amanda State Memorial
Wapakoneta, Ohio 45895

A blockhouse fort was erected in this area by General Harrison during the War of 1812; its purpose was to protect one of a series of supply depots necessary for his campaign to recapture Detroit from the British. Memorial obelisk.

Harrison Headquarters
570 W. Broad Street
Columbus, Ohio 43216
(614) 469-1300

Harrison Headquarters is a building that served as headquarters for William Henry Harrison when he served in the army during the War of 1812. This building is now utilized as the research library of the Ohio Genealogical Society. Closed to the public.

William Henry Harrison Statue
Garfield Place
Cincinnati, Ohio 45202

An equestrian statue by Louis T. Rebisson depicts William Henry Harrison as an Indian fighter, wearing the full dress of a general of the US Army.

See also: **Belle Air** (p. 20); **Virginia Governors Mansion** (p. 76); **Old Talbott Tavern** (p. 100); **Jed Prouty Tavern** (p. 107); **Sherwood Forest** (p. 113); **Bedford Springs** (p. 133).

John Tyler

Tenth President
1841–1845

Born March 29, 1790, Charles City, Virginia
Died January 18, 1862, Exchange Hotel, Richmond, Virginia
Burial Site: Hollywood Cemetery, Richmond, Virginia

Greenway
John Tyler Memorial Highway
Charles City, Virginia 23030

    The Colonial home in which Tyler was born is still standing, but privately owned and not open to the public. There is a marker on Route 5 near the house.

Sherwood Forest
14501 John Tyler Memorial Highway
Charles City, Virginia 23030
(804) 829-5377

    President John Tyler's retirement estate on the James River was named Sherwood Forest as Tyler considered himself a political Robin Hood.

It is the longest frame house in the nation and features a first-floor ballroom and the rocking chair of the Grey Lady, the only ghost known to grace a presidential home. The house, filled with valuable family artifacts, remains a working plantation, home of Tyler descendants for over one-hundred-fifty years. The house had once been the property of the Harrison family and it is probable that William Henry Harrison resided in it briefly. Open to the public.

Cedar Grove
Providence Forge, Virginia 23140

John Tyler and Letitia Christian were married in her family's home on March 29, 1813. The 2½-story brick house dates from 1810, with a wing added in 1916. Closed to the public.

Church of the Ascension
5th Avenue and 10th Street
New York, New York

Letitia Tyler died in the White House in 1842. John Tyler remarried on June 26, 1844, taking Julia Gardiner of New York as his bride. They were married at the Church of the Ascension.

The Finnie House
James Semple House
Francis Street
Williamsburg, Virginia 23185
(757) 447-8679

John Tyler attended the College of William and Mary where he boarded in a house owned by James Semple. The house is an excellent example of a Roman country home adapted for town use. It has been restored as part of Colonial Williamsburg. Open to the public.

Woodburn
Virginia SR 618
Charles City , Virginia 23030

John Tyler built a striking Palladian home in 1815 and lived in it until 1831. It remains in good condition, but is privately owned and is closed to the public.

Tyler Mansion
27 Tyler Street
Staten Island, New York 10307

A Greek Revival house was the residence of Tyler's mother-in-law,

Mrs. Gardiner, and it became a frequent vacation spot for the Tyler family. Closed to the public.

See also: **Virginia Governors Mansion** (p. 76); **Liberty Hall** (p. 90); **Jed Prouty Tavern** (p. 107); **Westover Church** (p. 109).

James Knox Polk

Eleventh President
1845–1849

Born November 2, 1795, Pineville, North Carolina
Died June 15, 1849, Nashville, Tennessee
Burial Site: Tennessee State Capitol, Nashville, Tennessee

James K. Polk Memorial
Box 475
Pineville, North Carolina 28134
(704) 889-7145

A Visitor Center and several replicated farm buildings stand on some twenty-one acres of the nearly-four-hundred-acre farm where President James K. Polk was born. Exhibits and interpretation features life on the farm and the most significant events in the Polk presidency — the war with Mexico, the annexation of California, and the establishment of an independent Treasury. The Memorial is a North Carolina State Memorial Site and is administered by the State Division of Archives and History. Open to the public.

Polk Ancestral Home
Box 741
301 West 7th Street
Columbia, Tennessee 38401
(615) 388-2354

James K. Polk's father prospered on the frontier and built a fine home where James lived until his own marriage. The house, a two-story Federal of hand-made bricks, is owned by the State of Tennessee and maintained by the Polk Memorial Association. The home of Polk's sisters next door serves as a Visitor Center for a museum and tours. Open to the public.

Childress Home
College Street
Murfreesboro, Tennessee 37131

James K. Polk married Sarah Childress in her family's home on January 1, 1824. The house has been demolished and replaced by a hotel.

First Presbyterian Church
4815 Franklin Road
Nashville, Tennessee 37220
(615) 383-1815

First Presbyterian was the Polk family church following James K. Polk's retirement from the presidency. Polk, himself, was not a believer in organized religion but happily accompanied his wife to services.

South Building
University of North Carolina
Chapel Hill, North Carolina 27599-3265

James K. Polk roomed in South Building for his entire college career, 1815–1818, probably living in a third-floor room. The building is still in use as the main administration building of the University. Closed to the public.

Rally Hill
West 8th Street
Columbia, Tennessee 38401

Rally Hill was owned by James K. Polk's brother-in-law, James Walker, and Polk visited frequently. It is currently unoccupied and closed to the public.

Gower House
US Route 60 and Water Street
Smithland, Kentucky 42081

Gower House, a two-story brick building, was originally an inn catering to travelers along the Ohio River. Its guests included James K. Polk and Zachary Taylor. It is currently under restoration and closed to the public.

See also: **Dickson-Williams Mansion** (p. 93); **Carnton Mansion** (p. 98); **Chester Inn** (p. 98); **Shepards Inn** (p. 98); **Netherland Inn** (p. 99); **Hale Springs Inn** (p. 100); **The Pillars** (p. 100); **Presidential Memorial** (p. 104); **Bedford Springs Hotel** (p. 133).

Zachary Taylor

Twelfth President
1849–1850

Born November 24, 1784, Montebello, Virginia
Died July 9, 1850, Washington, DC
Burial Site: Zachary Taylor National Cemetery, Louisville,
Kentucky

Montebello
Highway 33
5 miles west of Gordonsville, Virginia

      Zachary Taylor's family was on its way to a new life in Kentucky when it stopped briefly for a real new life — Zachary's birth. The actual site of the birth is in dispute, the evidence obscure. The State of Virginia has concluded, however, that the Montebello estate was the most likely site, and that possibly it took place in a secondary house on the property. Closed to the public. There is a marker.

Springfield
5608 Apache Road
Louisville, Kentucky 40207

Zachary Taylor lived with his parents in Louisville until receiving an army commission in 1808. It is thought that he and Margaret Smith married in the family home on June 21, 1810, although it has been suggested that the ceremony took place at Margaret's sister's house on Harrods Wood Creek. It is likely, however, that several of the Taylor children were born in the Apache Road house. The house is privately owned. Closed to the public.

Zachary Taylor's Military Career

Fort Howard
Chestnut Street
Green Bay, Wisconsin 54304
(414) 494-6868

Fort Howard was one of a small series of forts on the frontier — the center of a settlement of American pioneers. Zachary Taylor was stationed at Fort Howard in 1816 and became post commander shortly after. Fort Howard is part of a municipal museum complex owned by the City of Green Bay. Open to the public.

Fort Selden (1821–1822)
Natchitoches, Louisiana 71457

Taylor established Fort Selden in 1821 and spent the winter of 1821–1822 at the fort that was on the border of a neutral strip between the United States and Spanish Mexico. The site is identifiable and some stonework remains. The property is privately owned and closed to the public.

Fort Jesup State Monument
Many, Louisiana 71449
(318) 256-4177

Taylor established Fort Jesup in 1822, utilizing it as the jumping-off spot for his march into newly-annexed Texas. The Monument of 22 acres includes officer's quarters reconstructed as a Visitor Center. Open to the public.

Pentagon Barracks (1822–1824, 1827–1828, 1840–1841, 1847)
Baton Rouge, Louisiana 70801
(504) 342-1866

The Pentagon Barracks became a US Army installation in 1819 and has had innumerable manifestations, currently as Louisiana state offices and apartments. The State utilizes part of one building as an interpretive historical center. Open to the public.

Historic Fort Snelling (1828–1829)
Saint Paul, Minnesota 55111
(612) 726-1171

Built on a commanding bluff above the Mississippi and Minnesota rivers, Fort Snelling was the last United States outpost on the "western wilderness," a symbol of American ambition in the west of the 1820s. The fort has been restored. Open to the public.

Second Fort Crawford (1828–1829)
717 S. Beaumont Road
Prairie de Chien, Wisconsin 53821
(608) 326-6960

Fort Crawford is the site of a Medical Museum dedicated to the history of army medicine. Open to the public.

Jefferson Barracks Historic Park (1836–1837)
533 Grant Road
Saint Louis, Missouri 63125
(314) 544-5714

Jefferson Barracks is a 424-acre county park that was once part of an army post. Both Zachary Taylor and Ulysses S. Grant served here. Open to the public.

Okeechobee Battlefield (1837)
US Route 441, 4 miles southeast of
Okeechobee, Florida 34972

Colonel Zachary Taylor won a decisive victory over the Seminole Indians at Okeechobee on December 25, 1837. The success brought him promotion to brevet brigadier general. Closed to the public.

Fort Gibson Military Park (1841)
Muskogee, Oklahoma 74401
(918) 478-2669

Fort Gibson, Oklahoma's first military installation, is currently a seventy-acre military park. Open to the public.

Fort Smith National Historic Site (1841–1844)
Box 1406
Fort Smith, Arkansas 72901
(800) 637-1477

This National Park Service Site incorporates the remains of two successive frontier forts and the courtroom of "Hanging" Judge Parker. When General Taylor was stationed here, Fort Smith was the base of operations from which the military could direct forced Indian migrations and suppress uprisings. Open to the public.

Fort Washita
Madill, Oklahoma 73446

Fort Washita was established by General Taylor in 1842 to protect the relocated Chickasaw and Choctaw Indians from the Plains Indians. Open to the public.

Fort Brown (1846)
Brownsville, Texas 78520

Fort Brown was established by General Taylor to confirm the Rio Grande as the boundary between Mexico and the United States. The site is now the campus of Texas Southmost College. Closed to the public.

Palo Alto Battlefield National Historic Site
FM 1847, 5½ miles north of
Brownsville, Texas 78520

Palo Alto was the site of the artillery duel which opened the Mexican War on May 8, 1845, the Americans under the command of General Zachary Taylor. Ulysses S. Grant as a young officer served on Taylor's staff. There is an historical monument.

Resaca de la Palma Battlefield
Paredes Line Road between Price Road and Coffee Post Road
Brownsville, Texas 78520

Resaca de la Palma was a continuation of the Palo Alto engagement, fought on May 9, 1846. There is a marker.

Fort Zachary Taylor
Key West, Florida 33040
(305) 292-6713

Fort Zachary Taylor was built in 1845–1846 as part of Florida's coastal defense system. It has been reclaimed and is maintained by the State of Florida. Open to the public.

See also: **Berkeley Springs** (p. 21); **Locust Grove** (p. 90); **Gower House** (p. 118).

Millard Fillmore

Thirteenth President
1850–1853

Born January 7, 1800, Locke, New York
Died March 8, 1874, Buffalo, New York
Burial Site: Forest Lawn Cemetery, Buffalo, New York

Millard Fillmore Birthplace
Locke, New York 13092

Millard Fillmore was born in a log cabin on a rugged farm in the nearly-frontier country of the Finger Lakes district of New York. The original cabin is no longer standing. There is a marker.

Millard Fillmore Log Cabin
Fillmore Glen State Park
Moravia, New York 13118
(315) 497-0130

This replication of the Fillmore log cabin was placed on the grounds of a lovely recreational park four miles from his actual birth site in Locke.

Biographer Robert Scarry has noted, *It is hoped that this cabin will serve as an inspiration to young people . . . in that it exemplifies the American dream, that a person from humble surroundings can rise to hold the highest office in the land.* Open to the public.

Judge Powers House
Smith Street
Moravia, New York 13118

Millard Fillmore and Abigail Powers were probably married in the home of her brother on February 5, 1826. The house is a two-story frame with a small front porch. Closed to the public.

Fillmore House Museum
Shearer Avenue
Box 472
East Aurora, New York 14052
(716) 652-8875

East Aurora was the hometown of Millard and Abigail Fillmore from 1826 to 1830. The Aurora Historical Society has refurbished the small cottage they lived in during the 1820s into the style of the Fillmore occupancy. Open to the public.

Fillmore Home
Olean and Lapham
East Aurora, New York 14052

The Fillmore House was an early home for the Fillmores before they moved to the more permanent house on Shearer Avenue. Closed to the public.

Schuyler Mansion
32 Catherine Street
Albany, New York 12202
(518) 434-0834

Abigail Fillmore became ill at the inauguration of Franklin Pierce, and passed away in Washington on March 30, 1853. On February 10, 1858, the widowed Fillmore and Caroline Carmichael McIntosh were married in Schuyler Mansion, originally the residence of Philip Schuyler, noted Revolutionary War general and senator from New York. The house was noted for a previous wedding that had united Schuyler's daughter, Betsy, and Alexander Hamilton. Open to the public.

Judge Woods House
State Route 38A
Montville, New York 13118

In 1820 and 1821, Fillmore studied law with a Judge Wood and it is thought he lived in the Judge's home. Closed to the public.

Unitarian Universal Church
695 Elmwood Avenue
Buffalo, New York 14223
(716) 885-2136

Millard Fillmore attended Unitarian Universal when he lived in Buffalo before and after his presidency.

Memorial to Millard Fillmore

Millard Fillmore Statue
City Hall
Buffalo, New York 14202

A Millard Fillmore statue is situated diagonally across the street from the site of Fillmore's retirement home which has been demolished.

See also: **Berkeley Springs** (p. 21); **All Souls Church** (p. 94).

Franklin Pierce

Fourteenth President
1853–1857

Born November 23, 1804, Hillsborough, New Hampshire
Died October 8, 1869, Concord, New Hampshire
Burial Site: Old North Cemetery, Concord, New Hampshire

The Pierce Homestead
Routes 9 and 31
Hillsborough, New Hampshire 03244
(603) 478-3913

The actual house in which Franklin Pierce was born has not survived. A few months after his birth, however, the family moved into a handsome Colonial-style house nearby – a home of affluence reflecting Pierce's father's success as farmer, entrepreneur and politician. Spacious rooms, hand-stenciled walls and a second-floor ballroom indicated prosperity, good taste and gracious living. The ballroom, especially, became a local center for the discussion of public affairs during a period of maturation in America's democratic development and, not incidentally, the political development of Franklin Pierce. The Pierce Homestead, filled with family treasures, is maintained by the New Hampshire State Parks and Recreation Department. Open to the public.

McNeil Residence
Routes 9 and 31
Hillsborough, New Hampshire 03244

A handsome Colonial-style house was Franklin Pierce's first permanent home following his marriage to Jane Appleton. The young couple lived there before moving to Concord in 1838. The residence is privately owned and closed to the public.

The Pierce Manse
14 Penacook Street, Box 425
Concord, New Hampshire 00301
(603) 224-7668

A comfortable white Colonial-style house was considered Pierce's permanent residence while he practiced law in Concord, served in Congress, and fought in the War with Mexico. The house has been moved to an attractive city park where it is operated by the Pierce Brigade as a house museum. It is called "manse" simply to differentiate it from the homestead in Hillsborough. Open to the public.

Means Mansion
Amherst, New Hampshire 03031

On November 19, 1834, Pierce married Jane Appleton at the Means House, the home of her maternal grandmother. The house is an architecturally distinguished Federal structure. Closed to the public.

South Congregational Church
27 Pleasant Street
Concord, New Hampshire 00301
(603) 224-2521

Franklin Pierce and his wife were congregants in South Congregational, which dates to 1836. Following a disastrous fire in mid-century that destroyed the earlier building, the cornerstone of the present structure was laid in 1860.

Saint Pauls Episcopal Church
Concord, New Hampshire 00301

Following the death of his wife, Franklin Pierce returned to the church of his original faith. The building has been rebuilt on the site where a fire had destroyed the original.

Merrimack County Courthouse
163 N. Main Street
Concord, New Hampshire 00301
(603) 225-5451

Franklin Pierce tried many cases in the Merrimack County Courthouse when practicing law in Concord. The building dates from 1855. Open to the public.

Eagle Hotel
N. Main Street
Concord, New Hampshire 00301
(603) 636-1800

From its grand opening in 1852, the four-story brick Eagle Hotel has hosted Concord's social and political events. President Benjamin Harrison, Jefferson Davis, Charles Lindbergh and Eleanor Roosevelt have been guests, and local resident Franklin Pierce attended functions many times. The hotel is now the center of Eagle Square Marketplace. Open to the public.

Phenix Hall
40 N. Main Street
Concord, New Hampshire 00301

Phenix Hall was once the "rendezvous of gentlemen of the Whig party" and welcomed many famous people including Franklin Pierce. Phenix Hall was the site of a speech by Abraham Lincoln prior to his election in 1860. The Hall burned but was rebuilt in 1893, and is now a commercial building. Closed to the public.

Franklin Pierce's Military Career

Franklin Pierce had returned home to Concord following his service in Washington as congressman and senator when he enlisted in the army at the outbreak of the War with Mexico — as a private! His political prominence, however, almost immediately gained him a presidential appointment as a colonel and soon promotion to brigadier general. As a general, he led an army from Vera Cruz to join General Winfield Scott and assist in the capture of Mexico City. Overcoming Scott's doubts about his military abilities, Pierce proved to be an effective and courageous leader. In a strange twist of fate, Pierce defeated Scott for the presidency four short years later.

Franklin Pierce Statue
State House Grounds
Concord, New Hampshire 00301

Pierce's presidency was considered a failure, and his sympathy for the South turned his own hometown constituents against him. He had left New Hampshire as President-elect, but when he returned four years later there was not even a parade in his honor. The only monument to him is the statue at the New Hampshire State House.

James Buchanan

Fifteenth President
1857–1861

Born April 23, 1791, Stoney Batter, Pennsylvania
Died June 1, 1868, Lancaster, Pennsylvania
Burial Site: Woodward Hill Cemetery, Lancaster, Pennsylvania

Buchanan Historic Site
Mercersburg, Pennsylvania 17236
(717) 328-3116

The town of Mercersburg is the center of the Buchanan Historic District. James Buchanan's birthplace, a log cabin located a few miles from the town center, is marked by a monument in a state park. The cabin itself has been restored and moved to a permanent and protected location on the campus of Mercersburg Academy. Other sites in Mercersburg are a reflection of Buchanan's boyhood and early political history – part of a walking tour of the town. The Buchanan Hotel, for example, was once the Buchanan family home and store, and Buchanan launched his bid for the presidency with a speech given from the balcony of the Mansion House. Open to the public.

131

Wheatland

1120 Marietta Avenue
Lancaster, Pennsylvania 17603
(717) 392-8721

Wheatland is a gracious home built in 1828 by a wealthy Lancaster banker and named for its view of the rich wheat fields surrounding it. The house was purchased by Buchanan in 1848 at the time he was Secretary of State. It was restored to glory as *the beau ideal of a statesman's abode,* as described by Buchanan when he returned to Lancaster following his presidency. Buchanan loved his time at Wheatland and praised *the comforts and tranquillity of home as contrasted with the trouble, perplexities and difficulties of public life.* Wheatland is owned and operated by the James Buchanan Foundation for the Preservation of Wheatland. Open to the public.

First Presbyterian Church of Lancaster

140 Orange Street
Lancaster, Pennsylvania 17602
(717) 394-6854

James Buchanan considered the First Presbyterian, founded in 1742, as his home church. He owned a $600 pew which is marked in the sanctuary.

Church of the Epiphany

1317 G Street, NW
Washington, DC 20003
(202) 347-2635

James Buchanan was a parishioner of the Church of the Epiphany, situated a few blocks from the White House, although he sometimes attended National Presbyterian Church when in Washington.

Anderson House

US Soldiers and Airmens Home
Rock Creek Church Road
Washington, DC 20011

Anderson House, originally established as a retirement domicile for members of the armed forces, is a guest house and supervisor's lounge for the current, expanded facility. Due to its higher elevation (all of 300 feet!) it was utilized by presidents Buchanan, Lincoln, Hayes and Arthur as a sort of early "Camp David," — a place to get away from the stifling heat and humidity of downtown Washington. Closed to the public.

Buchanan Vacation Home
205 Howard Street
Cape May, New Jersey 08204

James Buchanan's physician brother owned a simple seaside cottage which Buchanan utilized as a vacation retreat. Closed to the public.

Bedford Springs Hotel
US Routes 220 and 30
Bedford, Pennsylvania 15522
(814) 623-1771

President Buchanan visited Bedford, renowned for its therapeutic waters, using it as the summer White House between 1857 and 1860. Other presidential guests included William Henry Harrison, James K. Polk, Zachary Taylor, James A. Garfield and Dwight D. Eisenhower. The hotel is undergoing major remodeling and plans are to reopen it in 2000.

Memorial to James Buchanan

James Buchanan Memorial
Meridian Hill Park
Washington, DC

A statuary group by Hans Shuler was a gift to the nation from Buchanan's niece, Harriet Lane, who served as White House hostess for the bachelor President during his term in office.

Abraham Lincoln

Sixteenth President
1861–1865

Born February 12, 1809, Hardin County, Kentucky
Died April 15, 1865, Washington, DC
Burial Site: Oak Hill Cemetery, Springfield, Illinois

Lincoln Birthplace National Historic Site
Sinking Spring Farm
2995 Lincoln Farm Road
Hodgenville, Kentucky 42748
(502) 358-3874

In 1911, President William Howard Taft dedicated an imposing neoclassical building of marble and granite as a memorial to Abraham Lincoln, grandiose for a simple man except for what laid within the walls of the memorial – the tiny two-room cabin in which Abraham Lincoln was born – a cabin that dramatically symbolizes the basic human values that sustained the great leader through America's darkest hours. The Memorial Building sits atop a hill approached by a flight of fifty-six steps, each representing one year of Lincoln's life. Granite columns above the entrance are inscribed with his most famous words — . . . *with malice toward none, with charity for all*. Open to the public.

Knob Creek Farm
US Route 31E
Hodgenville, Kentucky 42748
(502) 549-3741

When Abraham Lincoln was two years of age, his family moved from Sinking Spring Farm to Knob Creek, ten miles east, where they remained for the next six years. Their log cabin has been replicated near the original Knob Creek site. Open to the public.

Lincoln Boyhood National Memorial
Box 1816
Lincoln City, Indiana 47552
(812) 937-4541

In 1816, the Lincoln family moved once more, to Indiana, where their farm has been replicated as a living history farm operated by a costumed staff using authentic frontier implements demonstrating farming methods of the period. National Park Service Site. Open to the public.

Lincolns New Salem
RR 1, Box 144A
Petersburg, Illinois 62675
(217) 632-4000

After leaving the family farm to seek his fortune, Abraham Lincoln settled in New Salem where he clerked in a general store, worked as a surveyor, served the community as postmaster and studied the law. Lincoln was elected to the state legislature in 1834 and 1836, but upon receiving a law degree in 1839, he left for the state capital in Springfield. The town of New Salem went into decline shortly after but the State of Illinois has recreated the entire village of shops, stables, farm buildings, schools and churches to represent the time when Lincoln resided there. Open to the public.

Lincoln Log Cabin State Historic Site
RR 1, Box 172A
Lerna, Illinois 62440
(217) 345-6489

The Lincoln Log Cabin State Historic Site, an eighty-six-acre living historical farm, includes a reproduction of the last home of Lincoln's father and stepmother in the late 1840s. Lincoln had left home by then, but he visited periodically. This site is managed by the Illinois Historic Preservation Agency. Open to the public.

Farmington
3033 Bardstown Road
Louisville, Kentucky 40205
(502) 452-9920

Young Abraham Lincoln's closest friend was the son of Mr. and Mrs. Speed, who owned Farmington, and he stayed there as their guest for three weeks in 1841. Farmington is currently owned and operated by the Historic Homes Foundation as a house museum with fourteen fully-furnished period rooms. Open to the public.

Ninian W. Edwards House
Spring and Edwards Street
Springfield, Illinois 62701

Attorney Abraham Lincoln wed Mary Todd in the home of her sister on November 4, 1842. The original structure has been demolished but there is a marker at the site. A scale reconstruction of the Edwards House has been erected at the southeast corner of 8th and Capitol streets in Springfield.

Lincoln Home National Historic Site
413 South 8th Street
Springfield, Illinois 62701
(217) 492-4150

The home in which the Lincoln family lived for seventeen years before moving to Washington, DC, has been restored as part of a project to restore a four-square-block neighborhood to its likeness at the time of Lincoln's residency. Abraham Lincoln purchased the house, the only house he ever owned — a Greek Revival with oak framing and brown pine exterior — in 1844 for $1200 cash and a small lot valued at $300. As the Lincoln family grew with the addition of growing boys, the house was renovated and gradually expanded to become a distinguished two-story residence appropriate for a successful attorney, politician and father. National Park Service Site. Open to the public.

Lincoln Depot Museum
10th and Monroe
Springfield, Illinois 62701
(217) 544-8695

The depot was the site of Lincoln's farewell speech to the citizens of

Springfield in 1861 — the terminus of his funeral cortege in 1865. Open to the public.

Lincoln Family Pew
First Presbyterian Church
321 South 7th Street
Springfield, Illinois 62701
(217) 528-4311

The Lincoln family attended the First Presbyterian Church during their seventeen years of residence in Springfield, and the family pew is marked. There are also copies of original family papers on display in the church. Open to the public.

Lincoln-Herndon Law Offices
Old State Capitol State Historic Site
6th and Adams
Springfield, Illinois 62701
(217) 785-7961

Abraham Lincoln had a law practice in partnership with William Herndon. A second-floor office is part of the only surviving building from that era. The interior of the building contains a restored courtroom, Lincoln's office, exhibits and an audiovisual presentation. Open to the public.

Edwards Place
70 North 4th Street
Springfield, Illinois 62701
(217) 523-2631

The oldest house in the city of Springfield, circa 1831, was the site of political rallies in which Lincoln was a frequent participant. It is presently a house museum operated by the Springfield Art Association. Open to the public.

Lincoln Ledger
Marine Bank of Springfield
East Old Capitol Plaza
Springfield, Illinois 62701
(217) 525-9600

Abraham Lincoln was a depositor at the Marine Bank, and his account ledger is displayed in the lobby. Open to the public.

Illinois Governors Mansion
5th and Jackson
Springfield, Illinois 62701
(800) 545-7300

The Illinois Governors Mansion is a twenty-eight-room white brick Victorian located three blocks from the capitol that was built in 1855. Its records indicate that the Lincolns were frequent guests. Open to the public.

Metamora Courthouse State Historic Site
113 E. Partridge Street
Metamora, Illinois 61548
(309) 367-4470

Lawyer Abraham Lincoln, riding the law circuit, practiced in Metamora from 1844 to 1856. The courthouse has some original furnishings. Open to the public.

Postville Courthouse State Historic Site
914 5th Street
Lincoln, Illinois 62656
(217) 732-8930

This is a replica of a building that served as the Logan County Courthouse from 1839 to 1847 and was one of Lincoln's stops on the law circuit. The original building is in Greenfield Village, Dearborn, Michigan (p. 281). Open to the public.

Old State Capitol
315 West Gallatin
Vandalia, Illinois 62471
(618) 283-1161

Abraham Lincoln served in the Illinois legislature when it was based in Vandalia in 1836. The Old State Capitol is the last of three buildings to serve as Illinois State Capitol before Springfield was chosen as the permanent capital. The capitol building is a restoration. Open to the public.

Mount Pulaski Courthouse State Historic Site
Town Square
Mount Pulaski, Illinois 62548
(217) 792-3919

Mount Pulaski was headquarters of the 8th Judicial District of

Illinois which Lincoln served as a traveling attorney from 1847 through 1853. The courthouse is a restoration. Open to the public.

Bryant Cottage State Historic Site
146 East Wilson Street
Bement, Illinois 61813
(217) 678-8184

Bryant Cottage is a four-room, period-furnished house where Abraham Lincoln and Stephen A. Douglas met to plan their famous senatorial debates in 1858. The Cottage is maintained by the Illinois State Department of Conservation. Open to the public.

Lincoln-Douglas Debates, 1858

In 1856, attorney Abraham Lincoln joined the newly-formed Republican Party, a coalition of antislavery groups backing presidential candidate John C. Fremont. Lincoln, although holding no elective office himself, campaigned strenuously and became a national leader of the party. In 1857, he attacked Senator Stephen A. Douglas for his position on slavery, leading to Lincoln's nomination to face Douglas in the Senate race of 1858 and provoking what have become the most famous head-to-head philosophical debates in American political history. All have appropriate markers.

Washington Park, Ottawa, August 21

Douglas and State Streets, Freeport, August 27

Jonesboro, September 15

Charleston, September 18

Knox College, Galesburg, October 7

Quincy, October 13

Broadway and Market Streets, Alton, October 15

Cooper Union
Cooper Square
7th Avenue and 4th Street
New York, New York 10003
(212) 254-6300

Cooper Union was the site of a Lincoln speech on February 27, 1860, which established him as a serious presidential contender. The building housed Peter Cooper's pioneer effort to provide free education and has served as a place for public debate on important issues for over a century. Open to the public.

Lincoln-Tallman Restorations
440 N. Jackson Street
Janesville, Wisconsin 53545
(608) 752-4519

Abraham Lincoln visited the Tallman House, an opulent 26-room Italianate villa, in 1859. The owner, William Tallman, was a wealthy attorney and abolitionist. The house, currently operated by the Rock Island Historical Society, is part of a two-house restoration project. Open to the public.

Archer House Hotel
717 Archer Avenue
Marshall, Illinois 62441
(217) 826-8023

The famous Archer House has been visited by Presidents Abraham Lincoln and Grover Cleveland. Open to the public.

Woonsocket City Hall
169 Main Street
Woonsocket, Rhode Island 02895
(401) 762-6400

Edward Harris, a prominent wool manufacturer, constructed a neo-classical building to house the Harris Institute. The building was subsequently converted to a public building. Abraham Lincoln spoke from its front steps during his 1860 presidential campaign. Open to the public.

Moore Home State Historic Site
4th Street Road
Charleston, Illinois 61920
(217) 3345-6489

On the evening before leaving Illinois for his inauguration in 1861, President-elect Abraham Lincoln dined with his stepmother and her daughter, Mrs. Matilda Moore, at the latter's home. Open to the public.

Mary Todd Lincolns Home
578 West Main Street, Box 132
Lexington, Kentucky 40205
(606) 233-9999

An attractive, upper middle-class Georgian was the family home of

Lincoln's wife, and the Lincolns visited on many occasions. The house contains original furnishings from Mary Todd's residency. The house has been restored and is maintained by the Kentucky Mansions Preservation Foundation, Inc. Open to the public.

Quarters Number 1
Fort Monroe
Hampton, Virginia 23651
(757) 727-3973

Fort Monroe was the longest continuously-controlled Union stronghold nearest to Richmond during the Civil War and was the place where Confederate President Jefferson Davis was incarcerated following the conflict. President. Lincoln stayed at Fort Monroe in May, 1862, during an inspection visit. Open to the public.

Thomas Wallace House
Market and Halifax
Petersburg, Virginia 23860
(804) 541-2060

President Abraham Lincoln and General Ulysses S. Grant met on the porch of the Wallace House to discuss terms for the surrender of the Confederate army in 1865. The house is owned and operated as a house museum by the Virginia Preservation Foundation. Open to the public.

Harlan House
101 W. Broad Street
Mount Pleasant, Iowa 52641
(319) 385-8021

James A. Harlan was a United States Senator and Secretary of the Interior in President Lincoln's cabinet. Lincoln's eldest son, Robert, married Harlan's daughter, Mary, and they and their three children spent many summers in Harlan's opulent mid-19th century home. The house has been refurbished with some original pieces, plus Lincoln memorabilia. Visitors are intrigued by the height marks of the Lincoln grandchildren, still visible on the front door. Operated by Iowa Wesleyan College. Open by appointment.

Fort Stevens
13th Street between Piney Branch Road and Rittenhouse Street
Washington, DC 20011

Fort Stevens was part of a series of seventeen forts surrounding Washington during the Civil War; the only one to be challenged, repulsing

Confederate General Jubal Early's attack on July 11–12, 1864. The fort was visited by President Lincoln during the assault. Open to the public.

Gettysburg National Cemetery
Gettysburg, Pennsylvania 17325
(717) 334-6274

President Lincoln's famous Gettysburg address was delivered at the dedication ceremonies of the National Cemetery on November 19, 1863. Open to the public.

Frederick Presbyterian Church
115 W. 2nd Street
Frederick, Maryland 20701
(301) 663-5338

The Frederick Presbyterian Church was founded in 1780 and the present church building was completed in 1825. The church, like so many others in both the North and South, served as a military hospital during the Civil War. It is known that President Lincoln visited the wounded from nearby battles at the Frederick Church. The sanctuary features a Moller pipe organ, banners of the Presbyterian faith and Roman arch stained glass windows.

New York Avenue Presbyterian Church
1313 New York Avenue, NW
Washington, DC 20005
(202) 393-3700

The New York Avenue Presbyterian Church in downtown Washington was organized in 1803 by stonemasons who had worked on "The President's House," now called The White House. President Abraham Lincoln was a communicant and his pew and hitching post are extant, as is the original manuscript of his proposal to abolish slavery. The present brick church building dates from 1951.

Fords Theatre National Historic Site
511 10th Street, NW
Washington, DC 20004
(202) 426-6824

President Lincoln was felled by an assassin's bullet on April 14, 1865, as he was attending a performance at Fords Theatre. The stricken President was removed to the Petersen House across the street where he expired the next morning. The refurbished theater and the Petersen House are a National Park Service Site. Open to the public.

Hildene
Route 7A
Manchester, Vermont 05254
(802) 362-1788

Hildene, built in 1905, was the summer home of Abraham Lincoln's son, Robert Todd Lincoln, and the home of other Lincoln descendants until 1975. The twenty-four-room Georgian-style structure is a magnificent, informal mansion, filled with original furnishings and Lincoln memorabilia. The house is governed by the Friends of Hildene, Inc. Open to the public.

Lincoln Memorial
Lincoln Memorial Circle
The National Mall
Washington, DC 20242
(202) 619-PARK

The Lincoln Memorial, a Classical structure of exquisite beauty and dignity, houses a striking statue of the Great Emancipator sculpted by Daniel Chester French. National Park Service Site. Open to the public.

Lincoln Trail State Memorial
Lawrenceville, Illinois 62439

A twenty-five-acre state park marks the place where the Thomas Lincoln family entered Illinois in 1830. The site features a statue of youthful Abraham Lincoln leading the family wagon caravan.

Decatur
Decatur Convention and Visitor Center
202 East North Street
Decatur, Illinois 62523
(217) 423-7000

The Lincoln family lived in the Decatur area in 1830. There are statues and appropriate markers throughout the city and on the Millikin College campus commemorating events in Abraham Lincoln's life. A replica of the courthouse where he practiced law is displayed on its original site, now called Lincoln Park.

Abraham Lincoln Statue
Grant Park
Chicago, Illinois 60505

Grant Park features a statue of a seated, thoughtful Lincoln, rendered by Augustus Saint-Gaudens.

Abraham Lincoln Statue
Lincoln Park
Chicago, Illinois 60504

Augustus Saint-Gauden's statue of a standing Lincoln is displayed in Lincoln Park, as is a statue of Ulysses S. Grant.

Emancipation Monument
Lincoln Park
East Capitol Street
Washington, DC

A group of sculptures placed in Lincoln Park in 1876 depicts Abraham Lincoln holding the Emancipation Proclamation, with a freed slave at his feet. Former slaves posed for the monument and paid for its execution. The sculptor was Thomas Ball.

Great Moments with Mr. Lincoln
Disneyland
Anaheim, California 92802
(714) 999-4565

An audio-animatronic representation of Abraham Lincoln speaks words taken from his speeches and writings. Open to the public.

Illinois State Historical Society Library
Old State Capitol Building
Springfield, Illinois 62701
(217) 782-4836

The Library of the Illinois State Historical Society houses a large collection of books on Illinois history, Lincoln and the Civil War. A Lincoln Room contains artifacts once owned by Mary Todd Lincoln and busts of the Great Emancipator rendered by various artists. The Lincoln Collection – considered to be third in size only to the National Archives and the Library of Congress in the number of manuscripts it contains – includes a copy of the Gettysburg Address and a signed copy of the Emancipation Proclamation. Open to the public.

The Little Brick House
621 Saint Clair Street
Vandalia, Illinois 62471
(618) 283-2728

The Little Brick House is a simple 19th-century Italianate residence decorated with furnishings of the period (1820–1839) when Vandalia was the capital of Illinois. The house displays memorabilia associated with figures from Illinois' early history, including Abraham Lincoln. Open to the public.

Macon County Historical Society Museum
5580 N. Fork Road
Decatur, Illinois 62523
(217) 422-4919

The Macon County Museum houses an exhibit center containing historical artifacts. A Prairie Village with period buildings preserves Macon County's rich heritage, the most prominent building being the Macon County log courthouse in which attorney Abraham Lincoln practiced in 1838. Open to the public.

Lincoln Prairie Shrine
Mentor Graham House
Blunt, South Dakota 57522
(605) 962-6445

Mentor Graham was a village schoolmaster in New Salem who tutored Abraham Lincoln, and who is generally credited with teaching the future President his succinct style of speaking and writing. Graham's prairie home has been restored and furnished in the style of the 1880s through the efforts of the South Dakota Historical Society. Operated by the Town of Blunt. Open to the public .

Lincoln Monument State Memorial
Lincoln Statue Drive
Dixon, Illinois 61021

The memorial marks the site of the Dixon Blockhouse where Jefferson Davis, Zachary Taylor and Abraham Lincoln met as soldiers during the Black Hawk War in 1832. A small park has a statue of youthful Abraham Lincoln in semi-military garb. Open to the public.

Chicago Historical Society Museum
Clark at North
Chicago, Illinois 60614
(312) 642-4600

The Chicago Historical Society, one of the most respected historical institutions in the nation, has an impressive collection concentrating on the history of Illinois, including many original Lincoln items. Open to the public.

Vermilion County Museum
116 N. Gilbert
Danville, Illinois 61834
(217) 442-2922

Abraham Lincoln spoke from the balcony of the Fithian house during his 1858 senatorial campaign. The house has been converted to a museum. Open to the public.

Montgomery County Historical Society Courthouse Museum
3rd and Main
Dayton, Ohio 45402
(937) 628-6271

The Courthouse in Dayton was the site of a speech by Abraham Lincoln in 1859. Open to the public.

Lincoln Memorial Shrine
125 West Vine Street
Redlands, California 92373
(909) 798-7632

A distinguished marble building was built by industrialist Robert Watchorn in 1931 to house his personal collection of Lincoln memorabilia — the only such tribute to Lincoln west of the Mississippi. Open to the public.

The Lincoln Museum
66 Lincoln Square
Hodgenville, Kentucky 42748
(502) 358-3163

A small museum on the Hodgenville town square displays life-sized wax figures in dramatic representations of important events in Lincoln's life, including the Lincoln-Douglas debates and the Gettysburg Address, among others. Open to the public.

Abraham Lincoln Statue
Lincoln Square
Hodgenville, Kentucky 42748

In 1904, Larue County was given permission by the Kentucky State Legislature to commission a statue of Abraham Lincoln to be placed in Hodgenville. A. A. Weinman, a disciple of Augustus Saint-Gaudens, won the competition, and his bronze figure of Lincoln remains to this day the centerpiece of Hodgenville's town square.

The Lincoln Museum
200 East Berry Street
Fort Wayne, Indiana 46802
(219) 455-3864

A full-service museum with hundreds of artifacts and an extensive library of Lincolniana is owned and operated by the Lincoln National Corporation as a tribute to the man whose name they proudly carry. Open to the public.

Abraham Lincoln Statue
Lincoln National Corporation
Harrison Street
Fort Wayne, Indiana 46802

An original cast-bronze statue, "Abraham Lincoln: The Hoosier Youth," executed by Paul Manship in 1932, stands outside the corporate offices of the Lincoln National Corporation. Except for Mount Rushmore and the Lincoln Memorial, it is the largest representation of Abraham Lincoln in America, standing twenty-two-feet tall.

The Abraham Lincoln Museum
Lincoln Memorial University
Cumberland Gap Parkway
Harrogate, Tennessee 37752
(615) 869-6237

Lincoln Memorial University was founded by General O. O. Howard, an admirer of Lincoln, to serve the people of southern Appalachia, its expressed philosophy ". . . to provide the public with a moving and creative portrayal of Lincoln's dramatic commitment to the American way of life and confront each of us with the need to reaffirm that commitment." The Lincoln Museum is housed in a handsome brick building on campus. Open to the public.

Lincoln College Museum
300 Keokuk Street
Lincoln, Illinois 62656
(217) 732-3155

On August 27, 1853, the first lots were sold in a new real estate development to be named Lincoln in honor of Attorney Abraham Lincoln, who proceeded to christen the town with watermelon juice! A marker at the corner of Broadway and Chicago streets commemorates the deed, and a museum on the nearby campus of Lincoln College contains many mementos which include the original town plat signed by Lincoln. Open to the public.

Abraham Lincoln Statue
Lincoln College
Lincoln, Illinois 62656

The exterior of the McKinstry Library on the campus of Lincoln College is graced by Merrell Gage's dramatic sculpture called "Lincoln, the Student."

The Lincoln Room Museum
12 Lincoln Square
Gettysburg, Pennsylvania 17325
(717) 334-8188

Installation Chairman Judge David Wills invited President Lincoln to Gettysburg to "give a few remarks" at the dedication of a National Cemetery on November 19, 1863, a few short months after the climactic Battle of Gettysburg that had taken place in July of that year. The President polished his speech in an upstairs bedroom of the Wills home that has been converted into a museum of memorabilia that includes a life-sized wax figure of the President at work, sitting at a tiny writing table. Open to the public.

Civil War Library and Museum
1805 Pine Street
Philadelphia, Pennsylvania 19103
(215) 735-8196

A research library and museum housed in a building of the Civil War era located in the heart of downtown Philadelphia. Contents include Civil War books and artifacts with one room dedicated solely to the life and times of Abraham Lincoln. Open to the public.

Union Pacific Historical Museum
1416 Dodge Street
Omaha, Nebraska 68102
(402) 271-5457

The Union Pacific Historical Museum documents the history of this railroad from 1862 to the present. Among the railroad artifacts on display is the funeral car that brought President Lincoln's body home to Springfield, Illinois, in 1865. Operated by Union Pacific Corporation. Open to the public.

Lincoln Collection
University of Delaware
Newark, Delaware 19713
(302) 831-8123

More than 2,000 items relating to the life of Abraham Lincoln are on display in a museum on the campus of the University of Delaware. Open to the public.

Lincoln Train Museum
Gettysburg, Pennsylvania 17325
(717) 334-5658

Visitors to the Lincoln Train Museum "ride and listen" to White House reporters and guests as they all accompany the President over the same railroad route Abraham Lincoln took from Washington to Gettysburg for his speaking engagement. Open to the public.

Lincoln Gettysburg Address Exhibit
National Park Cyclorama Building
Gettysburg, Pennsylvania 17325
(717) 334-1124

The Gettysburg Address is recreated by a Lincoln impersonator in an inspiring live performance. Open to the public.

Gettysburg Railroad Steam Train
106 N. Washington Street
Gettysburg, Pennsylvania 17325
(717) 334-6932

An actual steam train journey through the rolling Pennsylvania countryside features various theme rides, one of which is a "Ride with Lincoln." Open to the public.

Lincoln Heritage House
US Route 31W at Freeman Lake Park
Elizabethtown, Kentucky 42701
(502) 769-3916

One of the two log buildings in Freeman Lake Park was built in 1805 by owner Hardin Thomas and his friend Thomas Lincoln, father of Abraham. A skilled cabinetmaker, Thomas Lincoln built the staircases and mantelpieces. Open to the public.

Old Fort Harrod State Park
Harrodsburg, Kentucky 40330
(606) 734-3314

One of the attractions in Old Fort Harrod Park is the Lincoln Marriage Temple housing the log cabin in which Abraham Lincoln's parents were married. During the summer season costumed local residents portray early settlers of Harrodsburg, the first permanent town west of the Alleghanies. Open to the public.

Abraham Lincoln Statue
Courthouse Lawn
Clinton, Illinois 61727

A life-sized statue created by Belgian artist Van den Bergen marks the site where, during the Illinois senatorial campaign of 1858, Lincoln delivered his famous aphorism, "You can fool all the people part of the time and part of the people all the time, but you cannot fool all the people all the time."

Lincoln Center for the Performing Arts
New York City, New York 10023
(212) 875-5350

Lincoln Center is a fourteen-acre complex of educational and artistic institutions which includes the Metropolitan Opera House, Avery Fisher Hall and the New York City Ballet. Open to the public.

Abraham Lincoln Statue
State Capitol
14th and H Streets
Lincoln, Nebraska 68508
(402) 471-0448

The foyer of the Nebraska State Capitol building contains a sculpture of Abraham Lincoln created by Daniel Chester French, the artist

150

who executed the statue in the Lincoln Memorial in Washington, DC. Open to the public.

Fort Abraham Lincoln State Park
State Route 1806
Mandan, North Dakota 58554
(701) 663-9571

Fort Abraham Lincoln was the military base from which General George Armstrong Custer left on his way into battle with the Sioux Indians, and history. The fort was abandoned in 1891 and remains mostly destroyed, although a reconstruction is planned. Museum. Open to the public.

Abraham Lincoln Statue
421 E. 4th Street
Cincinnati, Ohio 45215

A park area in downtown Cincinnati features a statue of the Great Emancipator by George Grey Bernard.

Abraham Lincoln Statue
State House
Capitol Square
Topeka, Kansas 66612
(913) 296-3966

The foyer of the Kansas State House displays a bronze statue of Abraham Lincoln by Merrell Gage.

Abraham Lincoln Statue
Federal Triangle
Washington, DC 20005

A statue of Lincoln, rendered by Lot Flannery, stands in front of the Washington City Hall.

See also: **Old Talbott Tavern** (p. 100); **Phenix Hall** (p. 129); **Anderson House** (p. 132); **Mount Rushmore** (p. 285).

Andrew Johnson

Seventeenth President
1865–1869

Born December 29, 1808, Raleigh, North Carolina
Died July 31, 1875, Carter Station, Tennessee
Burial Site: Andrew Johnson National Cemetery, Greeneville,
Tennessee

Andrew Johnson Birthplace
Mordecai Historic Park
Raleigh, North Carolina 27601
(919) 834-4844

    Andrew Johnson was born in a small house, utilized as a combined kitchen and dwelling, which was attached to Cassos Inn, where his father Jacob was employed as a hostler and his mother Polly as a seamstress. The house was purchased in 1904 by the Wake County Committee of the Colonial Dames of America and presented to the City of Raleigh in 1975. It has been refurbished and moved to Mordecai Historic Park near downtown Raleigh where it is managed by Capital Area Preservation. Open to the public.

Andrew Johnson National Historic Site
College and Depot Streets
Greeneville, Tennessee 37744
(423) 638-3551

The Andrew Johnson National Historic Site is divided geographically into three parts. One is a modern Visitor Center that houses the original Johnson tailor shop and oversees the first Johnson home located across the street. The second, a larger home in which Johnson retired following his presidency, is located about a mile away. The third, the Andrew Johnson National Cemetery where the President lies at rest, is located another mile away. At the President's request, his winding sheet was the American Flag, and his pillow the Constitution of the United States. All sections are open to the public.

Andrew Johnson Marriage Site
Greeneville or Warrensburg, Tennessee

Andrew Johnson and Eliza McCardle were married on May 17, 1827, but the exact location is unknown − it occurred either in Greeneville or Warrensburg, Tennessee.

Andrew Johnson Library and Museum
Tusculum College
Greeneville, Tennessee 37743
(423) 636-7320

Although he did not matriculate, Andrew Johnson felt close to Tusculum College and served on its Board of Trustees upon his retirement from the presidency. A replicated Andrew Johnson birth house was donated to Tusculum by his granddaughter, and is located just behind the Library which has been developed into a museum dedicated to Johnson's life and career. Open to the public.

Memorials to Andrew Johnson

Andrew Johnson Statue
Greeneville, Tennessee 37744

In June, 1995, the town of Greeneville dedicated a statue of President Johnson, presented as a gift from the estate of Johnson's granddaughter, Mrs. Margaret Johnson Patterson Bartlett. The statue is located across the street from the Visitor Center of the Andrew Johnson National Historic Site in downtown Greeneville.

See also: **Chester Inn** (p. 98); **Netherland Inn** (p. 99); **Hale Springs Inn** (p. 100); **Presidential Memorial** (p. 104).

Ulysses S. Grant

Eighteenth President
1869–1877

Born April 27, 1822, Point Pleasant, Ohio
Died July 23, 1885, Mount McGregor, New York
Burial Site: Grant's Tomb, New York, New York

Grants Birthplace
Routes 52E and 322
Point Pleasant, Ohio 45143
(513) 553-4911

Ulysses S. Grant was born in the bedroom of a tiny frame house of white Allegheny pine set high on the banks of the Ohio River twenty-five miles southeast of Cincinnati. The house, consisting only of a kitchen, living room and bedroom, is owned by the State of Ohio and maintained by the Ohio Historical Society which has restored and furnished the house with historic memorabilia including the actual cradle in which the infant "Lys" slept. The family stayed in Point Pleasant only a year before moving on to Georgetown, Ohio. Open to the public.

155

Grants Boyhood Home
217 East Grant Street
Georgetown, Ohio 45121
(513) 378-4222

When Ulysses Grant was still an infant, his family moved thirty miles southeast from Point Pleasant to Georgetown where his father founded a tannery and built a two-story brick house with only one room downstairs and one upstairs. As the family fortunes improved a kitchen, parlor and two bedrooms were added. In 1982, dedicated preservationists completed a restoration of the home, their intention being to preserve its future as a house museum furnished in period style. The Grant House is the centerpiece of a modern walking tour of Georgetown that includes views of father Jesse Grant's tannery, two schoolhouses attended by Ulysses, the Brown County Courthouse and other buildings of historic interest. Open to the public.

Grant Memorial Building
Ohio State Routes 125 and 133
Bethel, Ohio 45106
(513) 753-7141

In 1845, the Grant family moved to Bethel, Ohio, ten miles west of Georgetown. Ulysses returned for visits whenever possible. When he received orders to report to the West Coast for military duty he brought his wife, Julia, to Bethel where their son was born. The Grant Memorial building displays memorabilia from the mid-1880s. Open to the public.

Dent Townhouse
4th and Cerre Streets
Saint Louis, Missouri 63102

Ulysses S. Grant married Julia Dent in the Dent's residence on August 22, 1848. The house has been demolished.

U. S. Grant House
Michigan State Fairgrounds
State Fair and Woodward
Detroit, Michigan 48203
(313) 368-1000

In 1849, Ulysses S. Grant was stationed at Fort Wayne in Detroit, where Mrs. Grant resided with him in a small frame house at 1369 East Fort Street. In 1936, the house was moved to its present location at the State Fair Grounds where it may be inspected during the fair.

156

Ulysses S. Grant National Historic Site
7400 Grant Road
Saint Louis, Missouri 63123
(314) 842-1867

A two-story frame house named "White Haven" was owned and used by Grant's father-in-law, Saint Louis businessman Frederick Dent, as a summer residence. This is where Ulysses S. Grant proposed to Dent's daughter, Julia. Grant returned to his wife and White Haven in 1854 upon his first retirement from the army. The National Park Service is currently conducting a vigorous program of research, rebuilding and refurbishing at White Haven. Open to the public.

Grants Farm
10501 Gravois Road
Saint Louis, Missouri 63123
(314) 843-1700

Shortly after Ulysses S. Grant returned to White Haven in 1854, father-in-law Dent presented the Grants with a part of his White Haven property upon which Grant built "Hardscrabble," a small cabin facetiously named not only for the land but for the difficulty of the times. Hardscrabble has been preserved as part of Grants Farm, a 281-acre entertainment complex owned and operated by the Anheuser-Busch Company as a public service. The cabin may be observed from a tram circling the park. Open to the public.

Grants House
1121 High Street
Galena, Illinois 61036

The "Hardscrabble" farm effort failed in 1860 and the Grants moved to Galena where Grant worked in his family's store. He and Julia resided in a small house on High Street. Closed to the public.

J. R. Grant Leather Store
120 Main Street
Galena, Illinois 61036
(815) 777-3331

When the Grants moved to Galena in 1860, Ulysses worked for a brief time in a leather store owned by his father. The building collapsed in the early part of the century but was rebuilt using some of the original bricks. Open to the public.

General Grant House
309 Wood Street
Burlington, New Jersey 08016

General Grant sent his family here for safety during the Civil War. Closed to the public.

Grant Home State Historic Site
Bouthillier Street, Box 333
Galena, Illinois 61036
(815) 777-0248

Failing as a Missouri farmer, Ulysses S. Grant and his family moved to Galena in 1860 where he hoped to reverse his fortunes by working in a leather store owned by his father. Only a year later, however, he left home to rejoin the army as colonel of the Twenty-First Illinois Volunteer Infantry Regiment — and the rest is history. Upon General Grant's triumphant return from the Civil War, proud hometown citizens presented the Grants with a lovely home in the Italianate Bracketed style so popular at the time. The family resided there only briefly as Grant was called to Washington as president and thereafter made New York City his permanent residence. The Grant Home, set in one of America's best-preserved 19th-century towns, was purchased from the Grant estate by the State of Illinois which now maintains it as an outstanding example of post-Civil War decor and architecture. Open to the public.

Campbell House Museum
1508 Locust Street
Saint Louis, Missouri 63103
(314) 421-0325

A three-story brick townhouse where President and Mrs. Grant were entertained by its owner, wealthy fur trader Robert Campbell, remains intact, owned and operated by the Campbell House Foundation. Open to the public.

Tabor House
116 East 5th Street
Leadville, Colorado 80461
(719) 486-0551

The Tabor House is a two-story frame with barge-board trim that was built by silver king H. A. W. Tabor. It was restored as a museum in 1950. President and Mrs. Grant were guests in 1880. Open to the public.

Magnolia Mansion

Charles H. Galigher House
2700 Washington Avenue
Cairo, Illinois 62914
(618) 734-0201

The Magnolia Mansion, filled with Victorian antiques, was built by Charles H. Galigher as an Italianate showplace. It was the scene of a reception for President and Mrs. Grant in 1880. The mansion is operated by the Cairo Historical Society. Open to the public.

Scott-Grant House

3238 R Street
Washington, DC 20007

The Scott-Grant House, an ornate residence in the Georgetown area of Washington, was utilized by President and Mrs. Grant for relief during the summer since the air there was cooler than at the White House. The house is privately owned and currently unoccupied. Closed to the public.

The Old Tavern

Main Street
Grafton, Vermont 05146
(802) 843-2231

Modern-day Grafton has been called "Vermont's Cinderella," one of the most meticulously restored villages in New England. The Old Tavern, exquisitely refurbished, exemplifies the town's charm and ambiance. Celebrities who have stayed at The Old Tavern include Ralph Waldo Emerson, Henry David Thoreau, Rudyard Kipling, Ulysses S. Grant, Theodore Roosevelt and Woodrow Wilson. Open to the public.

Blaine House

162 State Street
Augusta, Maine 04330
(207) 287-3531

James G. Blaine, "The Man from Maine," was an influential politician who served as congressman, Speaker of the House, United States Senator and Secretary of State under two presidents. Among his guests on one occasion was President Grant, honored with a grand reception. The Blaine House now serves as Maine's Executive Mansion. Open to the public.

Excelsior Hotel
211 West Austin Street
Jefferson, Texas 75657
(903) 665-2513

The Excelsior was built as the home of Captain William Perry. Notables who have stayed in the hotel include Ulysses S. Grant and Rutherford B. Hayes. Some original documents and guest registers are displayed in the lobby. Open to the public.

Beehive House
75 East South Temple Street
Salt Lake City, Utah 84111
(801) 240-2671

The Greek Revival home of pioneer Brigham Young, governor of the Mormon State of Deseret and the Territory of Utah, was built in 1854. The name of the house was taken from its beehive-shaped cupola, the beehive symbolizing Mormon industry. The house has served as the official residence of Mormon presidents, and it has been restored to its original appearance at the time when Ulysses S. Grant had been a guest of Brigham Young. Open to the public.

Teller House Casino
120 Eureka Street
Central City, Colorado 80427
(303) 582-3200

At the height of the Colorado Silver Rush, thousands of people hurried west fostering boom towns, one of which was Central City. The Teller House Hotel was constructed as part of the town's success. President U. S. Grant stopped for a brief visit, and the sidewalk in front of the hotel was paved with silver ingots in his honor. Teller House has been converted to a casino with a separate museum section Open to the public.

Cookes Row
3007–3027 31st Street, NW
Washington, DC 20008

Cookes Row consists of four double Victorian houses designed by Starkweather and Plowman in 1868 for Henry Cooke, first governor of the District of Columbia. The two central buildings are in the Italian Villa style while the end houses are in the Second Empire style. The houses were considered the most luxurious residences in the city, with double walls, specially designed dumbwaiters, servant's bells and ventilating systems.

160

President Grant often visited his brother-in-law and private secretary, Colonel Dent, who lived in #3009. Closed to the public.

Mohegan Bluffs and Southeast Lighthouse
Block Island, Rhode Island 02807
(401) 466-5200

The lighthouse, once visited by President Grant, sits high on a two-hundred-foot-high bluff, its electric beam the most powerful on the east coast. Open to the public.

Church of the Presidents
1260 Ocean Avenue
Long Branch, New Jersey 07740

A gray Victorian Episcopal church in the Elberon section of Long Beach has welcomed seven presidents as worshippers — including Ulysses S. Grant, James A. Garfield, Chester A. Arthur, Benjamin Harrison, William McKinley, Rutherford B. Hayes and Woodrow Wilson. President Garfield attended the church while wounded, having been brought to the Jersey shore to escape Washington's heat after being shot by an assassin. The building, owned by a Long Branch historical organization, is unoccupied (1998) and in an advanced state of deterioration. Closed to the public.

Metropolitan Memorial Methodist Church
Nebraska and New Mexico Avenues
3401 Nebraska Avenue
Washington, DC 20016
(202) 363-4900

Metropolitan Memorial Methodist Church was the Washington church home of presidents Ulysses S. Grant and William McKinley. Grant was among the first trustees of the original church building at John Marshall Place where is found the name of ". . . Ulysses S. Grant, President of the United States and first Chairman of the Board."

Grant Cottage State Historic Site
Mount McGregor, Box 990
Saratoga Springs, New York 12866
(518) 584-4768

In 1885, ex-President Ulysses S. Grant journeyed to a simple vacation cottage in the Adirondack Mountains of New York with two purposes — one to find relief from the ravages of painful throat cancer and the other to finish his memoirs which he hoped would sell well enough to replenish a fortune lost in a financial swindle. The courageous President

Grant passed away only a few weeks after completing his memoirs. The State of New York has preserved the cabin "in time" — frozen as it was at the moment of Grant's death. Open to the public.

Ulysses S. Grant's Military Career

Fort Humboldt State Historic Park
3431 Fort Avenue
Eureka, California 95503
(707) 445-6567

Ulysses S. Grant was stationed at Fort Humboldt in 1854 as a young officer. The park contains logging and military exhibits of the period. Open to the public.

Benicia Arsenal Capitol Historic Park and Barracks
First and West G Streets
Benicia, California 94510
(707) 745-3385

The historic park contains remains of an arsenal complex dating to the mid-19th century. It was occupied and visited by many important military figures, including Ulysses S. Grant. Museum. Open to the public.

Officers Row
Fort Vancouver Barracks
1611–1616 E. Evergreen Boulevard
Vancouver, Washington 98661
(360) 696-7655

Officers Row is a stately collection of twenty-one Victorian-era homes built for US Army officers serving the local post, including such notables as Philip Sheridan, Ulysses S. Grant, George C. Marshall and Omar Bradley. At various times special receptions were held to honor visiting presidents Grant, Rutherford B. Hayes and Franklin D. Roosevelt. The Grant and Marshall homes are open to the public.

Grant House
Officers Row
E. Evergreen Boulevard
Vancouver, Washington 98661
(360) 694-5252

The Grant House was the first house on the Row, constructed originally as the commanding officer's quarters. Ulysses S. Grant never lived in the house, but visited often in his capacity as post quartermaster. The house was renamed in his honor after he achieved military and political success. Museum. Open to the public.

Madison Barracks
Sackets Harbor, New York 13685
(315) 646-2321

Ulysses S. Grant was stationed here twice in his early army career (1848–1849, 1851–1852.) The area is presently under private development. Closed to the public.

U. S. Grant House
Nolan Park
Governors Island, New York 10004

Ulysses S. Grant was stationed on Governors Island early in his military career. He resided in a house on Officers Row. Closed to the public.

Columbus-Belmont Civil War State Park
Columbus, Kentucky 43032
(502) 677-2327

During the early months of the Civil War, Columbus was the northernmost Confederate line of defense. General Grant assaulted this Confederate position on November 8, 1861. The attack failed, but Grant's aggressive, positive effort in this battle was not lost on President Lincoln, who was looking for generals who would fight. Museum. Open to the public.

Ryan House
1375 Locust Street
Dubuque, Iowa 52001
(515) 556-2733

The Ryan House, a Victorian home in which General Grant was a guest, is now a public restaurant. Open to the public.

Ross House
501 S. Muldrow
Mexico, Missouri 65265
(573) 581-3910

General Grant visited the Ross House, circa 1857, during the early part of the Civil War. It has furnished period rooms. Open to the public.

Fort Donelson National Military Park
Dover, Tennessee 37058
(615) 232-5349

General Grant's capture of Fort Donelson in February of 1862 was the first major Union victory of the war. This battle became particularly noted for Grant's famous ultimatum to the Confederates of *unconditional and complete surrender*. National Park Service Site. Open to the public.

Walter Place
331 West Chulahoma Avenue
Holly Springs, Mississippi 38625
(601) 252-2943

Holly Springs is a few miles southeast of Memphis, Tennessee. Walter Place is a large Greek Revival mansion used by General and Mrs. Grant in 1862. Open to the public.

Hunt-Phelan House
553 Beale Street
Memphis, Tennessee 38108
(901) 344-3166; (800) 350-9009

A Greek Revival masterpiece of a house was used by General Grant as headquarters preceding the Battle of Shiloh, and may be where he planned the Vicksburg campaign. The House has recently been renovated to reflect its original sparkling grandeur. Open to the public.

Cherry House
101 Main Street
Savannah, Tennessee 38372

David Robinson built this house around 1830 and presented it as a wedding gift to his daughter and son-in-law, W. H. Cherry. In the spring of 1862, Major General Grant appropriated it as headquarters preceding the Battle of Shiloh. The building is not open to the public but visitors may walk the grounds. The Grant Monument commemorating the battle is one block east of the Cherry House.

Shiloh Battlefield National Military Park
Box 61
Shiloh, Tennessee 38376
(901) 689-5275

The bloodiest battle of the Civil War was engaged on April 6 and 7, 1862, between the forces led by Ulysses S. Grant and Confederate generals

Albert Sidney Johnston and P. G. T. Beauregard. Over 24,000 young Americans were killed or wounded in the horrific action. Future President James A. Garfield was also a participant in the battle. National Park Service Site. Open to the public.

The Vicksburg Campaign

Vicksburg is the key — the war can never be brought to a close until that key is in our pocket, declared President Lincoln. In the spring of 1863, General Ulysses S. Grant began the actions which would deliver that key to Lincoln.

Grand Gulf Military Monument Park
Port Gibson, Mississippi 39150
(601) 437-5911

The Battle of Port Gibson began on May 1 with a skirmish near the A. K. Shaifer House (still standing.) Open to the public.

Port Gibson
Port Gibson Chamber of Commerce
Box 491
Port Gibson, Mississippi 39150
(601) 437-4351

General Grant declared Port Gibson "too beautiful to burn," and thus spared the homes and churches that form Port Gibson's picturesque historic district. Open to the public.

Raymond Battlefield
Routes 18 and 462
Raymond, Mississippi 39154

On May 12, an important battle was fought here as part of Grant's unstoppable march to Jackson and on to Vicksburg. Grant's headquarters was in the Waverly House, since destroyed. The battlefield and Confederate cemetery are open to the public.

Old Capitol
100 South State Street
Jackson, Mississippi 39202
(601) 359-6920

Jackson was the capital of Mississippi between 1839 and 1903. Its surrender to General Ulysses S. Grant in 1863 concluded his successful assault. Museum. Open to the public.

Governors Mansion
316 E. Capitol Street
Jackson, Mississippi 39180
(601) 359-3175

Following the surrender of the city of Jackson, the Governors Mansion was appropriated by Union troops as headquarters for generals Grant and William Tecumseh Sherman. Open to the public.

Battle of Champion Hill
Route 467
Edwards, Mississippi 39154

The decisive battle of the Vicksburg campaign was won by the Union on May 16. Except for one more skirmish to come, the road to Vicksburg had been opened. Grant's headquarters was in the Champion House, since destroyed. The Coker House, used as a field hospital, still remains although it is under restoration. Open to the public.

Battle of Big Black River Bridge
Near Exit 11, US Route 80
west of Vicksburg, Mississippi 39180

The final battle preceding the siege of Vicksburg was fought on May 17. Open to the public.

Rosalie
100 Orleans Street
Natchez, Mississippi 39121
(800) 647-6742

A stately mansion combining Georgian and Classical Revival styles served as a Union headquarters in 1863 and General Grant stayed in it at one time. Rosalie, owned and operated by the Daughters of the American Revolution, is a state shrine furnished with period pieces. Open to the public.

Vicksburg National Military Park and Cemetery
3201 Clay Street
Vicksburg, Mississippi 39180
(601) 636-0583

Reconstructed forts and trenches evoke memories of the 47-day siege of the city, terminated on July 4, 1863. The fall of Vicksburg cut the Confederacy in half, a situation that was instrumental in bringing about the eventual Union victory. The National Cemetery at the northern end of the park contains the graves of nearly 17,000 Civil War soldiers. National Park Service Site. Open to the public.

Civil War Earthworks at Tallahatchie Crossing
Abbeville, Mississippi 38601

Earthen artillery parapets, built as a link in the communications chain supplying Grant's troops, are visible at Tallahatchie Crossing.

Old Court House Museum
1008 Cherry Street
Vicksburg, Mississippi 39180
(601) 636-0741

The victorious General Grant paid a symbolic visit to the Court House on July 4, 1863, following the surrender of the city of Vicksburg. Museum. Open to the public.

Chickamauga and Chattanooga National Military Park
Box 2128
Fort Oglethorpe, Georgia 30742
(706) 866-9241

There are two battlefields where the Union and Confederacy fought for control of Chattanooga. Chickamauga, fought September 19 and 20, 1863, was a Confederate victory which merely postponed the inevitable. The Battle for Chattanooga, on November 23 and 24, ended with a Union victory. Ulysses S. Grant was the Union commander-in-chief, and future President James A. Garfield fought here as a young officer. National Park Service Site. Open to the public.

Carriage Inn
417 E. Washington
Charles Town, West Virginia 25414
(304) 728-8003

Generals Grant and Sheridan conducted a strategy session in the Carriage Inn in 1864. Carriage Inn is currently a Bed and Breakfast Inn. Open to the public.

Fredericksburg and Spotsylvania National Historic Site
US Route 1 and Sunken Road
Box 679
Fredericksburg, Virginia 22404
(540) 373-4461

The National Historic Site commemorates Chancellorsville, The

Wilderness and many other battles fought in the area. National Park Service Site. Open to the public.

Richmond National Battlefield Park
3215 E. Broad Street (Visitor Center)
Richmond, Virginia 23223
(804) 226-1981

From the beginning of the Civil War, "On to Richmond!" was the rallying cry for the Union, the capital of the Confederacy their primary objective for four years. In all, seven military thrusts were hurled at the beleaguered city before it finally capitulated. Richmond National Battlefield Park comprises ten park units that offer insight into the period and commemorate many battles – Cold Harbor, Drewrys Bluff, Gaines Mill, Malvern Hill, Beaver Dam Creek and others – all actions that lead to the Union capture of Richmond itself. National Park Service Site. Open to the public.

Petersburg National Battlefield
Box 549, Route 36
Petersburg, Virginia 23804
(804) 732-3531

The Union army waged a ten-month campaign in 1864–1865 to seize Petersburg, center of a rail network supplying Richmond and the army of Robert E. Lee. National Park Service Site. Open to the public.

Hopewell and City Point
201–D Randolph Square
Hopewell, Virginia 23860
(804) 352-8987

General Grant's headquarters during the Petersburg siege was in a large home prophetically named Appomattox Manor. The entire Hopewell area was part of the Petersburg battlefield. Open to the public.

Appomattox Court House National Historic Park
Box 218
Appomattox, Virginia 24552
(540) 352-8987

Appomattox is where Confederate General Robert E. Lee surrendered to Ulysses S. Grant, ending the Civil War. The tiny village of Appomattox has been reconstructed, including the McLean House where the formal signing of the surrender papers took place. National Park Service Site. Open to the public.

Henry C. Bowen House
Roseland Cottage
State Route 169
Woodstock, Connecticut 06281
(860) 928-4074

Roseland Cottage, facing the Woodstock Town Green, is an architectural anomaly — one of the most important surviving examples of Gothic Revival style. Roseland was built by the influential founder/publisher of *The Independent,* Henry C. Bowen, who hosted an annual July 4th gala attended at least once by every sitting president from Grant to McKinley. An outbuilding houses one of the first bowling alleys in the country, supposedly used by President Grant on one of his visits. Open to the public.

Memorials to Ulysses S. Grant

General Grant and Redwood Mountain Groves
Kings Canyon National Park.
Three Rivers, California 93271
(209) 561-3459

The General Grant Tree, standing proudly in Grants Grove, is the third largest of the known sequoias, 267 feet-high with a circumference of 107.6 feet. Open to the public.

Union Square Statuary
East end of the National Mall
Washington, DC

A bronze sculpture group depicts a mounted General Grant leading a group of Union cavalry and ground troops. The grouping is 252 feet in length and faces the reflecting pool at the foot of the Capitol steps. National Park Service Site.

See also: **William H. Seward House** (p. 93); **Jefferson Barracks Historic District** (p. 121); **Palo Alto Battlefield** (p. 122); **Thomas Wallace House** (p. 141); **Lincoln Park** (p. 143).

Rutherford B. Hayes

Nineteenth President
1875–1879

Born October 4, 1822, Delaware, Ohio
Died January 17, 1893, Fremont, Ohio
Burial Site: Spiegel Grove, Fremont, Ohio

Rutherford B. Hayes Birthplace
East William Street
Delaware, Ohio 43015

The brick house in which Rutherford B. Hayes was born no longer stands. There is a marker.

Hayes Presidential Center
Spiegel Grove State Park
Fremont, Ohio 43420-2796
(419) 332-2081

Spiegel Grove is a gracious twenty-five-acre estate that includes a modern library-museum, the Hayes gravesite and a stately thirty-three-room, brick and wood mansion filled with precious antiques. Hayes' uncle built the

170

house, naming it Spiegel Grove, using the German word for "mirror" to describe the reflection of pools of water after a rain. The complex is administered jointly by the Hayes family, the Ohio Historical Society and the Rutherford B. Hayes and Lucy Webb Hayes Foundation. Open to the public.

Mrs. Maria Webb Residence
141 W. 6th Street
Cincinnati, Ohio 45219

Rutherford B. Hayes and Lucy Webb were married at the Maria Webb residence, the home of the bride's mother, on December 30, 1852. The newlyweds lived with Mrs. Webb until the spring of 1854. The house has been demolished.

Kenyon Building
Kenyon College
Gambier, Ohio 43022

Rutherford B. Hayes boarded in a gable room when attending Kenyon College, 1838–1842. The structure burned but has been reconstructed. Closed to the public.

Ohio State Capitol
Broad and High Streets
Columbus, Ohio 43211
(614) 466-2125

Future presidents Rutherford B. Hayes and William McKinley both served as Governor of Ohio in the capitol building, constructed circa 1861 and considered one of the finest examples of Greek Doric architecture in the United States. Its library contains historical documents, portraits and other works commemorating Ohio's governors and US Presidents from Ohio. Open to the public.

Foundry United Methodist Church
1500 16th Street, NW
Washington, DC 20002
(202) 332-4010

Lucy Hayes was a devout Methodist, and the President accompanied her to services at Foundry United Methodist Church during his presidency. She was a member of the Methodist Church in Fremont, Ohio, and he was a regular there as well, although he had no wish to join any organized church.

First Brethren Church

216 S. Park Avenue
Fremont, Ohio 43420
(419) 332-0531

The building originally housing the Fremont Methodist Church was destroyed by fire but rebuilt shortly before Lucy Hayes' death. A stained glass window in the building, currently used by another denomination, was a gift from President Hayes in memory of his wife.

The Old Mansion

Benefit and John Streets
Providence, Rhode Island 02096

In 1877, President Hayes made a triumphal tour of New England. On June 28 he stopped in Providence, Rhode Island, where he was greeted with great fanfare and affection. He stayed overnight at a private mansion. Closed to the public.

Rutherford B. Hayes' Military Career

Camp Jackson

2900 Sullivant Avenue
Columbus, Ohio 43204

During the Civil War, Major Rutherford Hayes headed the Twenty-Third Ohio Volunteer Infantry which trained here. The only remains are the camp cemetery, now under the jurisdiction of the Veterans Administration. Future president James A. Garfield also served at Camp Jackson.

Fort Scammon

Charleston, West Virginia 25301

The remains of earthworks built by men under Hayes' command are still visible at Fort Scammon.

Giles County Courthouse

Pearlsburg, Virginia 23134

In May, 1862, the courthouse square in Pearisburg, Giles County, in western Virginia was the scene of an encounter between Union and Confederate troops. Lt. Colonel Hayes was the senior Union officer present.

172

Carnifex Ferry Battlefield State Park
Summersville, West Virginia 26651
(304) 872-3773

The Twenty-Third Ohio Volunteer Infantry commanded by Rutherford B. Hayes fought at Carnifex, September 10, 1862.

South Mountain
near Hagerstown, Maryland 21740

Lt. Colonel Rutherford B. Hayes was wounded in a fierce battle at South Mountain on September 14, 1862.

Cedar Creek Battlefield
Strasburg, Virginia 22657

Colonel Rutherford B. Hayes commanded a division under General Philip Sheridan whose army defeated Confederate General Jubal Early at Cedar Creek on October 19, 1864. Closed to the public.

Sandusky
Sandusky Drive
Lynchburg, Virginia 24502

In 1864, Sandusky served as Union headquarters for General David Hunter, whose staff included two future presidents — Rutherford B. Hayes and William McKinley. James A. Garfield also served at Sandusky. Hayes left the army a Brevet Major General. Closed to the public.

See also: **Anderson House** (p. 132); **Excelsior House Hotel** (p. 160); **Henry C. Bowen House** (p. 169).

James A. Garfield

Twentieth President
March, 1881–September, 1881

Born November 19, 1831, Cuyahoga, Ohio
Died September 19, 1881, Elberon, New Jersey
Burial Site: James A. Garfield Monument, Cleveland, Ohio

James A. Garfield Birthplace
4350 S. O. M. Center Road
Moreland Hills (now Chagrin Falls)
Cuyahoga County, Ohio 44022

James A. Garfield was born in a frontier log cabin that was destroyed long ago. There is a marker.

Garfield House
6825 Hinsdale Street
Hiram, Ohio 44234

Lucretia Garfield bought a house while husband James was in military service. After the war they lived in Hiram while he served as president of Western Reserve Eclectic Institute, now Hiram College. It remained their principal residence during Garfield's early congressional career. Closed to the public.

Lawnfield
8095 Mentor Avenue
Mentor, Ohio 44060
(216) 255-8722

When serving in the United States Congress, James A. Garfield purchased a rundown farmhouse that evolved over the years into a thirty-room mansion, now filled with original furnishings and Garfield memorabilia. Lawnfield is operated by the Western Reserve Historical Society under the aegis of the National Park Service. The house is currently under renovation with a planned reopening in 1998.

Rudulph Home
Hiram, Ohio 44234

On November 11, 1858, James Garfield and Lucretia Rudulph were married in her parents' home. The newlyweds often boarded with her family, and spent two summers with the Rudulphs before acquiring Lawnfield. The Rudulph house no longer stands.

Williams College
Williamstown, Massachusetts 01267

James A. Garfield roomed in #16 South College and #23 East College during his undergraduate days at Williams. Both buildings are owned by the college. Closed to the public.

Campbell Mansion
SR 67
Bethany, West Virginia 26032
(304) 829-4258

Alexander Campbell's twenty-four-room showplace house was host to many prominent figures, including President James Garfield. Eighteen of the rooms are furnished in period style. Open to the public.

National City Christian Church
14th and Massachusetts Avenues, NW
Washington, DC 20005
(202) 232-0323

President Garfield was an ordained minister of the Disciples of Christ, and attended National City Christian Church during his time in Washington as President, as did President Lyndon Johnson later.

Garfield Place
Second Place
Prestonsburg, Kentucky 41653

Garfield Place, named in Garfield's honor during his presidency, was used as military headquarters by Colonel Garfield at an engagement at Middle Creek near Prestonsburg on January 10, 1862. Closed to the public.

Memorials to James A. Garfield

James A. Garfield Statue
Maryland Avenue and 1st Street, NW
Washington, DC 20002

The Garfield statue, at the foot of the Capitol steps, is the only memorial to President Garfield in the nation's capital.

James A. Garfield Statue
The Promenade
Long Branch, New Jersey 07740

On July 2, 1881, President Garfield was accosted and shot by a demented office-seeker in the Baltimore and Potomac Railroad Station in Washington. After several weeks of recuperation he was transported to a vacation home on the New Jersey shore in hopes that fresh ocean air and atmosphere would aid his recovery. However, he died in Elberon, New Jersey on September 19. The President has been honored by the seashore community with a statue in nearby Long Branch.

See also: **Berkeley Springs** (p. 21); **Church of the Presidents** (p. 161); **Shiloh National Military Park** (p. 164); **Chickamauga and Chattanooga National Military Park** (p. 167); **Henry C. Bowen House** (p. 169); **Camp Jackson** (p. 172); **Sandusky** (p. 173).

Chester A. Arthur

Twenty-First President
1881–1885

Born October 5, 1830, Fairfield, Vermont
Died November 18, 1886, New York, New York
Burial Site: Rural Cemetery, Albany, New York

Chester A. Arthur State Historic Site
Route 36
Fairfield, Vermont 05455
(802) 828-3226

    Chester A. Arthur was born in a tiny two-room manse, just down the hill from the Baptist church where his father was pastor. The house, which has been replicated by the State of Vermont as a place of historical interest, has two rooms downstairs with a loft above. Open to the public.

Arthur Residence
7 Elm Street
Perry, New York 14530

    The Arthur family resided in Perry from 1835 to 1837. The Elm

Street house is one of the few existing homes used by the itinerant Arthur family as they moved from one parsonage to another. Closed to the public.

The Baptist Church of Perry
77 N. Main Street
Perry, New York 14530
(716) 237-2768

Elder William Arthur served the Perry parish from 1833 to 1837. Part of the original structure, circa 1820, remains as part of today's church building.

Arthur Residence
22 Woodlawn Avenue
Greenwich, New York 12834

The Reverend Arthur was pastor in Greenwich, then known as Union Village, from 1839 to 1844. Closed to the public.

Arthur Residence
626 1st Avenue
Lansingburgh (Troy), New York 12182

The Arthur family lived in Troy from 1846 to 1849. The house has survived, although much altered from its earlier form. Closed to the public.

First Baptist Church of Troy
82 Third Street
Troy, New York 12180
(518) 273-8561

Reverend Arthur served the Troy (at that time the Lansingburgh) parish from 1846 to 1849. The two-hundred-year-old First Baptist Church building is still in use.

Arthur Residence
123 Lexington Avenue
New York, New York 10016

Chester A. Arthur resided in a brownstone building in New York when he served in a variety of administrative jobs during the Civil War, and then as a private attorney and an active participant in the New York political machine. It was in his home that he took the oath of office upon the death of President Garfield and where he retired following his presidency. The building has been converted to offices and apartments. Closed to the public.

Calvary Church
Park Avenue South and 21st Street
New York, New York 10010

Chester A. Arthur married Ellen Herndon in Calvary Church on October 25, 1859.

See also: **Anderson House** (p. 132); **Church of the Presidents** (p. 161); **Henry C. Bowen House** (p. 169).

Grover Cleveland

Twenty-Second President
1885–1889

and

Twenty-Fourth President
1893–1897

Born March 8, 1837, Caldwell, New Jersey
Died June 24, 1908, Princeton, New Jersey
Burial Site: Princeton Cemetery, Princeton, New Jersey

Grover Cleveland Birthplace State Historic Site
207 Bloomfield Avenue
Caldwell, New Jersey 07006
(973) 226-1810

      Grover Cleveland was born in the manse of the First Presbyterian Church served by his pastor father. The simple frame house of 2½ stories is similar to many of the period, with a gabled roof and clapboard siding. The church no longer stands, but the house has been refurbished to represent the time of the Cleveland occupancy. Museum. Open to the public.

Grover Cleveland Boyhood Home
109 Academy Road
Fayetteville, New York 13066

Grover Cleveland's minister father served a Fayetteville church from 1841 until 1850, and the family resided in a house near the church. Closed to the public.

Grover Cleveland Boyhood Home
22 Utica Street
Clinton, New York 13323

The Cleveland family residence from 1850 to 1853 is closed to the public.

Grover Cleveland Boyhood Home
9573 Main Street
Holland Patent, New York 13323

The last pastoral post of Grover Cleveland's father was a church in Holland Patent, but Reverend Cleveland died less than a month after settling in there in 1853. Cleveland's mother and sister remained in Holland Patent and Grover visited often after leaving home for college. Closed to the public.

First Presbyterian Church of Holland Patent
Box 703
Holland Patent, New York 13354
(315) 865-5754

The 1840 church served so briefly by Reverend Cleveland has survived.

Westland
15 Hodge Road
Princeton, New Jersey 08540

Westland was the retirement home of President Cleveland from 1897 until his death. This is an impressive Victorian house set in a lovely grove of trees. Closed to the public.

The Blue Room
The White House
Washington, DC 20500

On June 2, 1886, President Grover Cleveland married Frances

Folsom. This was the only wedding of a president that has been held in the White House.

Cleveland Honeymoon Cottage
Deer Park Hotel Road
Deer Park, Maryland 21550

The little resort town of Deer Park was a popular vacation retreat for many prominent people including Presidents Ulysses S. Grant and Benjamin Harrison. The cottage where President Cleveland honeymooned in 1886 still exists, but is closed to the public.

First Presbyterian Church
Mason and Breckinridge Streets
Buffalo, New York 14213

First Presbyterian was Grover Cleveland's home church when he lived in Buffalo.

New York State Capitol
Governor Nelson A. Rockefeller Empire State Plaza
Albany, New York 12220
(518) 474-2418

Presidents Grover Cleveland, Theodore Roosevelt and Franklin D. Roosevelt served New York as governor. All worked in the capitol building, built in the late 1800s. Carvings on the "Million Dollar Staircase" depict famous people in American history. Open to the public.

New York Executive Mansion
138 Eagle Street
Albany, New York 12202

As Governor of New York (1882–1884), Grover Cleveland occupied a large 1860 brick Victorian mansion that has been the residence of New York governors since 1877. It has been enlarged and improved through the years and, although damaged by fire in 1961, has been restored and continues to serve as the Executive Mansion. Open on a limited basis.

Acorn Lodge
Duncan Lake, Box 144
Ossippee, New Hampshire 03864
(603) 539-2151

Grover Cleveland was a great sportsman and he used Acorn Lodge as a fishing camp following his presidency. Some Cleveland memorabilia remains on hand at Acorn Lodge, owned and operated by Mr. Ray Terry as a bed and breakfast inn. Open to the public.

Cleveland House
Cleveland Road
Tamworth, New Hampshire 03886

Cleveland House is a lake country retreat used by the retired President Cleveland from 1904 to 1906. Closed to the public.

Arcade and Attica Railroad
2787 Main Street
Arcade, New York 14009
(716) 496-9877

The Arcade and Attica Railroad operates an historical and educational fifteen-mile steam train ride through the attractive New York countryside. Vintage railroad cars are on display, including the private presidential carriage used by Grover Cleveland. Open to the public.

East Broadtop Railroad
Rockhill Furnace
Huntington County, Pennsylvania 17249
(814) 447-3011

The only remaining narrow-gauge railroad in the east is currently operated as a ten-mile excursion through the rolling hills of central Pennsylvania. One of the wooden coaches is reported to have been used by President Cleveland when on a fishing trip. Open to the public.

Arbor Lodge State Historical Park
Nebraska City, Nebraska 68410
(402) 873-7222

The home of J. Sterling Morton, secretary of agriculture in the Cleveland cabinet, is the centerpiece of a sixty-five-acre park — the fifty-two-room Neocolonial mansion host to President Cleveland. Open to the public.

Historic Fontaine House
680 Adams Avenue
Memphis, Tennessee 38105
(901) 526-1469

A fine example of French Victorian style and craftsmanship, the 1870 Fontaine House has been restored. Grover Cleveland was entertained here. Open to the public.

Belle Meade Plantation
5025 Harding Road
Nashville, Tennessee 37205
(615) 356-0501

This 1853 Greek Revival mansion is noted for its curving stairway and high ceilings. Grover Cleveland slept here while on a western tour. Open to the public.

Memorial to Grover Cleveland

Cleveland Memorial Tower
Princeton University
Princeton, New Jersey 08540

A finely-detailed 173-foot tower adjoins Princeton University's Gothic quadrangle. Although Grover Cleveland did not attend Princeton, he lived in town and served the University as a Trustee.

See also: **Archer House Hotel** (p. 140); **Henry C. Bowen House** (p. 169).

Benjamin Harrison

Twenty-Third President
1889–1893

Born August 20, 1833, North Bend, Ohio
Died March 13, 1901, Indianapolis, Indiana
Burial Site: Crown Hill Cemetery, Indianapolis, Indiana

Benjamin Harrison Birthplace
William Henry Harrison Home
Symmes and Washington Avenues
North Bend, Ohio 45052

Benjamin Harrison was born in a red brick house belonging to his grandfather, William Henry Harrison, President of the United States when Benjamin was seven years of age. The house burned in 1858 and the property passed from the family. There is a marker.

185

President Benjamin Harrison Home
1230 North Delaware Street
Indianapolis, Indiana 46202-2598
(317) 631-1898

The impressive Harrison home is in the Italianate style, although the addition of a spacious porch reflects the Colonial Revival style popular in the 1890s. Benjamin Harrison's wife, Caroline, was a talented, professionally-trained artist whose work, especially in ceramics, is displayed in the house. The sixteen room house was President Harrison's permanent home from 1875 until his death in 1901 and was where he conducted his famous "front porch" campaign for the presidency in 1888. The Benjamin Harrison Foundation, Inc. currently operates the home as a house museum. Open to the public.

Dr. John W. Scott House
Campus and High Streets
Oxford, Ohio 45056

Benjamin Harrison and Caroline Scott married on October 20, 1853, in the home of her father. The house has been demolished.

Saint Thomas Episcopal Church
5th Avenue and 53rd Street
New York, New York 10019

Caroline Harrison died in 1892 and the widowed Benjamin Harrison took Mary Dimmick as his bride on April 6, 1896. Saint Thomas burned in 1905 but was replaced in 1914.

Congress Hall Hotel
251 Beach Drive
Cape May, New Jersey 08204
(609) 884-8421

Congress Hall is a "Grand Dame" hotel facing the beach in historic Cape May, the nation's oldest seaside resort, a picturesque town containing over six hundred Victorian gingerbread homes dating to the 19th century. President Benjamin Harrison used Congress Hall as a summer White House. Open to the public, in season.

Berkeley Lodge
Second Lake
near Old Forge, New York 13420

In 1895, President Harrison built a rustic "getaway" cabin on the shore of Second Lake in the isolated Chain o' Lakes sector of the upper Adirondacks resort area north of Utica, New York. Closed to the public.

Benjamin Harrison's Military Career

Kennesaw Mountain National Battlefield
Box 1167
Marietta, Georgia 30061
(770) 427-4686

Two major engagements of the Atlanta campaign took place in the Marietta area on June 20 and July 2, 1864. Benjamin Harrison, a capable brigade commander under General Joseph Hooker, took part in the action and participated in the entire Atlanta campaign, from Dalton through the capture of Atlanta. He left the army as a General. National Park Service Site. Open to the public.

See also: **Church of the Presidents** (p. 161); **Henry C. Bowen House** (p. 169).

William McKinley

Twenty-Fifth President
1897–1901

Born January 19, 1843, Niles, Ohio
Died September 14, 1901, Buffalo, New York
Burial Site: McKinley National Memorial, Canton, Ohio

William McKinley Birthplace
36 South Main Street
Niles, Ohio 44446

    The McKinley Federal Savings and Loan occupies a commercial building on the site of William McKinley's birth — a small two-story frame house that was destroyed by fire in 1935. There is a marker.

First Presbyterian Church
(Now Christ United Church)
530 W. Tuscarawas Street
Canton, Ohio 44071

    William McKinley and Ida Saxton were married on January 25, 1871. The church building has been much altered. Open to the public.

The Saxton-Barber House
331 Market Street, South
Canton, Ohio 44702
(330) 454-3426

William McKinley's father-in-law, John Saxton, owned a house occupied by the McKinleys from 1873 to 1892. It has been lovingly restored and converted to offices for the Stark County Foundation which has plans to open the "National First Ladies Library," a computer-assisted research center, on the premises. It will include museum displays and is scheduled to open for public visitation in June, 1998.

McKinley National Memorial and Museum
800 McKinley Monument Drive, NW
Canton, Ohio 44701
(330) 455-7043

108 marble steps lead up to a magnificent mausoleum high above Canton, one of the most impressive and imposing presidential memorials in the country. The double-domed structure, sheathed with Milford granite, is supported by more than two million bricks. The ninety-six-foot-high memorial is the final resting place for William and Ida McKinley and their two daughters who died in infancy. The McKinley Museum, serving the intellectual appetite of Stark County, is at the foot of the stairway. Open to the public.

Lambert Castle
Paterson, New Jersey 07501
(973) 881-2761

Lambert Castle, in the Garret Mountain Reservation overlooking Paterson, was built in 1892 by Catholina Lambert, a wealthy silk manufacturer. The elaborate stone building, the home of the Passaic County Historical Society Museum, features period rooms and changing historical exhibits. President McKinley was entertained here on several occasions when it was a private home. Open to the public.

Moore-Woodbury House
416 Pearl Street
Burlington, Vermont 05401

A Federal-style brick building was home to Urban Woodbury, mayor of Burlington and later governor of Vermont. Famous visitors included William McKinley, Theodore Roosevelt and William Howard Taft. The house is now an apartment complex. Closed to the public.

Church of the Savior
120 Cleveland Avenue, SW
Canton, Ohio 44702
(216) 455-0153

William McKinley was a life-long member and active participant in the affairs of the First Methodist Church of Canton, and his commemorative pew remains in the sanctuary. The name change to Church of the Savior was effected in 1968 at the time of Church unification.

William McKinley's Military Career

William McKinley joined the Twenty-Third Ohio Volunteer Infantry as an enlisted man. His commanding officer was Rutherford B. Hayes, making the Twenty-Third the only military unit to have two future presidents in its ranks.

Antietam National Battlefield
Box 158
Sharpsburg, Maryland 21782
(301) 432-5124

Sergeant William McKinley fought valiantly in the bloody battle at Antietam which took place on September 17, 1862. He is remembered with a McKinley monument at Antietam, one of the few Civil War monuments honoring an enlisted man. Open to the public.

Fishers Hill
near Winchester, Virginia 22601

Union forces under General Philip Sheridan defeated the Confederates at Fishers Hill on September 22, 1864, in a battle in which William McKinley participated.

Buffington Island State Park Monument
Portland, Ohio 45770
(614) 297-2630

Buffington was the site of one of the few Civil War battles fought in the state of Ohio. William McKinley was a participant.

McKinley Memorial Library
40 North Main Street
Niles, Ohio 44446
(330) 652-1704

An imposing structure of Classic Greek architecture has an open central court flanked by a museum of McKinley memorabilia on one side and the Niles Public Library on the other. The central atrium features an Italian marble garden and a larger-than-life statue of William McKinley surrounded by busts of outstanding national and local political figures. Open to the public.

William McKinley Statue
State Capitol
Broad and High Streets
Columbus, Ohio 43211
(614) 466-2125

An heroic bronze statue of McKinley stands on the grounds of the capitol where he served as Governor of Ohio from 1892 to 1896.

Mount McKinley
Denali National Park and Preserve
Box 9
McKinley Park, Alaska 99755

Denali is an Indian word for "The High One" and this highest peak in North America stands 20,230 feet above sea level — the centerpiece of a huge wilderness expanse established as McKinley National Park in 1917 to honor the President who had been assassinated in 1901. The park was combined with the Denali National Monument in 1980 to form Denali National Park and Preserve.

See also: **Church of the Presidents** (p. 161); **Metropolitan Memorial Methodist Church** (p. 161); **Henry C. Bowen House** (p. 169).

Theodore Roosevelt

Twenty-Sixth President
1901–1909

Born October 27, 1858, New York, New York
Died January 6, 1919, Oyster Bay, New York
Burial Site: Youngs Memorial Cemetery, Oyster Bay,
New York

Theodore Roosevelt Birthplace National Historic Site
28 East 20th Street
New York, New York 10003
(212) 260-1616

    Theodore Roosevelt was born in a narrow, four-story brownstone in midtown New York City. The house was demolished in 1916, but through the efforts of a dedicated group of preservationist women, using original blueprints, the house was completely replicated following Roosevelt's death. The house is a vivid representation of prosperous city living in the middle of the 19th century, with more than forty percent of the furnishings being original Roosevelt pieces. National Park Service Site. Open to the public.

Roosevelt Residence
6 West 57th Street
New York, New York 10019

The Roosevelt family moved "uptown" in 1873, residing in an apartment where young Theodore stayed on visits home from Harvard. In 1880, Roosevelt and his bride, Alice Lee, stayed there until they took their own apartment in 1882. The building has been extensively altered and is currently used for commercial purposes. Closed to the public.

Sagamore Hill National Historic Site
20 Sagamore Hill Road
Oyster Bay, New York 11771-1899
(516) 922-4447

A rambling frame and brick Queen Anne-style building of twenty-two rooms filled with Theodore Roosevelt's books, paintings, flags, hunting trophies — and his personality — was his permanent home from 1885 until his death — and the summer White House throughout his presidency. The Theodore Roosevelt Association acquired the fully-furnished house in 1950 and subsequently donated it to the federal government for maintenance. National Park Service Site. Open to the public.

Brookline Unitarian Church
Brookline, Massachusetts 02146

Roosevelt married Alice Lee of Chestnut Hill, Massachusetts, on October 27, 1880.

Christ Episcopal Church
Oyster Bay, New York 11771
(516) 922-6377

The Episcopal church home for the Roosevelt family has been altered greatly since the Roosevelt residency at nearby Sagamore Hill although there is a corner dedicated to the distinguished family. The President's pew has been retained and marked.

Saint Georges Church
Hanover Square
London, England

On February 14, 1884, Theodore Roosevelt's mother and his young wife, Alice, passed away of unrelated illnesses, a remarkable and tragic coincidence. On December 2, 1886, widower Roosevelt married Edith Carow in London in Saint Georges Church.

Maltese Cross Cabin
Theodore Roosevelt National Park
Medora, North Dakota 58645
(701) 623-4466

Theodore Roosevelt visited North Dakota on a hunting trip in 1883, impressed enough to invest in ranch land. Upon the deaths of his wife and mother in 1884 he returned to North Dakota, hoping to ease his grief by indulging in the rugged outdoor life of a cowboy. He constructed a three-room rough log cabin as a ranch and hunting headquarters. The original cabin has been relocated adjacent to the Visitor Center of the Theodore Roosevelt National Park. National Park Service Site. Open to the public.

Roosevelt Residence
1820 Jefferson Place, NW
Washington, DC 20036

In 1889, Theodore Roosevelt became a member of the Civil Service Commission. He and wife Edith rented a house at that time, remaining there until 1892. The house is now a combination office/apartment. Closed to the public.

Roosevelt Residence
1215 19th Street, NW
Washington, DC 20036

During his service on the Civil Service Commission, the Roosevelts lived in this house from 1892 until he returned to New York City in 1885 to become Police Commissioner. Privately owned. Closed to the public.

North Creek Railroad Station
Box 156
North Creek, New York 12853-0156
(518) 251-3661

Vice President Roosevelt was vacationing at a remote lodge in the Adirondacks when he was notified that the condition of President McKinley, shot by an anarchist in Buffalo, had worsened. Roosevelt made a harrowing ride by buckboard to the North Creek Railroad Depot where he learned that McKinley had succumbed. Roosevelt boarded a waiting train which took him to Buffalo where he was inaugurated and began his dramatic journey into presidential history. In 1990, a dedicated group of preservationists began a campaign to save the deteriorating station and by 1998 the depot building, circa 1874, was in the last stages of restoration as an historical museum. Open to the public.

Theodore Roosevelt Inaugural National Historic Site
Ansley Wilcox House
641 Delaware Avenue
Buffalo, New York 14202
(716) 884-0095

When President McKinley was assassinated in 1901, Vice President Roosevelt rushed to the scene where he was hurriedly sworn into office in the home of a friend. The house has been fully restored. Open to the public.

Roosevelt Residence
736 Jackson Place, NW
Washington, DC 20006

The Roosevelts resided in a townhouse on Lafayette Square during a White House renovation in 1902. Closed to the public.

Pine Knot
State Route 712
Keene, Virginia 22946

When he wished to escape the pressure, or weather, of Washington, President Roosevelt retreated to Pine Knot, a rustic cabin without electricity, indoor plumbing, or modern facilities located in the deep woods south of Charlottesville. The cabin is owned by the Theodore Roosevelt Association which opens it only to specially pre-arranged groups.

Christ Church, Glendower
900 Glendower Road
Keene, Virginia 22946
(804) 286-3437

Each Sunday morning when in residence at Pine Knot, President and Mrs. Roosevelt walked one-half-mile across their back field to Christ Church (Episcopal) for services. The neoclassical red brick structure of Jeffersonian influence has been described by one architectural historian as *a perfect little building.*

Midland Railway
Baldwin City, Kansas 66006
(913) 594-6982

Midland Railway was constructed in 1867, the first railroad south of the Kansas River. Using passenger coaches typical of the early 1900s, the railroad today provides excursion trips through woods, farmland and over a two-hundred-foot bridge. The railroad's 1906 Santa Fe Depot building was visited by presidents Theodore Roosevelt and William Howard Taft. Open to the public.

Grace Reformed Church
1405 15th Street, NW
Washington, DC 20005
(202) 387-3131

Theodore Roosevelt regularly attended this church when in Washington, including during his time in the White House.

Equinox House Historic District
Main and Union
Manchester, Vermont 05254
(802) 362-4114

The center of Manchester Village is dominated by a complex of resort buildings which have been attracting tourists since the early 1800s. Among the regular visitors have been Mrs. Abraham Lincoln, Mrs. Ulysses S. Grant, Theodore Roosevelt and William Howard Taft.

Wave Hill House
West 249th Street and Independence Avenue
New York, New York 10471
(718) 549-2055

The centerpiece of a twenty-eight-acre estate overlooking the Hudson River, Wave Hill has been the home of Mark Twain, Theodore Roosevelt (1870–1871) and Arturo Toscanini. The historical property contains a manor house, horticultural garden and environmental education center. Wave Hill is owned by the City of New York and is operated by the Wave Hill Foundation. Open to the public.

Theodore Roosevelt's Military Career

At the outbreak of the Spanish-American War in 1898, Theodore Roosevelt resigned as Assistant Secretary of the Navy to accept an appointment as a lieutenant colonel in a national volunteer cavalry regiment, the "Rough Riders," which he had helped organize. His bravery and leadership during their service in Cuba vaulted Roosevelt into the national limelight.

Menger Hotel
204 Alamo Plaza
San Antonio, Texas 78205
(210) 223-4361

Colonel Theodore Roosevelt billeted in the Menger while The Rough Riders assembled in San Antonio during the Spanish-American War. The Menger was also host to presidents Grant, Taft and McKinley. Open to the public.

Roosevelt Park
Mission Road south of downtown
San Antonio, Texas 78234

The Rough Riders trained in San Antonio, in what has been transformed into a city park. There is a marker.

Rough Riders Memorial and City Museum
725 Grand Avenue
Las Vegas, New Mexico 78234
(505) 425-8726

Forty percent of The Rough Riders were from New Mexico, a fact remembered with a memorial and museum. Theodore Roosevelt attended a reunion of the group in 1899. Open to the public.

Tampa Bay Hotel
University of Tampa
401 W. Kennedy Boulevard
Tampa, Florida 33606-1490
(800) 733-4773

A building that has been refurbished and renamed H. B. Plant Hall was headquarters for the army that was positioning to invade Cuba during the Spanish-American War. Theodore Roosevelt and his officers stayed there prior to their embarkation. The Hall is utilized as an elegant classroom building for the University of Tampa. Open to the public.

Theodore Roosevelt Island
George Washington Memorial Highway
Turkey Run Park
McLean, Virginia 22101

Visitors cross a footbridge to reach an island in the Potomac River where nature trails lead to a wooded sanctuary dominated by an imposing statue of environment-conscious President Roosevelt. The statue is flanked by stone tablets upon which are inscribed Roosevelt's tenets on nature, manhood, youth and government. National Park Service Site. Open to the public.

Roosevelt Arch
Box 168
Yellowstone National Park, Wyoming 82190

The Roosevelt Arch, an opening through uncut basaltic rock with natural stone towers rising fifty-two feet on either side, serves as the Montana entrance to Yellowstone National Park at the town of Gardiner. President Theodore Roosevelt dedicated the arch in 1903.

Theodore Roosevelt Memorial Obelisk
Maria's Pass
Glacier National Park, Montana

A sixty-foot granite shaft was built as a monument to the President who made forest conservation a national policy. The obelisk is owned by the United States Forest Service.

Bucky O'Neill Monument
Courthouse Plaza
Prescott, Arizona 86301

Captain William "Bucky" O'Neill, the first volunteer in the Spanish-American War, was the major organizer of the First US Volunteer Cavalry, the military unit known as The Rough Riders. The Rough Riders was later commanded by Theodore Roosevelt.

Theodore Roosevelt Bird Sanctuary and Trailside Museum
East Main Street at Cove Road
Oyster Bay, New York 11771
(516) 922-3200

A memorial to Theodore Roosevelt and a series of exhibits of Long Island animal and plant life are featured in a nature museum near Roosevelt's home, Sagamore Hill. The President is interred in Youngs Memorial Cemetery abutting the Sanctuary. Open to the public.

Theodore Roosevelt Monument
Mount Roosevelt
US Route 85
Deadwood, South Dakota 57732

Shortly after Theodore Roosevelt's death in 1919, Sheriff Seth Bullock constructed a stone tower on a mountain overlooking Deadwood, the first monument in the nation to honor the President who had spent so much time in western South Dakota.

Theodore Roosevelt Dam and Lake
Salt River, SR 88
Globe, Arizona 85501

The first major project completed under the Reclamation Act of 1902 was one of the finest accomplishments of Theodore Roosevelt's administration. The highest all-masonry dam in the world impounds the waters of Roosevelt Lake.

Theodore Roosevelt Memorial Building
American Museum of Natural History
79th Street and Central Park West
New York, New York 10023
(212) 769-5100

The Theodore Roosevelt Memorial Building opened in 1936, its facade resembling a triumphal arch. The collections within memorialize Roosevelt's fascination with nature. Open to the public.

See also: **Corner of Celebrities** (p. 81); **The Old Tavern** (p. 159); **New York Executive Mansion** (p. 182); **New York State Capitol** (p. 182); **Moore-Woodbury House** (p. 189); **Hazelden** (p. 202); **Mount Rushmore** (p. 285).

William Howard Taft

Twenty-Seventh President
1909–1913

Born September 15, 1857, Cincinnati, Ohio
Died March 8, 1930, Washington, DC
Burial Site: Arlington National Cemetery, Arlington, Virginia

William Howard Taft National Historic Site
2038 Auburn Avenue
Cincinnati, Ohio 45219
(513) 684-3262

    William Howard Taft was born in a first-floor bedroom of a sturdy and roomy two-story brick house, perfect for a well-to-do family in the middle of the 19th century, especially a family with three active sons. In 1961, the house, then owned privately, was purchased by the Taft Memorial Association which transferred the property to the federal government as a National Historic Site in 1969. The ground floor is furnished and appears as it did during the Taft residency, and the upper floor contains museum galleries with displays highlighting Taft's many careers. Museum. National Park Service Site. Open to the public.

Farnum College, Room 158
Old South College
Yale University
New Haven, Connecticut 06520

Farnum College was William Howard Taft's dormitory during his undergraduate days at Yale. The building is still in use by the University. Closed to the public.

Herron Home
Pike Street
Cincinnati, Ohio 45202

William Howard Taft and Helen Herron were married in her parents' home in Cincinnati on June 19, 1886. The house has been demolished.

The Quarry
1763 East McMillan Street
Cincinnati, Ohio 45214

Newlyweds William and Helen Taft moved into a new home following their marriage, residing there until he was called to Washington as Solicitor General of the United States. Privately owned. Closed to the public.

First Unitarian Church of Cincinnati
536 Linton Street
Cincinnati, Ohio 45219
(513) 281-1564

Alphonso Taft, father of William Howard Taft, served First Unitarian as Chairman of the Board of Trustees — the entire Taft family was active in church affairs. William Howard was a senior at Yale when he was elected president of the Church's Youth organization and laughingly remarked in later years that the election success was the beginning of his presidential aspirations.

Taft Residence
1603 K Street, NW
Washington, DC 20006

A modest house was used by the Tafts when he was Secretary of War in the cabinet of Theodore Roosevelt, 1904–1909. Closed to the public.

Hazelden
c/o George Ade Memorial Association
Box 102
Kentland, Indiana 47951
(219) 275-6161

George Ade was the beloved and famous Hoosier humorist and author of *Fables in Slang*. Taft launched his 1908 presidential campaign in a rally at Ade's estate Hazelden, attended by 25,000 supporters. Hazelden, a Tudor mansion on a 417-acre estate, also hosted Theodore Roosevelt, Warren G. Harding and Calvin Coolidge. Hazelden is operated by the George Ade Memorial Association. Guided tours by appointment.

Stetson Cottage
37 Bradlee Road
Marblehead, Massachusetts 01945

The cottage used by the Tafts in the summer of 1909 was originally located in Beverly, Massachusetts, but has been moved, complete with one surviving wing, to Marblehead . Closed to the public.

Parramatta Estate
70 Corning Street
Beverly, Massachusetts 01915

A large house where the Tafts spent long vacations in 1910, 1911 and 1912 has been converted to apartments. Closed to the public.

Taft Residence
Hillcrest (1913)
367 Prospect Street
New Haven, Connecticut 06511

Following his presidency, William Howard Taft returned to his alma mater, Yale, as a visiting professor of law. The Tafts resided in a Victorian house. Closed to the public.

Taft Residence
2029 Connecticut Avenue, NW
Washington, DC 20008

Ex-President Taft continued to serve the nation, including co-chairmanship of the National War Labor Boar, during World War I. At that time the Tafts rented an apartment on Connecticut Avenue. Closed to the public.

Taft Residences
113 Whitney Avenue (1919–1921)
60 York Avenue
New Haven, Connecticut 06511

Following his service on the War Labor Board, the Tafts returned to New Haven where they bought a house on Whitney, then sold it when he was appointed Chief Justice of the United States Supreme Court. Before returning to Washington, however, they lived briefly on York Avenue. Closed to the public.

Elton Island
Thimble Islands
Branford, Connecticut 06045

A graceful Victorian house on an island in Long Island Sound was used by the Taft family as a vacation retreat when they lived in nearby New Haven. Closed to the public.

Taft Residence
2215 Wyoming Avenue, NW
Washington, DC 20008

William Howard Taft bought a comfortable brick house in 1921 when he was appointed Chief Justice of the United States Supreme Court by President Warren G. Harding. It remained Taft's principal residence until 1930. It is currently the Embassy of the United Arab Emirates. Closed to the public.

Museums

Heritage Plantation
Grove and Pine
Sandwich, Massachusetts 02563
(508) 888-3300

A collection of vintage automobiles at Heritage Plantation includes the first official presidential limousine, which was used by President Taft. Open to the public.

Taft Museum
4th and Pike
Cincinnati, Ohio 45202
(513) 241-0343

The Taft Museum is housed in a magnificent mansion purchased and refurbished by Charles Phelps Taft, elder half-brother of William Howard Taft. Charles Taft reportedly provided significant financial backing for Taft's run for the presidency, and Taft accepted the 1908 Republican presidential nomination from the front porch of the house. Open to the public.

See also: **All Souls Unitarian Church** (p. 94); **Moore-Woodbury House** (p. 189); **Midland Railway** (p. 195); **Equinox House Historic District** (p. 196).

Woodrow Wilson

Twenty-Eighth President
1913–1921

Born December 28, 1856, Staunton, Virginia
Died February 3, 1924, Washington, DC
Burial Site: Washington National Cathedral, Washington, DC

Woodrow Wilson Birthplace and Museum
18–24 Coalter Street
Staunton, Virginia 24401
(540) 885-0897

    Woodrow Wilson was born in the manse of the Presbyterian church served by his minister father. It was not a simple parsonage, but a large, imposing townhouse in the Greek Revival style − a rectangular brick building with a two-story, pillared portico reminiscent of Jefferson's Monticello. Its twelve spacious rooms are filled with Wilson memorabilia, including the cradle in which infant "Tommy" slept. The property is owned by the Woodrow Wilson Birthplace Foundation which recently purchased a chateau-style house two doors away and converted it into a Wilson museum. Open to the public.

205

Boyhood Home of President Woodrow Wilson
419 7th Street
Augusta, Georgia 30903
(706) 724-0436

Reverend Wilson moved his family to Augusta, Georgia, in October, 1857, where they remained until 1870, residing for most of those years in a church manse — a 2½-story brick house with a separate outside structure used as a kitchen and servant's quarters. A rear porch extended the full width, and a stable was located in the rear of the lot. The property has recently been purchased, refurbished and opened for visitation by Historic Augusta, Inc. Open to the public.

First Presbyterian Church of Augusta
642 Telfair Street
Augusta, Georgia 30903

Robert Mills, architect of the Washington Monument and the US Treasury Building, designed a landmark church in Augusta in 1809. This church was used a a military hospital during the Civil War and, later, was served by Woodrow Wilson's father.

Woodrow Wilson Boyhood Home
1705 Hampton Street
Columbia, South Carolina 29201
(803) 252-3964

In 1870, Reverend Wilson accepted a call to Columbia — as pastor of the First Presbyterian Church combined with a professorship at the Columbia Theological Seminary. The family moved into a simple two-story frame house purchased by Mrs. Wilson with an inheritance, the first house the family had ever owned. The Wilsons remained in Columbia for only two years (1870–1872) before moving on. The Wilson House is owned by the Historic Columbia Foundation and operated as part of a four-house historic district. Open to the public.

First Presbyterian Church of Columbia
1324 Marion Street
Columbia, South Carolina 29201
(803) 799-9062

Woodrow Wilson's father, while serving the First Presbyterian Church in Columbia, South Carolina, proudly confirmed his son Woodrow as a member.

Witherspoon Hall
Princeton University
Princeton, New Jersey 08540

Woodrow Wilson lived in Witherspoon Hall while an undergraduate student at Princeton, 1875–1879. Closed to the public.

University of Virginia
Charlottesville, Virginia 22908–9018

Woodrow Wilson spent time at the University of Virginia as a resident rector — living in room 158, House F, 31 West Range — while attending law school from 1879 to 1880. Closed to the public.

Presbyterian Manse
Oglethorpe and Whitaker
Savannah, Georgia 31406

Woodrow Wilson and Ellen Axson were married on June 24, 1885, in a house owned by her grandfather. The structure was demolished in 1928.

Old Baptist Parsonage
Gulph Road
Bryn Mawr, Pennsylvania 19010

Woodrow Wilson was appointed President of Bryn Mawr College in 1887 and lived in a parsonage on the campus. Closed to the public.

Wilson Residences
72 and 82 Library Place
Princeton, New Jersey 08540

After his experience at Bryn Mawr, Woodrow Wilson taught at Wesleyan University in Middletown, Connecticut, before accepting a position at his alma mater as Professor of Jurisprudence and Political Economy in 1896. The homes in Princeton are University-owned. Closed to the public.

Prospect
Princeton University
Princeton, New Jersey 08540

The Woodrow Wilson family resided in University-owned Prospect when he served as President of Princeton from 1902 to 1910. The house is presently a dining hall for the faculty of Princeton University. Closed to the public.

New Jersey State House
121 W. State Street
Trenton, New Jersey 08608
(609) 292-4661

Woodrow Wilson's success as President of Princeton University brought him to the attention of the state's political hierarchy. After extracting a promise of non-interference in policy-making, he was elected governor in 1910, a post that became an important stepping-stone to the presidency. The New Jersey State House, built about 1792 and crowned with a gold dome is the second-oldest state capitol in continuous use. It is a landmark structure of rare architectural importance. The building has undergone many changes since its construction. Open to the public.

Wilson Residence
25 Cleveland Lane
Princeton, New Jersey 08540

The State of New Jersey did not have a Governor's Mansion at the time of his service, so Governor Woodrow Wilson leased a home in Princeton. Closed to the public.

The Princeton Inn
Nassau Street
Princeton, New Jersey 08540
(609) 921-7500

Woodrow Wilson and his family stayed at the Princeton Inn for a short time following his election as Governor of New Jersey. Open to the public.

Galt House
1308 20th Street, NW
Washington, DC 20036

Mrs. Ellen Wilson died in The White House on August 6, 1914. President Wilson remarried on December 18, 1915, in the home of his bride, Mrs. Edith Bolling Galt. The house has been demolished.

Central Presbyterian Church
15th and 16th Streets at Irving, NW
Washington, DC 20010

Central Presbyterian was the Washington church home for President Wilson. The building is no longer in use as a church. Closed to the public.

Woodrow Wilson House Museum
2340 S Street, NW
Washington, DC 20008
(202) 387-4062

Anticipating retirement, President and Mrs. Wilson bought a handsome, four-story, neo-Georgian residence in an exclusive section of Washington. He passed away here in 1924. Mrs. Wilson remained in the home until her death in 1961, bequeathing the house and its furnishings to the National Trust for Historic Preservation which operates it as an historic house museum. Open to the public.

Woodrow Wilson Hall
Monmouth College
Cedar and Norwood Avenues
West Long Branch, New Jersey 07764
(908) 571-3400

A magnificent fifty-three-room mansion called "Shadow Lawn" was used by President Wilson as a summer White House. The mansion was featured in the motion picture *Annie* as the home of Daddy Warbucks. It was the victim of a fire, but was rebuilt in 1927 and now is the property of Monmouth College. Open to the public.

The Dixie White House
767 E. Beach Boulevard
Pass Christian, Mississippi 39571

The Dixie White House acquired its name in 1913 when President Woodrow Wilson visited. The dignified two-story structure, circa 1854, has divided front steps characteristic of many houses of the period. The open ground floor is screened with ironwork banisters; the columns are covered with ornamental plaster. The second floor is frame with a gallery across the front and arched windows extending from floor to ceiling. Closed to the public.

Memorials to Woodrow Wilson

Wilson Dam
Tennessee River, off US Route 72
Florence, Alabama 35630

Wilson Dam was an important hydroelectric facility begun during the administration of Woodrow Wilson — a symbol of the major controversy that took place over the role of the federal government in electric power matters. Closed to the public.

Woodrow Wilson International Center for Scholars
Smithsonian Institution
1000 Jefferson Drive, SW
Washington, DC 20560

The Woodrow Wilson International Center for Scholars is a living institution that preserves the memory of Woodrow Wilson through its pursuit of causes to which he was strongly devoted.

See also: **The Homestead** (p. 77); **The Old Tavern** (p. 159); **Church of the Presidents** (p. 161).

Warren G. Harding

Twenty-Ninth President
1921–1923

Born November 2, 1865, Blooming Grove, Ohio
Died August 2, 1923, San Francisco, California
Burial Site: Harding Memorial, Marion, Ohio

Warren G. Harding Birthplace
Highways 97 and 288
Blooming Grove, Ohio 44878

Warren Harding, the son of a doctor, was born in a small saltbox cottage in Blooming Grove, Ohio. The house was demolished in 1896. There is a marker at the site.

Second Harding Home
State Highway 97
Blooming Grove, Ohio 44878

Close by the birthplace marker in Blooming Grove is a small frame house believed to be the second Harding family home for a short period, although this has not been substantiated. Closed to the public.

Blooming Grove Baptist Church
Blooming Grove, Ohio 44878

Blooming Grove was Warren Harding's home parish as a child. It is rumored, though unconfirmed, that, when President, he attempted to purchase his boyhood home, together with the church!

Third Harding Home
South and Main Streets
Caledonia, Ohio 43314

When Warren Harding was five, his family moved into a white, two-story frame house in Caledonia, used as both home and office by Harding's farmer-doctor father. Warren lived with his family until he entered college. Closed to the public.

President Hardings Home
380 Mount Vernon Avenue
Marion, Ohio 43302
(614) 387-9630

After graduating from college, Warren Harding dabbled in both law and real estate, finally settling on journalism for a career. Not yet twenty, he purchased the *Marion Star* which he published until he left for The White House. Harding married Florence Kling DeWolfe on the veranda of their simple frame home on July 8, 1891, and they lived there until moving to Washington in 1921. The house is typically midwestern and contemporary, reflecting the popular styling of the time − 2½-stories painted green with white trim, with pots of petunias and geraniums on the porch. The house, maintained as it was at the time of the Harding residency, is owned and operated by the Harding Memorial Association. Open to the public.

Trinity Baptist Church
South Main Street
Marion, Ohio 43302

Trinity Baptist was Warren Harding's place of worship for the many years he resided in Marion.

Harding Residence
2314 Wyoming Avenue, NW
Washington, DC 20008

A 2½-story home was purchased by the Hardings in 1917 when he served in the United States Senate. Closed to the public.

Calvary Baptist Church
755 Eighth Street, NW
Washington, DC 20012
(202) 347-8355

President Warren G. Harding was a congregant at Calvary.

Harding Railroad Car
Alaskaland Park
Fairbanks, Alaska 99709
(907) 459-1087

A special observation car, part of a train that carried President Harding on an Alaska tour in 1923, is on display at Alaskaland, an historical theme park. Open to the public.

Southeastern Railway Museum
3966 Buford Highway
Box 1261
Duluth, Georgia 30126–1267
(770) 476-2013

The *Superb* is a 1911 Pullman car, the last remaining "heavy car," owned by the Atlanta chapter of the National Railroad Historical Society, and displayed in refurbished glory. The car was used by President Harding on his ill-fated "Voyage of Understanding" in 1923 that took him from Washington, DC, to Tacoma, Washington, where he embarked for Alaska. The car took him back down the west coast to San Francisco where he passed away. The car bore the President's body back to the nation's capital and on to his final resting place in Marion, Ohio. Open to the public.

See also: **Hazelden** (p. 202).

Calvin Coolidge

Thirtieth President
1923–1929

Born July 4, 1872, Plymouth Notch, Vermont
Died January 5, 1933, Northampton, Massachusetts
Burial Site: Plymouth Cemetery, Plymouth, Vermont 05056

Plymouth Notch Historic District
Vermont Route 100A
Box 79
Plymouth, Vermont 05056
(802) 672-3773

Plymouth Notch is a recreated New England village built around the heritage of Calvin Coolidge — a room behind the country store in which he was born, the family home where he took the presidential oath of office from his notary public father, Union Christian Church where the devout family worshipped and the simple country cemetery where generations of Coolidges are buried. The complex of actual and replicated buildings is owned and operated by the State of Vermont. Open to the public.

Goodhue Home

312 Maple Street
Burlington, Vermont 05401

Calvin Coolidge married Grace Goodhue at the home of her parents on October 4, 1905. Closed to the public.

Coolidge Residence

21 Massasoit Street
Northampton, Massachusetts 01060

Calvin Coolidge left Vermont to find fame and success in Massachusetts, beginning as an attorney and politician in Northampton. In 1906, the newlywed Coolidges rented half of a double house which they continued to lease until he retired from the presidency. Closed to the public.

Masonic Building

25 Main Street
Northampton, Massachusetts 01060

A brick, Italianate office building, circa 1898, contained Calvin Coolidge's law office on the second floor. He probably maintained the office from 1898 until 1919 when he was elected Governor of Massachusetts. Closed to the public.

Edward Congregational Church

Main Street
Northampton, Massachusetts 01060
(413) 584-5500

The Coolidges were active members of Edward Church during their residency in Northampton.

Massachusetts State House

Beacon Street
Boston, Massachusetts 02133
(617) 727-3676

Calvin Coolidge served as Governor of Massachusetts from 1918 to 1920 when he became the vice-presidential nominee of the Republican Party. The facade of the Massachusetts State House, designed by Charles Bulfinch in 1795, remains almost unchanged. The interior halls are filled with statues, historical paintings, transparencies of battle flags and other relics. Open to the public.

White Court Estate
Swampscott, Massachusetts 01907

White Court Estate, President Coolidge's summer White House in 1925, is a twenty-six-room wooden building. Closed to the public.

White Pine Camp
White Pine Road, Box 61
Paul Smiths, New York 12970
(518) 327-3030

White Pine Camp was constructed in 1907 for New York businessman Archibald White, a thirty-five-acre rustic lakeside complex containing twenty separate buildings, including the owner's cabin, a dining hall, sleeping cabins, a tennis house, indoor bowling alleys and a Japanese teahouse, all representative of the vacation opulence of the era. White Pine's most famous guest was President Calvin Coolidge who made White Pine the vacation White House for ten weeks in 1926. Beginning to deteriorate in the early 1990s, White Pine was restored and refurbished as a museum with exhibits on White Pine's unique history and the Adirondack "Great Camps." Open to the public.

Patterson Mansion
15 Dupont Circle
Washington, DC 20036

President and Mrs. Coolidge resided in the Patterson Mansion for six months in 1926 while the roof of the White House was under repair. Patterson is an elaborate four-story showplace of thirty rooms, presently occupied by the Washington Club. Closed to the public.

First Congregational Church
10th and G Streets
Washington, DC 20001
(202) 628-4317

President and Mrs. Coolidge worshipped at the First Congregational Church when residing in Washington. The building has been much altered, little reflecting the period of the Coolidge attendance.

Cedar Island Lodge
Highland, Wisconsin 53543

Cedar Island Lodge, an estate owned by a wealthy businessman, was used by President Coolidge as a vacation retreat in 1928. Closed to the public.

State Game Lodge
Custer State Park
Custer, South Dakota 57730
(605) 255-4541

An elaborate state-owned hotel and restaurant served as the summer White House for President Coolidge in 1927. Open to the public.

The Beeches
16 Hampton Terrace
Northampton, Massachusetts 01060

In 1930, Calvin and Grace Coolidge purchased The Beeches, a 2½-story, shingled house in Northampton where the former President passed away in 1933. Closed to the public.

Museums

Calvin Coolidge Memorial Room
Forbes Library
20 West Street
Northampton, Massachusetts 01060
(413) 584-8399

The Forbes Library is the only public library that houses a presidential collection — Calvin Coolidge's original personal papers and microfiches of his complete presidential papers. The Memorial Room also contains souvenirs, mementos and displays delineating Coolidge's career as Governor of Massachusetts, Vice President and President of the United States. Open to the public.

Black River Academy Museum
14 High Street
Ludlow, Vermont 05149
(802) 228-5050

Calvin Coolidge graduated from the Black River Academy, a preparatory school, in 1890. The Academy museum, devoted to the history of Ludlow and the Black River Valley, includes a special Coolidge section. Open to the public.

See also: **Hazelden** (p. 202).

Herbert Hoover

Thirty-First President
1929–1933

Born August 10, 1874, West Branch, Iowa
Died October 20, 1964, New York, New York
Burial Site: Herbert Hoover National Historic Site
West Branch, Iowa 52538

Herbert Hoover National Historic Site
West Branch, Iowa 52538
(319) 643-2541

The Herbert Hoover National Historic Site is a sprawling two-hundred-acre complex – a modern Visitor Center opens to a restored portion of 19th-century West Branch that includes Herbert Hoover's first schoolhouse, the original Quaker Meeting House, his father's blacksmith shop and Herbert Hoover's tiny birth house, a single bedroom and a kitchen/living room flanking a central chimney. The modern Herbert Hoover Library and Museum is located within the park and the gravesite of Herbert and Lou Hoover is on a slope overlooking the village of West Branch. National Park Service Site. Open to the public.

Herbert Hoover Presidential Library and Museum
West Branch, Iowa 52538
(319) 643-5301

The dominating feature of the National Historic Site is the Library and Museum devoted to scholarly research and the career of Herbert Hoover, "the great Humanitarian," his wife and partner Lou Henry Hoover, and their fifty years of devoted public service. The Library and Museum is one of the presidential libraries administered by the National Archives and Records Administration. Open to the public.

Osage Agency House
621 Granview Street
Pawhuska, Oklahoma 74056

One summer following father Jesse Hoover's death, son "Bertie" traveled to Pawhuska, Indian Territory, to live with his aunt Agnes and her husband, Laban Miles, government agent to the Osage and Kaw Indian nations. The house is a lovely old mansion. Closed to the public.

Hoover-Minthorn House
115 S. River Street
Newberg, Oregon 97132
(503) 538-6629

In 1884, newly-orphaned Herbert Hoover was sent to Oregon to live with his aunt and uncle, Henry and Laura Minthorn. The Minthorns had lost their own son and warmly welcomed the young eleven-year-old Iowan as their own. The Minthorn home has been fully-restored and is owned and operated by the Colonial Dames of America, Oregon. Open to the public.

Minthorn House
Hazel and Highland
Salem, Oregon 97132

The Minthorns and young Hoover moved from Newberg to Salem in 1888 where Herbert left school to work for several years until he left for Stanford University in 1891. The house is still standing, although it is much altered from the time of the Minthorn residency. Closed to the public.

Encina Hall
Stanford University
Palo Alto, California 94309

Herbert Hoover roomed in Encina Hall when he was an undergraduate in the first class to graduate from Stanford University. Encina Hall is still in use by the University. Closed to the public.

Herbert Hoover House
1079 12th Street
Oakland, California 94606

Upon college graduation, Herbert Hoover moved in with his brother and sister in Oakland, California. Closed to the public.

Henry Home
Pacific Street
Monterey, California 93940

Herbert Hoover and Lou Henry became man and wife on February 10, 1899. The ceremony took place in the bride's family home which has been demolished.

Hoover Residence
2300 S Street, NW
Washington, DC 20008

When Herbert Hoover was named Secretary of Commerce in 1921, he purchased a handsome brick house – the family residence until he entered the White House in 1929. Since 1953, the Burmese Embassy has been located in this house. Closed to the public.

Friends Meeting House
2111 Florida Avenue, NW
Washington, DC 20008
(202) 483-3310

President Hoover worshipped at the Meeting House when residing in Washington, including his term at The White House.

Camp Hoover
Shenandoah National Park
Route 4, Box 348
Luray, Virginia 22835

President Hoover, who was independently wealthy, bought mountain property which he developed into a presidential retreat – then donated it to the federal government upon his retirement. The area is a part of Shenandoah National Park and is open, but the surviving camp buildings are closed to the public.

Lou Henry Hoover House
623 Mirada Road
Stanford University Campus
Palo Alto, California 94309

A home designed by Mrs. Hoover was completed in 1920, but was seldom used due to their stay in Washington, DC, and extensive world travels. However, the Hoovers returned to it after the President's term was completed. Following Mrs. Hoover's death in 1944, the President donated the house to Stanford University where it is still used as the home for the University's president. Closed to the public.

Hoover Apartment
Waldorf Towers
Waldorf-Astoria Hotel
New York, New York 10017

The Waldorf was Herbert Hoover's residence from 1944 until his death in 1964. The apartment is closed to the public.

Saint Bartholomews Church
Park Avenue
New York, New York 10017

Absent a local Friends Meeting House, Hoover worshipped at Saint Bartholomews during his long residency in the Waldorf Towers.

Memorials to Herbert Hoover

George Fox College
Newberg, Oregon 97132
(503) 538-8383

Herbert Hoover attended George Fox College, then called Pacific College, before matriculating at Stanford. A campus academic building houses some Hoover memorabilia. Open to the public.

Hoover Institutions on War, Revolution and Peace
Hoover Tower
Stanford University
Palo Alto, California 94309
(415) 723-2053

The Institute was founded by Herbert Hoover in 1919, and contains documents forming the basis for research study. There are also exhibits highlighting the lives of Herbert and Lou Hoover, with emphasis on their fifty-year partnership of national and international service. Open to the public.

Hoover Dam
Lake Mead National Recreation Area
near Las Vegas, Nevada
(702) 293-8367

Hoover Dam, 726 feet-tall, one of the highest dams ever constructed, was built from 1931 to 1935. It is considered one of the engineering wonders of the United States. Museum. Open to the public.

Herbert Hoover Building
National Headquarters
Boys' Clubs of America
321 E. 111th Street
New York, New York 10026

Herbert Hoover took a passionate interest in the Boys' Clubs, serving as National Chairman for twenty-eight years, from 1936 until his death. Open to the public.

Franklin D. Roosevelt

Thirty-Second President
1933–1945

Born January 30, 1882, Hyde Park, New York
Died April 12, 1945, Warm Springs, Georgia
Burial Site: Franklin D. Roosevelt National Historic Site,
Hyde Park, New York

Franklin D. Roosevelt National Historic Site
519 Albany Post Road
Hyde Park, New York 12538
(914) 229-9115

The centerpiece of the Roosevelt National Historic Site is Springwood Mansion, the famous Hudson River Valley house where President Franklin D. Roosevelt was born and raised. The seventeen-room house has been added to, refurbished and improved upon since 1882, the improvements including the ramps built to accommodate the disabled President's wheelchair. President and Mrs. Roosevelt are entombed in the gorgeous Rose Garden on the grounds. A separate fieldstone building houses the Roosevelt Library. National Park Service Site. Open to the public.

Franklin D. Roosevelt Library and Museum
511 Albany Post Road
Hyde Park, New York, 12538
(914) 229-8114
(800) FDR-VISIT

The Franklin D. Roosevelt Library and Museum adjacent to the National Historic Site, the first great presidential library and museum, was inspired by an idea of President Roosevelt. The President donated land from the Hyde Park estate for its location and it was built with private funds before being turned over to the National Archives and Records Administration. The building is constructed of native blue fieldstone from Dutchess County. Open to the public.

Saint James Episcopal Church
Hyde Park, New York 12538

Saint James was President Roosevelt's "home" sanctuary, where he worshipped as a youngster and served the church as a warden for many years.

Top Cottage
Duchess Hill
Hyde Park, New York 12538
(914) 229-5321

Top Cottage, located five miles up the Hudson from the Roosevelt National Historic Site, was designed by FDR as a personal retreat and future retirement office. The three-bedroom fieldstone house, completed in 1939, was used for entertaining and high-level wartime meetings although the president never lived in it. The Franklin and Eleanor Roosevelt Institute is currently (1998) in negotiation with its now-private ownership to restore the property and make it accessible for visitation. Closed to the public.

Roosevelt Campobello International Park
Box 97
Lubec, Maine 04652
(506) 752-2922

The Roosevelt family vacation retreat in New Brunswick, Canada, is where Roosevelt succumbed to infantile paralysis in 1921. The "cottage," restored to its appearance at that time, is administered by a joint United States-Canadian Commission. Open to the public.

Saint Annes Anglican Church
Welshpool, Campobello Island
New Brunswick, Canada

Saint Annes was the vacation home church for the Roosevelt family when in residence at Campobello.

Parish-Ludlow Houses
6–8 East 76th Street
New York, New York 10021

Franklin Roosevelt married his distant cousin, Anna Eleanor Roosevelt, in the home of a cousin on March 17, 1905. She was given in marriage by her uncle, President of the United States Theodore Roosevelt. Closed to the public.

Roosevelt Residence
125 East 36th Street
New York, New York 10016

Newlyweds Franklin and Eleanor Roosevelt lived in a townhouse for three years after returning from a European honeymoon. Closed to the public.

Roosevelt Residence
49 East 65th Street
New York, New York 10021

Roosevelt's mother, Sara, built a comfortable five-story stone and brick townhouse as a wedding gift for Franklin and Eleanor, then erected a matching one for herself next door. The houses remained in the family until 1941 when they became headquarters for a Hunter College student association. Closed to the public.

Roosevelt Residence
2131 R Street, NW
Washington, DC 20008

In 1913, President Woodrow Wilson appointed Franklin D. Roosevelt Assistant Secretary of the Navy, a job he fulfilled with tireless efficiency. The Roosevelts moved into a spacious seventeen-room townhouse in 1917 where they remained until 1921. The house is now the Embassy of Mali. Closed to the public.

FDRs Little White House
Route 1, Box 10
Warm Springs, Georgia 31830
(706) 655-3511

Franklin D. Roosevelt, searching for relief from the debilitating physical effects of polio, visited the Warm Springs Institute frequently. Eventually, he built his own six-room bungalow among whispering Georgia pines surrounded by azaleas, dogwood and mountain laurel. This was the cottage in which the president died on April 12, 1945, and has been frozen in time; the exhibits even include the unfinished portrait for which he was posing at the time of his death. FDRs Little White House is thus memorialized as a shrine to the great president and wartime leader of the free world. Museum. Open to the public.

Chapel of the Warm Springs Institute
Warm Springs, Georgia 31830

When in residence at Warm Springs, President Roosevelt worshipped at the Warm Springs Chapel.

Saint Thomas Episcopal Church
18th and Church Streets, NW
Washington, DC 20036

Saint Thomas was President Roosevelt's place of worship in Washington.

Kenwood
Thomas Jefferson Memorial Foundation, Inc.
Box 316
Charlottesville, Virginia 22902
(804) 984-9684

Kenwood is a seventy-eight-acre estate across the road from Monticello on land once owned by Thomas Jefferson. The main residence was built between 1939 and 1941 for Major General Edwin M. "Pa" Watson, senior military aide to President Roosevelt. Roosevelt visited Kenwood several times, most notably for four days in 1944 awaiting news of the Normandy invasion. General Watson had a guest cottage, "The Little White House," built for the President who stayed in it only one night, preferring the social life and activity in the main house. Kenwood is owned by the University of Virginia which leases it to the International Center for Jefferson Studies as a headquarters and office complex. Closed to the public.

Potomac
FDR Pier
Foot of Clay Street, North end of Jack London Square
Oakland, California
(510) 839-7533

The *Potomac* was President Roosevelt's "Floating White House." The 165-foot vessel was used for relaxation and the entertainment of important dignitaries. In August, 1941, the *Potomac* was used to transport Roosevelt to his clandestine meeting with Prime Minister Churchill off the coast of Newfoundland where the principles of the Atlantic Charter were forged. The ship, completely refurbished, is owned and operated by a private corporation, and is open for dockside inspection, harbor tours and available for charter throughout the spring and summer months.

Eleanor Roosevelt National Historic Site
Val-Kill
519 Albany Post Road
Hyde Park, New York 12538
(914) 229-2115

Val-Kill is the first National Historic Site honoring a president's wife. Val-Kill was the name of a hideaway cottage on the Hyde Park estate where Mrs. Roosevelt could escape the constant political activity at Springwood. Open to the public.

Memorial to Franklin D. Roosevelt

Roosevelt Memorial Stone
9th Street and Pennsylvania Avenue
Washington, DC

The first memorial to FDR in the nation's capital is a desk-sized block of stone placed on a triangular piece of ground near the National Archives.

Franklin D. Roosevelt Memorial
The National Mall
Washington, DC
(202) 619-PARK

On May 2, 1997, dedication ceremonies were held for the Franklin D. Roosevelt Memorial on the National Mall. This newest Memorial joins those for Washington, Jefferson and Lincoln and serves as a tribute to Roosevelt's great contributions to humanity and a dramatic reflection of the historic continuity of the American heritage and spirit. The FDR Memorial is situated between the Lincoln and Jefferson memorials near Cherry Tree Walk on the Tidal Basin and consists of four outdoor galleries, each depicting a term in office. The President and the American people are represented in ten bronze sculptures and FDR's inspirational words carved in red Dakota granite amid waterfalls and quiet pools. National Park Service site. Open to the public.

See also: **Berkeley Springs** (p. 21); **Beekman Arms Hotel** (p. 45); **New York State Capitol** (p. 182); **New York Executive Mansion** (p. 182).

Harry S Truman

Thirty-Third President
1945–1953

Born May 8, 1884, Lamar, Missouri
Died December 16, 1972, Kansas City, Missouri
Burial Site: Harry S. Truman Library and Museum,
Independence, Missouri

Harry S Truman Birthplace State Historic Site
1009 Truman Avenue
Lamar, Missouri 64759
(417) 682-2279

Harry S Truman was born in a bedroom of a tiny 1½-story farmhouse with four rooms downstairs and two upstairs; a smokehouse and a well stood outside. The boy was named just plain "Harry," the S was added as an adult when he felt it more dignified to have a middle initial. The Trumans were in Lamar briefly, and moved to Belton, Missouri, when Harry was one year old. The birth house was purchased in 1957 by the United Auto Workers who had it restored and refurbished before presenting it to Missouri as a State Historic Site. Open to the public.

229

C. K. Frank Farm
Belton, Missouri 64103

Upon leaving Lamar in 1885, Harry Truman's father farmed in Belton where the family resided until 1887. Privately owned. Closed to the public.

Harry S Truman National Historic Site
223 North Main Street
Visitor Center
Independence, Missouri 64050
(816) 254-9929

In 1890, the Truman family moved to Independence where young Harry was educated. He graduated from Independence High School in 1901 and left Independence for Kansas City at that time. In 1919, after his army career, he returned to Independence and made that his permanent home. The Harry S Truman National Historic Site encompasses a number of attractions associated with President Truman and his life in Independence:

Truman Residences

619 S. Crisler Street (1890–1896)
909 W. Waldo Street (1896–1902)
902 W. Liberty Street (part of 1902)

Harry Truman and his family lived in three modest homes. These are now part of a walking tour, and the exteriors are visible from the street. Closed to the public.

Clinton Pharmacy
Courthouse Square

Harry Truman was employed as a "soda jerk" when he was a high school student. Open to the public

Jackson County Courthouse
Courthouse Square

Harry Truman worked at a political appointment as a county judge from 1923 to 1925 and again from 1927 to 1935. He supervised a rebuilding of the Jackson County Courthouse that gave it an appearance resembling Independence Hall in Philadelphia. His office suite has been restored. Open to the public.

Trinity Episcopal Church
409 N. Liberty Street

Harry Truman married his high school sweetheart, Bess Wallace, on June 28, 1919.

The Truman Home
219 N. Delaware

The famous home of Harry and Bess Truman is a fourteen-room Victorian with seven bedrooms, high-ceilinged parlor, music room and large dining room. The house had been Bess Truman's childhood home, and it remained in the Truman family until her death in 1962. Harry Truman resisted change and the house received minimal modernization over the years, thus the house has remained "Harry Truman Comfortable." Mrs. Truman bequeathed the property to the nation and the house is now a National Historic Site administered by the National Park Service. Open to the public.

Missouri Pacific Depot
600 West Grand Avenue

In 1948, President Truman made a famous campaign "whistle-stop" railroad trip through the nation, a trip which many historians believe tipped the election scales in his favor. The journey ended at the Missouri Pacific Depot in his "hometown." The depot has been converted to a small museum commemorating the event. Open to the public.

Truman Farm Home
12301 Blue Ridge Boulevard
Grandview, Missouri 64030
(816) 254-9929

In 1906, Harry Truman rejoined his father in Grandview to help him work the farm of his maternal grandfather, Solomon Young. Harry continued to manage the farm after his father died in 1914. The farm has recently been made part of the Truman National Historic Site, operated by the National Park Service. Closed to the public.

First Baptist Church
Grandview, Missouri

Harry Truman was a life-long member of the First Baptist Church in Grandview.

Truman Kansas City Residences
2108 Park Street
2650 East 29th Street
Kansas City, Missouri 64128

Between the time of his high school graduation and return to the Grandview farm, Harry Truman lived and worked in Kansas City in a variety of clerical jobs — railroad timekeeper, newspaper mail room worker, bank clerk and bookkeeper. Closed to the public.

Harry S. Truman Library and Museum
US Route 24 and Delaware Street
Independence, Missouri 64050
(816) 833-1400

Part of the modern Presidential Library system administered by the National Archives, the site includes a comprehensive museum devoted to Harry Truman's life and presidency. Open to the public.

Washington, DC Residences

Washington, DC residences of Harry S Truman

As is true for most members of Congress, Harry Truman and his wife had no permanent home in Washington, DC. Instead, they lived in several hotel suites and small apartments.

Tilden Gardens Apartments (1935–1936)
3016 Tilden Street, NW

Sedgwick Gardens (1936)
3726 Connecticut Avenue, NW

The Carroll Arms (1937)
301 1st Street, NW

Warwick Apartments (1938)
3051 Idaho Street, NW

Tilden Gardens (1938)
3000 Tilden Street, NW

3930 Connecticut Avenue, NW (1940)

4701 Connecticut Avenue, NW (1941–1945)

The Trumans were residing in an apartment at 4701 Connecticut at the time Mr. Truman became President.

First Baptist Church
16th and O Streets, NW
Washington, DC 20036
(202) 387-2206

First Baptist was the Washington church attended by presidents Harry S Truman and Jimmy Carter.

Casa Marmac Hotel
1500 Reynolds Street
Key West, Florida 33041

Following his presidency, Harry S Truman stayed at the Casa Marmac when vacationing in Key West.

Presidential Suite
Muelebach Hotel
West 12th and Baltimore Streets
Kansas City, Missouri 64105
(816) 421-6800

Thirteen presidents have been guests at the prestigious Muelebach. Harry S Truman used it often as senatorial and presidential campaign headquarters. The Presidential Suite contains a grand piano donated by Margaret Truman. The Muelebach is currently open as part of a Marriott Hotel complex in downtown Kansas City.

Harry S Truman's Military Career

Harry S Truman joined the National Guard in 1905. When the United States entered World War I in 1917, he was commissioned a first lieutenant in the field artillery. He led Battery D of the 129th Field Artillery, 35th Division, and served with distinction in France where he participated in the Vosges, Saint Michel, and Meuse-Argonne campaigns. Well respected by his men, he remained close to them through the years, even after the veteran "redleg" (artilleryman) captain became Commander in Chief of a nation at war.

Little White House Museum
111 Front Street
Key West, Florida 33041
(305) 294-9911

   The Commandant's home at the US Navy's submarine base in Key West was used by President Truman as a vacation White House. President Eisenhower used the building as an office in 1955 but, refusing to sleep in Trumans' bed, resided elsewhere. During the Cuban Missile Crisis, President Kennedy met in Key West with British Prime Minister Macmillan. The naval base has closed but the Commandant's home is owned by a private corporation and maintained as an historical museum. Open to the public.

Belton Museum
512 Main Street
Belton, Missouri 64013
(816) 331-2321

   Permanent exhibits in the Belton Museum include those featuring famous Missourians Harry Truman, Carrie Nation and Dale Carnegie. Open to the public.

Harry S. Truman State Park
Warsaw, Missouri 65355
(816) 438-2216

   A Visitor Center overlooks the Harry S. Truman Dam that controls water flow into the Lake of the Ozarks, centerpiece of the Harry S. Truman State Park. Open to the public.

Independence
US Air Museum
Old Wright Field
Springfield Pike
Dayton, Ohio 45402
(937) 255-3284

   Independence, a Douglas DC-6, went into service on July 4, 1947, as the flying White House. This airplane was named for President Truman's home town and for the date of its commissioning. Open to the public.

Dwight D. Eisenhower

Thirty-Fourth President
1953–1961

Born October 14, 1890, Denison, Texas
Died March 28, 1969, Washington, DC
Burial Site: Eisenhower Center, Abilene, Kansas

Eisenhower Birthplace State Historic Park
208 East Day Street
Denison, Texas 75020
(903) 465-8908

Dwight D. Eisenhower was born in a small frame house across from the railroad where his father was employed. The family moved to Abilene shortly after "Ike's" birth and it was not until fifty years later that the general discovered his birth place actually had been Denison; he'd assumed it had been Tyler, Texas, where his older brothers had been born. Following World War II, a group of Denison citizens formed a foundation to purchase the Eisenhower house and refurbish it in period style. The entire block around the house has been transformed into a city park. Open to the public.

Dwight D. Eisenhower Boyhood Home #1

112 Southeast 2nd Street
Abilene, Kansas 67410

The Eisenhower family moved to Abilene shortly after Dwight's birth, to a cottage near the railroad where his father worked as an engine wiper. Privately owned. Closed to the public.

Eisenhower Center

201 Southeast 2nd Street
Abilene, Kansas 67410
(913) 263-4751

The Eisenhower Center contains five components.

Boyhood Home #2

The Boyhood Home #2 is a two-story frame house with a porch, unchanged since the death of President Eisenhower's mother in 1946. The house contains original furnishings which include the upright piano the boys (there were seven) learned to play and the big double beds in which they slept. Open to the public.

Place of Meditation

The Place of Meditation — a steepled sanctuary of quiet contemplation — is the final resting place for President and Mrs. Eisenhower and their infant son, Doud. Open to the public.

Eisenhower Museum

The Eisenhower Museum is a repository for Eisenhower history, with displays covering his childhood, army career and presidency. Open to the public.

Eisenhower Library

The Eisenhower Library, administered by the National Archives, contains Eisenhower's presidential papers. Closed to the public.

Visitor Center

The Visitor Center is the starting place for tours and information about the Eisenhower Center. There is a gift shop and a film exhibition. Open to the public.

Doud Home
750 Lafayette Street
Denver, Colorado 80218

Dwight Eisenhower and Mamie Doud were married in her parents' home on July 11, 1916. The house was later used as a presidential retreat. Closed to the public.

Dwight D. Eisenhower's Military Career

Fort Sam Houston
Infantry Post
San Antonio, Texas 78234
(210) 221-6117

Dwight D. Eisenhower spent two tours of duty at Fort Sam Houston, in 1915–1917 as a Lieutenant, and as Chief of Staff of the Third Army in 1941–1942. During his first tour he met and married Mamie Doud. He had lived in various bachelor's quarters, but moved to Building 617 and later Building 688 following the marriage. His home as Chief of Staff was a 2-story structure with a full-width veranda. There is a museum on the base, open to the public as part of a 550-acre historic district. The living quarters are closed to the public.

Eisenhower Residence
157–159 N. Washington Street (1918)
Gettysburg, Pennsylvania 17325

A large Greek Revival house was a temporary residence for the Eisenhowers in 1918 when Dwight was assigned to Gettysburg during World War I. Closed to the public.

Eisenhower Residence
237 Spring Avenue
Gettysburg, Pennsylvania 17325

The Eisenhowers had an apartment in a three-story building sometime in 1918. Closed to the public.

Wyoming Apartments (1927–1928, 1929–1936)
2022 Columbia Road, NW
Washington, DC 20009

The Eisenhowers rented an apartment here on two occasions when he was attending the Army War College. Closed to the public.

Generals Row
Quarters #1
Fort Myer (1942)
Arlington, Virginia 22204

General Eisenhower served in Washington as Chief of Staff of the Army from November, 1945, to February, 1948. An 1899 house has been the residence of the Chiefs of Staff since 1910. Closed to the public.

Wardman Park Hotel (1942–1945)
2660 Woodley Road, NW
Washington, DC 20008

General Eisenhower was in Washington for a few months in 1942 before he went to Europe. While he was Supreme Commander of Allied Forces, Mrs. Eisenhower remained in an apartment at Wardman Park, now the Sheraton Washington Hotel. Closed to the public.

Tallwood
708 E. Broad Street
Falls Church, Virginia 22046

In 1941 and 1942, General Eisenhower divided his living arrangements between Fort Myer and the home of his brother, Milton. Closed to the public.

Presidents House
Columbia University
60 Morningside Drive
New York City, New York 10027

General Eisenhower served as president of Columbia University from 1948 until Inauguration Day, 1953. The house is an architecturally-elaborate 21-room mansion. Closed to the public.

Fort Adams
Quarters #1
Harrison Avenue
Newport, Rhode Island 02840
(401) 841-0707

Quarters #1 is a two-story clapboard structure, dating from 1872, that served as a summer vacation home for President Eisenhower in 1958 and 1960 as it was the nearest suitable government property to the Newport

Country Club where he played golf. The mansion, on a hill overlooking Newport harbor, is currently part of Fort Adams State Park. Open to the public.

"Mamie's Cabin"
Augusta National Golf Club
2604 Washington Road
Augusta, Georgia 30903

The Augusta National, site of the Masters Golf Tournament, was a favorite vacation spot for President and Mrs. Eisenhower. When in residence in Augusta they lived in a white frame cottage specially built for them in 1952. Closed to the public.

Surgeons House
51 Front Street
Key West, Florida 31792

In 1955, President Eisenhower resided at the Navy base in Key West while recuperating from his second heart attack. He used the Commandants House for his office, but slept in the Surgeons House down the street. Closed to the public.

Jacqueline Cochran Estate
Palm Desert, California 92261

Former President Eisenhower was granted use of a guesthouse on the estate of the famous aviatrix during his winter golfing vacations, 1961–1969. Closed to the public.

Eisenhower National Historic Site
Gettysburg, Pennsylvania 17325
(717) 334-1124

President Eisenhower was once quoted as saying *When I die, I am going to leave a piece of ground better than when I found it,* hopeful words from a career army officer and politician continually moving from one temporary home to another. His words came true, however, when he and Mamie bought a ramshackle farm and converted it to the famous Eisenhower farm nestled in the foothills of the Appalachians – a warm home of eight bedrooms, living room, dining room and a comfortable porch overlooking the Gettysburg Battlefield (and Ike's personal putting green). The house is filled with furniture, family pictures and decorative objects collected over thirty-nine years of marriage – as well as gifts from admirers around the world. Mrs. Eisenhower resided here until her death in 1979. National Park Service Site. Open to the public.

Gettysburg Presbyterian Church
208 Baltimore Street
Gettysburg, Pennsylvania 17325
(717) 334-1235

President Eisenhower was actively involved with the First Presbyterian Church when in residence in Gettysburg. His pew is marked.

Museums

National Railroad Museum
2285 S. Broadway
Green Bay, Wisconsin 54303
(414) 435-7245

General Eisenhower's World War II staff train has been transported from Europe and put on display at the National Railroad Museum. Open to the public.

Columbine II
US Air Museum
Old West Field
Springfield Pike
Dayton, Ohio 45402
(937) 255-3284

Columbine II was an advanced model of a Lockheed Constellation which served President Eisenhower as the flying White House from 1954 to 1960. It was named for the state flower of Colorado. Open to the public.

Mamie Doud Eisenhowers Birthplace
709 Carroll Street, Box 55
Boone, Iowa 50036
(515) 432-1896

Mrs. Eisenhower's childhood home is restored and furnished in the Victorian style. It houses a museum and a library with chronological displays and memorabilia depicting the first lady's life and family history. Open to the public.

See also: **Berkeley Springs** (p. 21); **Little White House Museum** (p. 234).

John F. Kennedy

Thirty-Fifth President
1961–1963

Born May 29, 1917, Brookline, Massachusetts
Died November 22, 1963, Dallas, Texas
Burial Site: Arlington National Cemetery, Arlington, Virginia

John F. Kennedy National Historic Site
83 Beals Street
Brookline, Massachusetts 02146
(617) 566-7937

John F. Kennedy was born in a simple six-room, two-story frame house on a quiet, tree-lined street in Brookline, a middle-class suburb of Boston. It was the family home from 1917 to 1921 when they moved to another house in the same neighborhood during which time the future president's father, Joseph, was an up-and-coming young executive. The Kennedy family re-purchased the Beals Street house in 1966, and the President's mother, Mrs. Rose Kennedy, supervised its reclamation and decoration to represent the time of the Kennedy occupancy. National Park Service Site. Open to the public.

Brookline Neighborhood

Brookline, Massachusetts 02146

Four sites important to the early Kennedy years are within walking distance of Beals Street: 131 Naples Road (now 51 Abbottsford Road,) where the family resided from 1921 to 1927; The Dexter and Edward Devotion Schools — schools attended by John and his older brother, Joseph; and Saint Aidans Church where John F. Kennedy was baptized in June, 1917. Saint Aidans is open to the public. The other sites are not, but are visible on a walking tour of the neighborhood.

Saint Aidans Catholic Church

158 Pleasant Street
Brookline, Massachusetts 02146
(617) 277-0799

The Kennedy Compound

Irving and Marchant Avenues
Hyannis, Massachusetts 02601

Joseph P. Kennedy rented a seaside house as a summer residence in 1926, purchased it three years later, then enlarged and remodeled it through the years. In 1956, John F. Kennedy bought an adjoining home and Robert Kennedy acquired one as well. At the time that Kennedy became President, the compound included three houses on six acres of beachfront — all three rambling white frame structures hidden behind high walls. Closed to the public.

Saint Marys Church

80 Memorial Boulevard
Newport, Rhode Island 02840
(401) 846-4926

Saint Marys was the site of the wedding of Senator John F. Kennedy and Jacqueline Bouvier on September 12, 1953.

Hammersmith Farm

Ocean Drive
Newport, Rhode Island 02840
(401) 846-0420

The summer home of Jacqueline Bouvier as a child was the site of the reception following her wedding to Senator John F. Kennedy. The house, built by her grandfather, is a twenty-eight-room shingle-style "cottage" representing Newport's grand social tradition and the informality of rural living. Hammersmith is the only working farm in the city of Newport. John and Jacqueline Kennedy and their children visited often. Open to the public.

John F. Kennedy Library and Museum
Columbia Point
Boston, Massachusetts 02125
(617) 929-4500

A magnificent modern structure designed by the distinguished architect, I. M. Pei, stands proudly beside the sea so loved by the martyred President Kennedy. Park-like surroundings and a unique view of Boston's historic skyline and harbor provide a setting capturing the modernity and vision of the man it honors. The Library is primarily a research facility, the Museum a treasure trove of artifacts, souvenirs, state gifts and historical displays delineating the John. F. Kennedy presidency and legacy. Administered by the National Archives. Open to the public.

Kennedy Residence
1095 North Ocean Boulevard
Palm Beach, Florida 33480

Joseph P. Kennedy bought a white stucco house in 1933 and it remained in the family for many years until sold to a private party in 1995. Closed to the public.

Kennedy Residence
122 Bowdoin Street, Apartment 36
Boston, Massachusetts 02108

A three-room apartment on Beacon Hill was John Kennedy's legal address from 1947 until his death. It is still owned by the Kennedy family. Closed to the public.

Washington, DC Residences

In 1947, John Kennedy took a seat in the United States House of Representatives and rented a house in Georgetown with his sister, Eunice. He lived in a number of homes, all in the Georgetown area until moving to the White House in 1961. All are closed to the public.

1528 31st Street, NW, Georgetown (1947–1949)

1400 34th Street, NW (1949–1951)

3260 N Street, NW (1952–1953)

3271 P Street, NW (1953)

3321 Dent Place, NW

Dent Place was the first home of John and Jacqueline Kennedy following their marriage. They leased it on December 15, 1953.

2808 P Street, NW (1957)

3307 N Street, NW (1958–1961)

A formal red brick Federal was the Kennedy home at the time he entered the White House.

Hickory Hill
1147 Chain Bridge Road
McLean, Virginia 22101

Hickory Hill was the permanent residence of Robert and Ethel Kennedy, although John and Jacqueline resided in it from mid-1955 until January, 1957. It remains Mrs. Ethel Kennedy's home. Closed to the public.

Glen Ora
Middleburg, Virginia 22117

In a search for privacy, John Kennedy rented a fine country estate from 1961 to mid-1963. Closed to the public.

Wexford
Atoka
Middleburg, Virginia 22117

The Kennedys built Wexford in 1963, but used it sparingly. Shortly after the President's assassination in November, 1963, Mrs. Kennedy sold the property. During the 1980 presidential campaign, Ronald and Nancy Reagan rented the house as their temporary Washington residence. Closed to the public.

Morton Downey Home
Squaw Island
West Hyannis, Massachusetts 02672

Even the Hyannis compound did not afford complete privacy from the onslaught of tourists, so President and Mrs. Kennedy rented the retreat of singer Morton Downey, in the western end of Hyannis to "get away from it all." Closed to the public.

Parish Churches

In addition to Saint Aidans, where he was baptized, and Saint Marys, where he married, John F. Kennedy attended several other churches in Hyannis, Palm Beach and Washington, DC, on a regular basis. He considered these to be his "hometown" parishes.

Saint Francis Xavier Church
Hyannis, Massachusetts 02601
(508) 775-5361

Saint Francis Xavier is the parish church for the Kennedy family when in residence in Hyannis.

Saint Anns Catholic Church
310 N. Olive
Palm Beach, Florida 33480
(407) 832-3757

Saint Edwards Catholic Church
142 N. County Road
Palm Beach, Florida 33480
(407) 832-0400

Saint Josephs Roman Catholic Church
15 Cedar Street
Bronxville, New York 10708
(914) 337-1660

Holy Trinity Roman Catholic Church
3513 N Street, NW
Washington, DC 20007
(202) 337-2840

Saint Stephens Martyr Roman Catholic Church
25th and Pennsylvania Avenues, NW
Washington, DC 20037
(202) 785-0982

Saint Matthews Cathedral
1725 Rhode Island Avenue, NW
Washington, DC 20036
(202) 347-3215

Saint Matthews Cathedral was the site of President Kennedy's funeral mass in 1963.

John F. Kennedy's Military Career

In 1941, John F. Kennedy was commissioned an ensign in the Navy, assigned to Washington, DC, and then to Charleston, South Carolina. Just after the attack on Pearl Harbor, his request for sea duty was granted and, after training in Rhode Island, he was placed in command of a PT Boat squadron in the Solomon Islands area of the South Pacific. A Japanese destroyer rammed and sank his craft, but despite a chronic back condition he helped his crew to safety. He was awarded the Purple Heart and the Navy and Marine Corps Medal for his heroic action. Kennedy finished his military career in hospitals and training facilities, and was discharged as a lieutenant.

Museums and Memorials to John F. Kennedy

The John F. Kennedy Hyannis Museum
397 Main Street
Hyannis, Massachusetts 02601
(508) 775-2201

The Hyannis Museum is devoted to President Kennedy's deep affection for Cape Cod and the lifestyle he enjoyed there. Open to the public.

The Sixth Floor Museum
411 Elm Street
Dallas, Texas 75202-3301
(214) 653-6666

On November 22, 1963, President Kennedy was killed by shots fired from the sixth floor of the Texas School Book Depository Building. The sixth floor of the Depository Building has been converted to a museum — a permanent educational exhibition examining the life, death and legacy of John F. Kennedy within the context of our national history and heritage. Open to the public.

John F. Kennedy Center for the Performing Arts
2700 F Street, NW
Washington, DC 20566
(202) 416-8341

A stately building, designed by Edward Durrell Stone, was authorized by Congress as a national cultural center. It houses the Eisenhower Theater, a concert hall, opera house, the American Film Institute Theater, the Terrace Theater, restaurants and gift shops. Open to the public.

John F. Kennedy Memorial Plaza
Maine, Commerce and Market Streets
Dallas, Texas

A tribute to the young President — who was assassinated only 200 yards away — was designed by Philip Johnson as a place of meditation, with high walls to block out traffic noise for those who wish to engage in spiritual contemplation. Open to the public.

JFK Memorial
Ocean Avenue
Hyannis, Massachusetts 02601

A circular fieldstone wall twelve-feet high faces a sparkling fountain and reflecting pool at this memorial. The wall is inscribed with the presidential seal.

John F. Kennedy International Airport
Queens, New York

"JFK Airport" was originally called Idlewild after the abandoned land upon which it was built — but the name was changed to honor President Kennedy following his assassination.

John F. Kennedy Space Center Visitor Center
Delaware North Park Services, Mail Code DNPS
Kennedy Space Center, Florida 32899
(407) 452-2121

Cape Canaveral was renamed to honor the young President who led our nation's early efforts in outer space. Public access is limited.

Military Park
Newark, New Jersey

Park statuary includes the monumental "Wars of America" by the famous sculptor Gutzon Borglum, and a bust of John F. Kennedy by Jacques Lipshitz.

Prospect Park
Brooklyn, New York
(718) 788-0055

Prospect Park contains a Quaker graveyard, gardens, trails, boating facilities and historic buildings. The north entrance, called Grand Army Plaza, features an arch commemorating Civil War heroes and a special memorial to John F. Kennedy.

See also: **Little White House Museum** (p. 234).

Lyndon B. Johnson

Thirty-Sixth President
1963–1969

Born August 27, 1908, Stonewall, Texas
Died January 22, 1973, Johnson City, Texas
Burial Site: LBJ Ranch, Stonewall, Texas

Lyndon B. Johnson National Historical Parks
Box 329
Johnson City, Texas 78636
(512) 868-7128

      Lyndon B. Johnson's grandfather built a small two-bedroom structure with an open hall, or "dog-trot," on his farm in Stonewall, Texas, near the Pedernales River, in 1889. That house is where Lyndon B. Johnson was born in 1908. It was demolished in 1930 but reconstructed at LBJ's request in 1965. The replicated birth house, Johnson's first schoolhouse, the modern LBJ Ranch House and the dignified Johnson gravesite are but one part of the National Historical Parks. The other is fourteen miles to the east, in Johnson City, a more urban town to which the family moved in 1913, and where Lyndon attended high school. Their house in Johnson City, a small one-story Victorian frame, has been restored and refurbished to its appearance circa 1925. National Park Service Site. Open to the public.

Trinity Lutheran Church
Stonewall, Texas 78671
(512) 644-2479

Trinity was President Johnson's home parish church.

Lyndon B. Johnson Library and Museum
2313 Red River Street
Austin, Texas 78705
(512) 916-5137

The Lyndon B. Johnson Library and Museum on the campus of the University of Texas is similar to the other great modern presidential libraries. The Library contains thirty-five million historical documents accessible to scholars and historians. The Museum provides public exhibits that track the political life of Lyndon Johnson. from his days as a young congressman to President of the United States and review his record as author of some of the most sweeping legislation in our history and victim of the national division caused by the Viet Nam War. Administered by the National Archives. Open to the public.

Alumni House
400 North LBJ Drive
Southwest Texas State University
San Marcos, Texas 78666
(512) 245-2371

Lyndon Johnson roomed in the home of the University's president when he was an undergraduate. Currently it is alumni headquarters for the University, but does contain a small museum with pictures and other Johnson memorabilia. Open to the public.

Welhausen School
Lane Street
Cotulla, Texas 78014
(210) 879-2326 (Chamber of Commerce)

In 1928–1929, between periods of study at college, Lyndon Johnson taught at Welhausen School, the student body then largely Mexican-American, and for a time he acted as its principal. Welhausen is now the home of Project Sunrise, an after-school program for at-risk children in the Cotulla area. There is a marker. Open to the public.

Saint Marks Episcopal Church
315 E. Pecan Street
San Antonio, Texas 78205
(210) 226-2426

On November 17, 1934, Lyndon B. Johnson and Claudia Taylor were married at Saint Marks. There is a marker.

Austin Residences

In 1933, Lyndon Johnson directed the Texas Division of the National Youth Administration. He and Lady Bird rented a home on San Pedro Street. Over the next fifteen years they owned or rented several houses in Austin while he served in the United States Congress. All sites are closed to the public.

2808 San Pedro (1935–1936)

4 Happy Hollow Lane (1937, 1939, 1941)

3119 Tom Green Street (1938–1939)

1901 Dillman (1948, 1951)

Washington Residences

When Lyndon Johnson first went to Washington as secretary to Representative Richard Kleberg in 1931, he lived in basement rooms at the Dodge Hotel, since demolished. When he returned with Lady Bird in 1935, they moved to rooms upstairs! Throughout his political career they showed upward mobility, from rented rooms to rented homes to their first owned house, that on 30th Street, where they lived until he became Vice President in 1961. When Johnson became Vice President, he and Lady Bird purchased "The Elms" from Mrs. Perle Mesta, and they were in residence at "The Elms" when Johnson became President. Closed to the public.

The Woburn (1934, 1939–1940)
1910 Kalorama Road, NW

The Kennedy-Warren (1937, 1940)
3133 Connecticut Avenue, NW

The Chatham (1938)
1707 Columbia Road, NW

Woodley Park Towers (1941–1942)
2737 Devonshire Place, NW

4921 30th Place, NW (1941–1961)

The Elms (1961–1963)
4040 52nd Street, NW

Memorials to Lyndon B. Johnson

Lyndon B. Johnson Memorial Grove on the Potomac
Lady Bird Johnson Park
Turkey Run Park
McLean, Virginia 22101

A living memorial — a park overlooking the Potomac vista of the nation's capital — features 500 white pines and slabs of Texas granite upon which Johnson quotations are inscribed. National Park Service Site. Open to the public.

Lyndon B. Johnson Space Center
NASA Clear Lake
2101 NASA Road
Houston, Texas 77058
(800) 972-0369

The Space Center, completed in 1963 and named for President Johnson in 1973, is the nerve center for America's space program — training, mission control, research and development. Public access is restricted.

LBJ School of Public Affairs
University of Texas at Austin
Drawer Y, University Station
Austin, Texas 78713
(512) 471-4962

See also: **National City Christian Church** (p. 175).

Richard M. Nixon

Thirty-Seventh President
1969–1974

Born January 9, 1913, Yorba Linda, California
Died April 22, 1994, New York, New York
Burial Site: Richard M. Nixon Library and Birthplace
Yorba Linda, California

Richard M. Nixon Library and Birthplace
18001 Yorba Linda Boulevard
Yorba Linda, California 92686
(714) 993-3393

Richard Nixon's fully-restored birth house, a small farmhouse built by his father, stands on its original site — but now at one end of an impressive nine-acre park featuring a spectacular formal "First Lady's Garden" and a one-hundred-thirty-foot-long Japanese reflecting pool. At the other end of the park is the magnificent Presidential Library and Museum, which includes fourteen thousand square feet of exhibit space, operated by the Richard Nixon Library and Birthplace Foundation. Open to the public.

First Baptist Church
Yorba Linda, California 92686

The First Baptist Church was built by Richard Nixon's father in 1915 as a Friends (Quaker) Meeting House, and is where Nixon received his first religious training.

Mission Inn
Riverside, California 92507

Richard Nixon and Patricia Ryan married at the Mission Inn on June 21, 1940.

Richard Nixon's Military Career

In 1942, not long after the outbreak of World War II, Richard Nixon moved to Washington to work for the Office of Price Administration. Even though his religion made him eligible for conscientious-objector status, he enlisted in the Navy during the summer, and was commissioned as a lieutenant, junior grade. He held a variety of assignments in supply and law — the highlight being a fourteen-month tour of duty in the Pacific.

La Casa Pacifica
The Western White House
Del Presidente Avenue
San Clemente, California 92674

La Casa Pacifica is a fourteen-room Spanish-style house acquired by President Nixon in 1969 — he visited throughout his presidency and returned to it following his resignation. Closed to the public.

California Residences

During his terms in Congress, Richard Nixon maintained a home in his congressional district, his stays limited by his service in Washington. The Anaconda Street home was his residence at the time he was elected to the United States Senate. All sites are closed to the public.

13211 East Walnut Street (1947)
Whittier, California

14033 Honeysuckle Lane (1951)
Whittier, California

15257 Anaconda Street (1953)
Whittier, California

Walter Lang Residence (1961–1963)
N. Bundy Drive
Beverly Hills, California

Washington Area Residences

Richard Nixon first served in Washington as a lawyer with the Office of Price Administration in 1942, when he rented a small apartment in Alexandria. When he returned after the war as a member of Congress, the Nixons rented rooms at the Broadmoor Hotel before moving on to private apartments and homes. They were living in a large Tudor on Forest Lane when he served his second term as Vice President. All sites are closed to the public.

The Broadmoor Hotel (1947)
3601 Connecticut Avenue, NW
Washington, DC

3538 Gunston Road (1947–1950)
Alexandria, Virginia

4801 Tilden Street, NW (1951–1967)
Washington, DC

4308 Forest Lane, NW (1957–1961)
Washington, DC

Nixon Compound
500 and 516 Bay Lane
Key Biscayne, Florida 33149

President Nixon bought two low-slung houses in late 1968 and used them as his southern vacation White House. They were sold in 1976. Closed to the public.

New York-New Jersey Residences and Office

Following his defeat for the presidency in 1960, Richard Nixon returned to California where he ran unsuccessfully for the office of Governor of California. In 1963, the Nixons moved to an apartment on Fifth Avenue in New York City when he went to work for a prestigious law firm and where they lived until he became president in 1969. After resigning the presidency in 1974, Nixon purchased a townhouse on East 65th Street in New York before opting for the suburban life of northern New Jersey, where he had houses in Saddle River and Woodcliff Lake and a condominium in Park Ridge. He was living at Park Ridge at the time of his death. His study at Park Ridge was taken apart and shipped to the Richard M. Nixon Birthplace and Library in Yorba Linda, California, where it has been reassembled to look the way it was on April 19, 1994, the day he had the stroke that led to his death. All sites are closed to the public.

810 Fifth Avenue, 5th Floor (1963–1969)
New York, New York

A twelve-room cooperative purchased in 1963 was Richard Nixon's residence until he was elected President.

142 East 65th Street (1980–1982)
New York, New York

A twelve-room, four-story townhouse was the Nixon family residence from 1980 until they moved to New Jersey.

15 Charleton Drive (1982–1990)
Upper Saddle River, New Jersey 07458

23 Sherwood Downs (1990–1994)
Park Ridge, New Jersey 07656

577 Chestnut Ridge Road (Office)
Woodcliff Lake, New Jersey 07675

Museums

Heritage of San Clemente
415 North El Camino Real
San Clemente, California 92672
(714) 369-1299

The Heritage of San Clemente was added to "Old Town" San Clemente in 1997 as is devoted to the history of the city. The displays include a complete photographic exhibit of Richard Nixon's years in San Clemente and his residency at La Pacifica, the Western White House. Open to the public.

Nixon Rooms
Wardman Library
Whittier College
13406 Philadelphia Street
Whittier, California 90608
(310) 907-4246

Two special rooms contain souvenirs, papers and other Richard Nixon memorabilia, especially of Whittier graduate Nixon's early legal and political career in California. Open to the public.

Gerald R. Ford

Thirty-Eighth President
1974–1977

Born July 14, 1913, Omaha, Nebraska

President Fords Birthsite Gardens
3202 Woolworth Avenue
Omaha, Nebraska 68103

President Ford's birth house no longer exists. However, a local philanthropist developed the site as a memorial park with busts of Gerald and Betty Ford, a decorative fountain, and a replica of the cupola of his birth house. The park is maintained by the City of Omaha. Open to the public.

Gerald R. Ford Presidential Library
1000 Beal Avenue
Ann Arbor, Michigan 48109
(313) 741-2218

The Gerald R. Ford Library is separated from its counterpart museum in Grand Rapids, although they are administered jointly by the National Archives. The Library, a two-story structure of glass and brick

258

filled with twenty million documents, is located on the campus of the University of Michigan, Ford's alma mater. Open to researchers only.

Gerald R. Ford Museum
303 Pearl Street
Grand Rapids, Michigan 49504
(616) 451-9290

The Gerald R. Ford Museum, sister institution to the Library in Ann Arbor, is a handsome triangular edifice on the west bank of the Grand River, a museum filled with displays and souvenirs pertinent to President Ford's long and distinguished career in public service. Open to the public.

Grace Episcopal Church
1815 Hall Street, SE
Grand Rapids, Michigan 49504

Gerald R. Ford married Elizabeth Bloomer in his home church on October 15, 1948.

Grand Rapids, Michigan Residences

Gerald R. Ford was born Leslie King, Jr., in Omaha. Shortly after his birth, he was taken by his mother to Grand Rapids in 1914, the year she divorced Mr. King. She remarried in 1916 and the youngster was given his stepfather's name. Several homes in which the family lived are extant, although President Ford considers the Union Avenue house as his "home," the place he lived in during his most formative years, from age eight to seventeen. All sites are closed to the public.

1960 Terrace Avenue SE (1915–1916)

630 Rosewood Avenue (1919–1921)

649 Union Avenue SE (1921–1930)

1011 Santa Cruz Drive (1934–1948)

1624 Sherman Street SE (1950–1979)

Washington Area Residences

Gerald Ford served in Congress with distinction for more than twenty years until he was called to the nation's highest office in 1974. During his congressional years, he retained his residences in Grand Rapids and rented several apartments and houses in Washington, DC, and Alexandria, Virginia. All sites are closed to the public.

259

Carlin Apartments (1948–1951)
2500 Q Street, NW
Washington, DC

1521 Mount Eagle Place (1951–1955)
Alexandria, Virginia

514 Crown View Drive (1955–1974)
Alexandria, Virginia

Immanuel on-the-Hill Church
3606 Seminary Road
Alexandria, Virginia 22304
(703) 370-6555

Immanuel-on-the-Hill was President Ford's church home when residing in Washington. Open to the public.

Gerald R. Ford's Military Career

Shortly after Pearl Harbor, Gerald R. Ford enlisted in the Navy as an ensign. He spent a substantial part of his tour of duty as an operations officer on the aircraft carrier USS *Monterey* in the Pacific. Early in 1946, he was separated as a lieutenant commander.

Retirement Homes

20775 Smoke Tree Lane
Thunderbird Heights
Rancho Mirage, California 92270

After leaving the White House, Gerald and Betty Ford rented a home where they resided for a year.

The Lodge
Vail, Colorado 81657

In 1968 the Fords purchased a condominium which they sold in 1979.

The Basshaus
Vail, Colorado 81657

From December, 1975, through September, 1982, the Fords rented a vacation residence which they used over the holidays and in the summer.

40–471 Sand Dune Road
Rancho Mirage, California 92270

The Fords current residence is protected by the Secret Service. Closed to the public.

James Earl Carter, Jr.

Thirty-Ninth President
1977–1981

Born October 1, 1924, Plains, Georgia

Jimmy Carter National Historic Site
Plains, Georgia 31780
(912) 824-7477

  The Jimmy Carter National Historic Site encompasses seventy-seven acres — almost all — of the town of Plains, Georgia, a living example of a small southern rural community where farming, church and school are essential values. The Site emphasizes places closely associated with President Carter and his life in the area both before and after he served as President. National Park Service Site. Open to the public.

Old Depot Visitor Center

  The Plains Railroad Depot, where Jimmy Carter launched his run for the presidency and which later served as headquarters for the national press covering the campaign, has been converted to a Visitor Center for the National Historic Site.

Wise Hospital
Hospital Street

Wise Hospital, renamed the Lillian G. Carter Nursing Center, was Jimmy Carter's birthplace. He holds the distinction of being the first president born in a hospital. Closed to the public.

Carter Boyhood Home
Old Plains Road
Archery, Georgia

Jimmy Carter's father bought a farm in Archery, a small town near Plains, in 1922, but the family didn't move in until 1928. They stayed on the farm for many years before moving back to Plains in 1949. The farmhouse is currently undergoing extensive structural reconstruction with plans to open it to the public in 1999.

Haunted House
Old Plains Highway

Jimmy and Rosalynn Carter and their three sons stayed in a small frame house for a few years (1956–1961) following Jimmy's discharge from the Navy. It is one of the oldest homes in the county although its "haunted" history is probably apocryphal. The house is unoccupied and in disrepair. Closed to the public.

Public Housing Unit 9A
Paschall Street and Thomas Street

Jimmy and Rosalynn Carter returned from Naval duty to Plains in 1953 to take over the family's peanut business following upon the death of Jimmy's father. They applied for public housing and were assigned unit 9A, part of a simple duplex still in use as public housing. Closed to the public.

Carter Residence
Woodland Drive

The official Carter residence is a large, comfortable, one-story brick ranch home protected by the Secret Service. Closed to the public.

Plains High School
300 North Bond Street

Jimmy Carter and Rosalynn Smith both matriculated here. The school has undergone extensive renovation and is open to the public with museum exhibits.

Plains United Methodist Church
Church Street and Thomas Street

Jimmy Carter married Rosalynn Smith in her home church on July 7, 1946.

Plains Baptist Church
Bond Street and Paschall Street

Jimmy Carter was baptized and received his first religious training at Plains Baptist Church.

Maranatha Baptist Church
Buena Vista Road

Maranatha was established when part of the congregation of Plains Baptist split off in the 1970s. Jimmy and Rosalynn Carter have been members of Maranatha since 1981 and are very active in its affairs. For example, President Carter teaches adult Sunday school on a regular basis.

Other attractions in Plains are Billy Carter's gas station, Miss Lillian's house and the Carter peanut warehouse (no longer owned by the Carter family.)

Carter Center
One Copenhill Avenue
Atlanta, Georgia 30307
(404) 331-3900
(404) 331-0296 (Museum)

A splendid office, museum and library complex overlooking Atlanta's skyline contains the offices of Jimmy Carter's diverse business and charitable interests and the Museum of the Jimmy Carter Library, administered by the National Archives. The Museum is filled with hands-on exhibits and other displays regarding the personal and political history of President Carter. Open to the public.

Georgia State Capitol
Washington Street
Atlanta, Georgia 30308
(404) 656-2844

Jimmy Carter served as Governor of Georgia from 1971 to 1975 in the capitol building patterned after the US Capitol. Gold leaf mined in northern Georgia covers the exterior dome. The interior houses museum displays. Open to the public.

Georgia Governors Mansion
391 West Paces Ferry Road, NW
Atlanta, Georgia 30308
(404) 261-1776

The Governors Mansion is a large Greek Revival building surrounded on all sides by a two-story columned veranda. Governor and Mrs. Carter resided there during his term in office, 1971–1975. Open to the public.

Jimmy Carter's Military Career

Jimmy Carter graduated from the United States Naval Academy in 1946. After a series of shore posts, he served at sea on board experimental radar and gunnery vessels as well as submarines. The highlight of his military service was participation in the nuclear submarine construction program, directed by the legendary Admiral Hyman G. Rickover.

Library

James E. Carter, Jr. Library
Georgia Southwestern College
Americus, Georgia 31709

Jimmy Carter was a freshman at Georgia Southwestern College in 1941 and 1942. The college honored its most famous student by naming the library after him.

See also: **First Baptist Church of Washington, DC** (p. 233).

Ronald Reagan

Fortieth President
1981–1989

Born February 6, 1911, Tampico, Illinois

Ronald Reagan Birthplace
111 Main Street
Tampico, Illinois 61283
(815) 438-2815

 Ronald Reagan was born in a cramped bedroom of a six-room, second-floor walkup apartment in Tampico, a small midwestern farming town. The Reagans remained in the apartment only a short time, moving at least twice in Tampico before moving to Dixon, Illinois, in 1920. Reagan's birthplace has been restored to approximate its 1911 appearance and the lower floor has been converted to a Reagan museum. Open by appointment.

Church of Christ
Freemont Street
Tampico, Illinois 61283

 Ronald Reagan's mother, Nell, was a Protestant and she took her son Ronald to Sunday School at the Church of Christ. Meanwhile, Ronald's father John, a Roman Catholic, accompanied Neil, the older son, to mass.

Ronald Reagan Boyhood Home
816 S. Hennepin Avenue
Dixon, Illinois 61021
(815) 288-3404

The Reagans moved to the middle-class, All-American town of Dixon, Illinois, in 1920 when Ronald was nine and he spent important formative years in this lively community that afforded many activities devoted to the development of young bodies, minds and spirits. The Reagan home was a two-story frame building of seven rooms – modest and comfortable. There was a barn outside where the Reagan boys raised rabbits, and a large vegetable garden. The house, restored to the time of the Reagan occupancy, is owned and maintained by the Ronald Reagan Home Preservation Foundation. The Reagans lived in other houses in Dixon, but the Hennepin Avenue house was considered "home." Open to the public.

Other Dixon, Illinois, Residences

All sites closed to the public.

338 W. Everett Avenue (1924–1931)

226 W. Lincolnway

107–108 Monroe Avenue

First Christian Church
Dixon, Illinois 61021

Mrs. Nell Reagan often taught Sunday School at the First Christian Church in Dixon, Illinois, the church where Ronald Reagan was baptized.

Ronald Reagan Presidential Library
40 Presidential Drive
Simi Valley, California 93065
(805) 522-8444

The Ronald Reagan Presidential Library is one of a series of presidential libraries and museums administered by the National Archives. This library stands high in the rugged mountains of Southern California, commanding a spectacular, sweeping view of the Simi Valley and surrounding foothills. It is a Spanish Mission-style complex of 135,000 square feet – the largest library in the Presidential Library system. The library portion houses all of President Reagan's personal and presidential papers. The public museum area chronicles his life and times with displays, souvenirs, pictures and audio-visual demonstrations. Open to the public.

Wee Kirk o' the Heather
Forest Lawn Memorial Park
Glendale, California 91205

Ronald Reagan and actress Jane Wyman were married at Wee Kirk-o'-the-Heather on January 26, 1940.

Little Brown Church in the Valley
4418 Coldwater Canyon Boulevard
Studio City, California 91604
(818) 761-1127

On March 4, 1952, Ronald Reagan married actress Nancy Davis at the Little Brown Church in the Valley.

Tau Kappa Epsilon House
Burton Avenue
Eureka, Illinois 61530

Ronald Reagan lived in his fraternity house most of the time he attended Eureka College. Closed to the public.

Des Moines, Iowa, Residences
After graduating from college, "Dutch" Reagan found work as a radio announcer in Des Moines. All sites closed to the public.

330 Center Street (Second floor)

400 Center Street (Ground Floor)

Hollywood, California, Residences
Ronald Reagan made his first trip to California as a play-by-play radio announcer for the Chicago Cubs baseball team that trained each spring on Avalon Island off the coast of southern California. One day off, on a lark and as a favor to an agent friend, Reagan screen-tested at Warner Brothers and, as they say, the rest is history. Reagan signed with the studio and was not to leave Hollywood again until elected Governor of California. When he was a contract player he lived in a series of "bachelor pads" in the Hollywood area. All sites are closed to the public.

Montecito Apartments
6650 Franklin Avenue

1326 Londonderry View (after marriage to Jane Wyman)

1128 Cory Avenue

9137 Cordell Drive

333 South Beverly Glen

1258 Amalfi Drive
Pacific Palisades, California

   Amalfi Drive was the first house owned by newlyweds Ronald and Nancy Reagan.

1669 San Onofre
Pacific Palisades, California

   The San Onofre house is a famous all-electric home featured on television — with appliances, heating, and progressive lighting provided by Ronald Reagan's television sponsor, General Electric. The house was sold when Reagan became President.

Yearling Row Ranch
Santa Monica Mountains
Agoura, California

   Yearling Row was Ronald Reagan's escape — a horse ranch that actor Reagan used to get away from the pressures of show business and his active presidency of the Screen Actors Guild. The ranch was sold to the 20th-Century Fox Film Corporation when Reagan was elected Governor of California.

Bel Air Presbyterian Church
Bel Air, California 90210

   Ronald and Nancy Reagan have been congregants at Bel Air for many years.

California Governors Mansion
Gallatin House
16th and H
Sacramento, California 95914
(916) 445-4209

The California Governor's Mansion is a Victorian Gothic frame mansion that was built for Albert Gallatin, local hardware merchant, in the 19th century. It was sold to the State of California and became home to thirteen governors. The Reagans moved in in 1966 even though the house had been declared unsafe as early as 1941! Horrified by the condition of the house, the Reagans moved into temporary quarters pending repair (or abandonment) of the existing mansion. Owned by the California Department of Parks and Recreation. Open to the public.

Reagan Sacramento Rental
1341 45th Street
Sacramento, California 95914

Nancy Reagan, horrified at the condition of the Governors Mansion, refused to remain there. While the state began to plan for a replacement, the Reagans moved into this Tudor home. Closed to the public.

California State Capitol
Bounded by 10th, 15th, L and N Streets
Sacramento, California 95914
(916) 324-0333

Governor Ronald Reagan served the people of California from 1966 until he was elected President in 1981. Open to the public.

Present Residences
After leaving the presidency, Ronald and Nancy Reagan retreated to their beloved California, splitting their time between a "modest" home in the exclusive Bel Air section of Los Angeles and the famous Reagan Ranch high in the mountains above Santa Barbara. Following President Reagan's diagnosis as having Alzheimer's Disease, the ranch was put up for sale in 1997. Both places are very private, protected by the Secret Service and closed to the public. Both sites are closed to the public.

668 Saint Cloud Road
Bel Air, California 90027

Rancho Del Cielo
Refugio Canyon
Santa Barbara, California

Santa Ynez Valley Presbyterian Church
1825 Alamo Pintado Road
Solvang, California 93463
(805) 688-6323

Ronald and Nancy Reagan sometimes worshipped in Santa Ynez when in residence at their nearby ranch.

Ronald Reagan's Military Career

Poor eyesight prevented Ronald Reagan from fighting duty. However, he served as an officer in the Air Corps in a variety of public relations and motion picture capacities in San Francisco and Hollywood.

Library

Meldrick Library
Eureka College
300 College Avenue
Eureka, Illinois 61530
(309) 467-6380

Ronald Reagan is a graduate of Eureka College where the campus library has accumulated a collection of Reagan memorabilia. Open to the public.

See also: **Wexford** (p. 244).

George Bush

Forty-First President
1989–1993

Born June 12, 1924, Milton, Massachusetts

George Bush Birthplace
173 Adams Street
Milton, Massachusetts 02187

George Bush was born in a makeshift delivery room in a Victorian house in a well-to-do suburb of Boston. The Bush family remained in residence for a year following George's birth. Closed to the public.

George Bush Boyhood Home
Grove Lane
Greenwich, Connecticut 06830

George Bush spent most of his boyhood in a large and roomy house in an exclusive section of Greenwich. Closed to the public.

First Presbyterian Church
Rye, New York 10580

George Bush and Barbara Pierce married on January 6, 1945.

Bush Summer Home
Walkers Point
Kennebunkport, Maine 04046

Walkers Point is the well-known vacation retreat for the Bush family, and is protected by the Secret Service. Closed to the public.

Saint Annes Episcopal Church
River and Windham
Windham, Maine 04062
(207) 892-8447

The Bush family worships at Saint Annes Church when vacationing in Kennebunkport.

Bush Residence
West Oak Drive
Houston, Texas 77056

George and Barbara Bush live in a home in a suburb of Houston. Protected by the Secret Service. Closed to the public.

Saint Martins Episcopal Church
717 Sage Road
Houston, Texas 77056
(713) 621-3040

George and Barbara Bush are active members of Saint Martins Episcopal Church.

George Bush Presidential Library
1000 George Bush Drive
Box 10410
College Station, Texas 77842-1145
(409) 862-2251

The George Bush Presidential Library, located on the campus of Texas A&M University, is the most recent addition to the system of presidential libraries administered by the National Archives and Record Service. Construction of this library was begun shortly after the President left office, and the dedication was held on November 5 and 6, 1997. Open to the public.

George Bush's Military Career

On his eighteenth birthday in 1942, George Bush enlisted in the Naval Reserve and was commissioned an ensign after completing flight training. At that time he was the youngest pilot in the Navy. He served valiantly for three years in the Pacific, and was shot down near the Bonin Islands. After four hours in the water he was rescued by a submarine. In 1945, Bush was discharged with honors that included the Distinguished Flying Cross and three Air Medals.

Museum

Nimitz Hotel
Admiral Nimitz State Historical Park
340 East Main Street
Fredericksburg, Texas 78624
(512) 997-4379

The Nimitz Hotel was built by the grandfather of Admiral Chester W. Nimitz. It has been converted to a museum of the War in the Pacific and features a George Bush Gallery. Open to the public.

William J. Clinton

Forty-Second President
1993–

Born August 19, 1946, Hope, Arkansas

Hope "Clinton Loop"
Hope Tourist Center
Box 596
Hope, Arkansas 71801
(800) 223-HOPE

Bill Clinton was born in the small town of Hope as William Jefferson Blythe, IV. His father was killed in an automobile accident three months before Bill's birth. The youngster was left in the care of his grandparents in Hope while his mother went to New Orleans to train for a nursing career. She returned to Hope to marry Roger Clinton, whose name young William eventually took as his own, The town of Hope has put together a drive-by tour of various local sites associated with President Clinton's birth and early years in Hope. Marked with appropriate signs, all are closed to the public, although a private foundation has purchased the house at 321 E. 13th Street. Renovation efforts are underway to restore it to its original 1946 appearance. Open to the public.

Julia Chester Hospital

The hospital where Bill Clinton was born has been razed.

Childhood Home
117 S. Hervey Street

Childhood home
321 E. 13th Street

Pre-School
601 E. 2nd Street

Elementary School
50 S. Spruce Street

Hot Springs " Clinton Loop"
Hot Springs Convention and Visitors Bureau
Box K
Hot Springs, Arkansas 71902
(800) 772-2489

The Clinton family moved to Hot Springs when young Bill was seven and, like Hope, Hot Springs has also put into place an automobile tour that leads past a number of places associated with Bill Clinton's formative years – homes, high school, church, and others. Each place is appropriately marked, although none is open to the public.

Park Place Baptist Church
721 Park Avenue
Hot Springs, Arkansas 71902

Bill Clinton was baptized at Park Place Baptist and was a steady congregant. The president's mother related that he never missed a Sunday. Often she had to work, so, on his own, he would pick up his Bible and walk to church.

Clinton Residence
930 California Boulevard
Fayetteville, Arkansas 72702-4216

On October 11, 1975, Methodist Minister Vic Nixon officiated at the marriage of Bill Clinton and Hillary Rodham in their home, now privately owned. Closed to the public.

Clinton Residence

5419 L Street
Little Rock, Arkansas 72201

On January 5, 1977, Bill and Hillary Clinton paid $35,000 for a buff brick home where they lived when Bill was Attorney General of Arkansas, 1977–1979. Closed to the public.

Arkansas Governors Mansion

18th and Center Streets
Little Rock, Arkansas 72201
(501) 376-6884

The Governors Mansion is a latter-day version of the Colonial Revival style, chosen to complement the Greek Revival architecture of the Old State House. The Clintons lived in the mansion during his first gubernatorial term, then from 1981 until his election as President in 1993. Closed to the public.

Clinton Residence

816 Midland
Little Rock, Arkansas 72201

Following his gubernatorial loss to Republican Frank White in 1980, the Clintons and their infant daughter moved to a two-story frame house, purchased for $112,000. Over the next two years, before his reelection to the governorship, Bill and Hillary Clinton returned to teaching and the practice of law. Closed to the public.

Immanuel Baptist Church

1000 Bishop Street
Little Rock, Arkansas 72201

When visiting Little Rock, President Clinton attends services at Immanuel Baptist, his home church for many years. Open to the public.

Arkansas State Capitol

West Capitol Avenue
Little Rock, Arkansas 72201
(501) 682-5080

Bill Clinton served four terms as Governor of Arkansas. The State Capitol building where he officiated is of white Arkansas marble, patterned after the US Capitol. Open to the public.

See also: **Saint Johns Episcopal Church** (p. 285).

A Selection of Museums, Churches and Other Sites Associated with Presidents

MUSEUMS

American Museum of Fly Fishing
Route 7A and Seminary Avenue
Manchester, Vermont 05254
(802) 362-3300

Fishing equipment belonging to presidents Herbert Hoover, Grover Cleveland, Dwight D. Eisenhower and Jimmy Carter is among the gear on display.

Anderson House Museum
2118 Massachusetts Avenue, NW
Washington, DC 20008
(202) 785-2040

Headquarters, library and museum of the Society of Cincinnati, founded by George Washington and others in 1783.

Antique Boat Museum
750 Mary Street
Clayton, New York 13624
(315) 686-4104

A collection of fresh water boats includes the personal craft of presidents Ulysses S. Grant and James A. Garfield.

Audrain County Historical Society and American Saddle Horse Museum
501 Muldrow Street
Mexico, Missouri 65265
(573) 581-3910

Named "Graceland," this 1857 home was visited by General Ulysses S. Grant during the early days of the Civil War. It is furnished in period.

Centre Hill Mansion Museum
Centre Hill Court
Franklin Street
Petersburg, Virginia 23804
(804) 733-2401

This 1823 Federal-style Centre Hill Mansion filled with period antiques was host to presidents John Tyler, Abraham Lincoln and William Howard Taft.

Daughters of the American Revolution Library
1776 D Street, NW
Washington, DC 20006
(202) 879-3229

A complete genealogical research facility devoted to America's colonial and revolutionary period is part of a thirty-three-room museum featuring the art, crafts and personalities of the times.

Genealogical Research Library
National Society of the Sons of the American Revolution
1000 South 4th Street
Louisville, Kentucky 40203
(502) 589-1776

The SAR Library contains more than 4000 genealogies and other records of the Revolutionary War and the Colonial period.

General Crook House Museum
Fort Omaha Campus
Metropolitan Community College
Omaha, Nebraska 68108
(402) 455-9990

General George Crook was commander of the Department of the Platte that included Iowa, Nebraska, Utah, Wyoming, Idaho and Montana during the Indian wars of the 1870s. Presidents Ulysses S. Grant and Rutherford B. Hayes were among the guests that Crook entertained in his two-story Italianate home complete with Victorian garden. The grounds and the house with its modern hands-on museum of Douglas County history are open to the public.

General James Mitchell Varnum Museum
57 Pierce Street
East Greenwich, Rhode Island 02818
(401) 884-1776

Brigadier General Varnum of the Continental Army was a confidante of George Washington who was entertained in Varnum's house along with Nathanael Greene and French generals Lafayette and Rochambeau. The house, circa 1773, is noted for its fine furniture and magnificent paneling along with an exquisite colonial garden. Open to the public.

Gold Coast Railroad and Museum
12450 SW 152nd Street
Miami, Florida 33196
(305) 253-0063

In addition to fascinating model railroads, the Gold Coast Railroad Museum features a collection of vintage rail cars, including Railroad Car #1, the "Ferdinand Magellan," the traveling office and home to presidents Franklin D. Roosevelt, Harry S. Truman, Dwight D. Eisenhower and Ronald Reagan. Open to the public.

Henry Ford Museum and Greenfield Village
20900 Oakwood Boulevard
Dearborn, Michigan 48121-1970
(313) 271-1620

A sprawling complex, 93 acres in size, is devoted to the 300 years of technological changes that moved America from an agrarian to industrial society. There are historical displays and items that include George Washington's folding camp bed, Abraham Lincoln's rocker from Fords

Theatre – and the original Postville (Logan County), Illinois, courthouse where Lincoln "rode the circuit." Also on display are Theodore Roosevelt's 1902 horse-drawn brougham and four modern presidential limousines – those of Franklin D. Roosevelt, Dwight D. Eisenhower, John F. Kennedy and Ronald Reagan.

Museum of American Political Life
University of Hartford
20 Bloomfield Avenue (SR 189)
West Hartford, Connecticut 06117
(860) 768-4090

Artifacts of every president are displayed, the emphasis being on political campaigns. The museum also examines different movements affecting American political attitudes – Womens' Rights, Temperance, Prohibition and the like.

Museum of American Presidents
130 N. Massanutten Street
Strasburg, Virginia 22657
(540) 465-5999

The private presidential collection of Mr. Leo Bernstein has been moved from its original location at the Ramada Inn in Luray to its own building in the historic town of Strasburg. Prominently displayed are James Madison's writing desk and a handsome chandelier from Montpelier. The museum is "dedicated to helping Americans, especially our youth, understand the principles upon which this nation was founded."

Parade of Presidents Wax Museum
Highway 16A, South
Keystone, South Dakota 57751
(605) 666-4455

This museum, located 2½ miles from Mount Rushmore, features wax figures of every president and other historical personages, each displayed in a setting representing a memorable event in American history.

Presidents Cottage Museum
The Greenbrier Hotel
White Sulphur Springs, West Virginia 24986
(304) 536-1110

The world-class Greenbrier resort hotel has hosted innumerable world leaders including presidents Martin Van Buren, Millard Fillmore,

Franklin Pierce, James Buchanan and John Tyler. The cottage in which they stayed has been converted to a small museum, open to guests of the hotel.

The Presidential Museum
622 North Lee Avenue
Odessa, Texas 79761
(915) 322-7123

This museum is devoted to a study of the office of the President, with exhibits and educational programs about the people who have held — or run for — the presidency. The displays include campaign paraphernalia, signatures and cartoons — and the famous Dishong Collection of First Lady dolls.

Springfield Armory National Historic Site
One Armory Square
Springfield, Massachusetts 01105
(413) 734-8551

The Springfield Armory Museum, founded in 1794, contains the largest array of military small arms in the world — everything from the sleek, long-barreled muskets of 1785 to the famous Springfield rifle to the M-1 of World War II and the M-16 of today. The museum also houses a collection of firearms donated by presidents John F. Kennedy, Dwight D. Eisenhower, Franklin D. Roosevelt and Woodrow Wilson.

Studebaker National Museum
525 S. Main Street
South Bend, Indiana 46601
(219) 284-9714

This museum is devoted to the history of American transportation. Featured items are carriages used by presidents Abraham Lincoln, Ulysses S. Grant and William McKinley.

Tennessee State Museum
James K. Polk Cultural Center
Deaderick Street
Nashville, Tennessee 37204
(615) 741-2692

A wide variety of exhibits depicts the history and heritage of Tennessee, home to presidents Andrew Jackson, James K. Polk and Andrew Johnson.

United States Army Quartermaster Museum
SR 36
Fort Lee, Virginia 23801
(804) 734-1854

This museum is devoted to the history of the Quartermaster Corps, displaying uniforms, weapons and equipment dating from 1775. There are individual items associated with Generals Franklin Pierce, Ulysses S. Grant and Dwight D. Eisenhower.

United States Naval Academy
Annapolis, Maryland
(410) 267-3363

President Jimmy Carter was a graduate of the United States Naval Academy. There is a naval museum on the campus. Open to the public.

United States Military Academy
West Point, New York 10966
(914) 938-2638

Two presidents, Ulysses S. Grant and Dwight D. Eisenhower, were graduates of the United States Military Academy. There is a military museum on the campus. Open to the public.

Wax Museum at Natural Bridge
Box 85
Natural Bridge, Virginia 24578
(800) 323-8843

This museum displays over 150 life replicas in scenes devoted to the history of the Shenandoah Valley, including a tribute to the several presidents born in Virginia.

CHURCHES

Washington National Cathedral
Massachusetts and Wisconsin Avenues, NW
Washington, DC 20016-5098
(202) 537-6200

The National Cathedral is one of the world's largest churches — an exemplification of classic Gothic architecture — symbol and modern representation of the nation's religious history. The cathedral, recently completed following decades of construction, is the burial site of President Woodrow Wilson.

Saint Johns Episcopal Church
"The Church of Presidents"
16th and H Streets
Washington, DC 20005
(202) 347-8766

A pew in Saint Johns Episcopal Church was reserved for President James Madison when the church opened in 1816, and it has remained reserved for every sitting president. Almost every Chief Executive has worshipped at Saint Johns as it fronts on Lafayette Park, directly across Pennsylvania Avenue from the White House. President Bill Clinton is a regular congregant.

National Presbyterian Church and Center
4101 Nebraska Avenue, NW
Washington, DC 20016
(202) 537-0800

This magnificent edifice serves as the National Church for Presbyterians, with meeting facilities available for all faiths. The Chapel of the Presidents and many stained glass windows depict modern humanity and biblical themes. The present structure was completed in 1967, the cornerstone laid by former President Dwight D. Eisenhower who had been baptized at National Presbyterian when it was located at 16th and N Streets. That 18th-century building had been the spiritual home for presidents Andrew Jackson, James Buchanan, Grover Cleveland and Benjamin Harrison as well as Eisenhower.

OTHER SITES

Mount Rushmore National Memorial
Box 268
Keystone, South Dakota 57751
(605) 574-2523

Mount Rushmore is the breathtaking sculpture of George Washington, Thomas Jefferson, Abraham Lincoln and Theodore Roosevelt carved into the granite face of a mountain, as executed by Gutzon Borglum. National Park Service Site.

285

Westover Plantation
7000 Westover Plantation Road
Route 2, Box 445
Charles City, Virginia 23030
(804) 829-2882

Connoisseurs consider the manor house at Westover to be the finest example of Georgian domestic architecture in this country. The mansion, built circa 1730, is a symbol of the high quality of building design attained during the Colonial period. A neighbor to Berkeley Plantation and other James River plantations, it is more than likely that many of the early Colonial elite visited Westover. Open on a limited basis.

Shirley Plantation
501 Shirley Plantation Road
Charles City, Virginia 23030
(804) 829-5121

Shirley has no rival in Queen Anne architectural distinction. A complete set of 18th-century brick buildings form a Queen Anne forecourt, unique to this country. The mansion has been home to the Carter family since 1723. Like the other James River mansions, the early Colonials undoubtedly visited. Open to the public.

Camp David
Naval Support Facility
Box 1000
Thurmont, Maryland 21788

Camp David, the famous presidential retreat located in the Blue Ridge Mountains of Maryland, dates to the administration of Franklin D Roosevelt at which time it was called "Shangri-La." Camp David is protected by the United States Marines. Closed to the public.

Historic Michie Tavern
Route 6, Box 7A
Charlottesville, Virginia 22901
(804) 977-1234

Historic Michie Tavern, one of Virginia's oldest homesteads, opened as a tavern in 1784 — hosting travelers along the stagecoach route south of Charlottesville. George Washington, Thomas Jefferson and other early Colonials undoubtedly refreshed themselves at Michie Tavern. Open to the public.

Federal Hall National Memorial
26 Wall Street
New York, New York 10005
(212) 264-8711

National Park Service Site. The present building was completed in 1842 as a federal customs house — erected on the site of the original Federal Hall, location of the trial of John Peter Zenger in 1735, the Convention of the Stamp Act Congress in 1765, meeting of the Second Continental Congress in 1785, and George Washington's first inauguration as President. A dignified statue of Washington dominates the entrance to Federal Hall. Open to the public.

Old Governors Mansion
420 High Street
Frankfort, Kentucky 40601
(502) 564-5000

This 1798 Georgian mansion is furnished in period. A number of illustrious guests have been welcomed, including seven presidents. It is currently utilized as the home of Kentucky's Lieutenant Governor. Open to the public.

Tudor Place
1644 31st Street
Georgetown Section
Washington, DC 20007
(202) 965-0400

Tudor Place is the finest mansion in Georgetown, one of the five most important houses in the city — a Neoclassical structure designed by Architect William Thornton around 1805 and built for Thomas Peter and his wife, Martha Parke Custis, granddaughter of Martha Washington. Many presidents and other distinguished visitors have been entertained at Tudor Place. The house was donated to a private foundation by the Peter family and opened to the public in 1988.

Hall of Fame for Great Americans
University Avenue at West 181st Street
Bronx, New York 10025
(718) 220-6312

A 630-foot colonnade houses bronze busts of ninety-seven famous Americans, including twelve presidents. Open to the public.

Hall of Presidents
Liberty Square
The Magic Kingdom
Walt Disney World
Lake Buena Vista, Florida 32830
(407) 824-2222

The Hall is a collection of audio-animatronic figures of every president — from Washington to Clinton — with spoken words taken from famous speeches and writings. Open to the public.

Hall of Presidents and First Ladies
Gettysburg, Pennsylvania 17325
(717) 334-5717

The presidents, meticulously reproduced in wax, relate the story of America in their own words, using simulated voices. Open to the public.

Forest Lawn-Memorial Park
6300 Forest Lawn Drive
Los Angeles, California 90068
(213) 254-7251

Forest Lawn in the Hollywood Hills is a 340-acre cemetery with sections dedicated to America's heritage — a full-sized replica of Boston's Old North Church and a fifteen-acre Court of Liberty that contains a reproduction of the Liberty Bell. The exterior of the Court features a 30 x 165-foot mosaic, "The Birth of Liberty," depicting epic moments in our nation's history. There is also a sixty-foot bronze and marble memorial to George Washington, a powerful bronze statue of Thomas Jefferson and a sculpture of Abraham Lincoln, executed by Augustus Saint-Gaudens. Open to the public.

Forest Lawn-Memorial Park
1712 South Glendale Avenue
Glendale, California 91209
(213) 241-4151

The "original" Forest Lawn contains its own piece of Americana including a reproduction of the "Church of the Hills," the old New England meeting house where Henry Wadsworth Longfellow worshipped, and a dramatic "Court of Freedom," its centerpiece one of the most inspiring sculptural representations of George Washington ever made — the second casting made from the mold of the statue standing at the Sub-Treasury Building in New York City. Open to the public.

Sequoia
Dry Dock
Norfolk Shipbuilding and Drydock Corporation
Norfolk, Virginia 23501
(804) 644-1200

This teak vessel served as the presidential yacht for every president from Hoover to Ford. It was sold by President Carter's administration in 1977 and is currently owned by the Norfolk shipyard, which is offering it for sale. Closed to the public.

USS *Williamsburg*
Drydock, Valdettaro Shipyards
Italy

The *Williamsburg* was used by President Harry Truman extensively during his administration as he preferred cruising on the Potomac to weekends at Shangri-La (Camp David). During his vacations in Key West, the ship was utilized for sailing, cooking and communications. A group of international investors has been formed to provide funding for the restoration of the *Williamsburg,* and recommissioning in Key West, Florida, in the near future. It will then be moved and used as a tourist attraction in Washington, DC.

WASHINGTON, DC

The White House
1600 Pennsylvania Avenue
(202) 456-7041 (Tour Information)

The White House is the oldest public building in the District of Columbia, the official residence of the President since November 1, 1800, when John and Abigail Adams moved into the still-unfinished "President's House." Its design was the result of a competition won by Irish-born James Hoban, whose entry was based on Leinster House in Dublin. The cornerstone was laid on October 23, 1792, by the Freemasons of the District of Columbia. President George Washington was in attendance. Open to the public.

Blair House
1651 Pennsylvania Avenue

Blair House is the official guest house for the United States government – most famous as the temporary home of the Truman family during an extensive overhaul of the White House. In 1950, President Truman escaped assassination when two Puerto Rican nationalists stormed Blair House. Closed to the public.

Pennsylvania Avenue National Historic Site
c/o Pennsylvania Avenue Development Corporation
Suite 1220 N
1331 Pennsylvania Avenue, NW
(202) 724-9068

A portion of Pennsylvania Avenue and the adjacent area between the Capitol and The White House encompasses Ford's Theatre, blocks of commercial buildings, the Old Post Office and other federal structures. The great inaugural parades and other demonstrations march down Pennsylvania Avenue.

Smithsonian Institution
1000 Jefferson Drive (Visitor Center)
(202) 357-2700

Known as "The Castle," the headquarters building is the oldest of the Smithsonian's fourteen museums and houses which include The National Zoo, National Air and Space Museum, National Museum of American History and the National Museum of Natural History. Open to the public.

National Portrait Gallery
8th and F Streets
(202) 357-2700

Among the best-known of the Smithsonian museums, the National Portrait Gallery is devoted exclusively to portraiture. A Hall of Presidents features portraits and descriptive material on the private and public life of every Chief Executive. Open to the public.

National Building Museum
401 F Street, NW
Washington, DC 20001
(202) 272-2448

On March 4, 1809, newly-inaugurated President James Madison hosted the very first Inaugural Ball, at Longs Hotel, located at East Capitol and 1st streets. Nowadays, the Inaugural Ball takes place at a number of hotels or other sites in the downtown area of Washington. The most popular site, however, has been the National Building Museum, official host from

1885 to 1909 and again in 1973, 1977 and 1981. The National Building Museum occupies one of the most impressive buildings in the capital; more than fifteen million bricks make up the exterior which is circled by a twelve-hundred-foot-long terra cotta frieze of Civil War soldiers on an endless march.

National Archives
7th and Pennsylvania Avenue, NW
(202) 501-5205

The National Archives and Records Administration preserves valuable national records. Among the objects displayed in its Exhibition Hall are the Declaration of Independence, the Constitution of the United States and the Bill of Rights. The Archives also administers nine of the modern presidential libraries distributed throughout the country. Open to the public.

United States Capitol
The National Mall
(202) 224-3121 (Tours)

The United States Capitol Building, situated atop Capitol Hill and dominated by a magnificent 180-foot-high white dome, is one of the most imposing structures in Washington, DC. It is here that the elected senators and representatives meet to shape legislative policies of the United States. Open to the public.

Presidents Park
518 6th Street, SE
(202) 547-1364

Presidents Park comprises the downtown Washington area that includes Lafayette Park, the White House and the South Lawn.

Riggs National Bank
1503 Pennsylvania Avenue

Presidential depositors at Riggs National Bank included Abraham Lincoln, Ulysses S. Grant and Theodore Roosevelt. Open to the public.

Woodley
3000 Cathedral Avenue, NW

A Federal-style house was a summer retreat for Martin Van Buren, John Tyler, James Buchanan and Calvin Coolidge. It is currently part of the Maret School. Closed to the public.

Library of Congress
Independence and I Streets
(202) 707-5458

The Library's nucleus was a personal collection of 6000 books donated by Thomas Jefferson after a small congressional collection was destroyed by the British during the War of 1812. One of the largest libraries in the world, the Library of Congress is housed in several buildings on Capitol Hill. The Thomas Jefferson Building is an impressive example of Beaux Arts Classicism. The James Madison and John Adams Buildings are to the south and east of the Jefferson Building. The Library is notable regarding presidents as it is the repository of the largest and most diverse collection of photographs and artwork documenting their careers. Open to the public.

The (New) Willard Hotel (Inter-Continental)
14th and Pennsylvania Avenue, NW
(202) 628-9100

The most notable of all Washington hotels was the elegant Willard, which became known as the "Residence of Presidents." The hotel, recently rebuilt, remains an excellent example of Beaux Arts architecture. Presidents Zachary Taylor, Millard Fillmore, Franklin Pierce, James Buchanan, Abraham Lincoln, Ulysses S. Grant, William Howard Taft, Woodrow Wilson, Warren G. Harding and Calvin Coolidge all lodged at the Willard. Coolidge had taken his first oath of office from his notary public father in Vermont, but due to some questions about its legality, he repeated the oath in a public ceremony at the Willard. Open to the public.

PHILADELPHIA, PENNSYLVANIA

Independence National Historical Park
313 Walnut Street
Philadelphia, Pennsylvania 19106
(215) 597-8974

Philadelphia served as the capital of the fledgling United States for a decade — a period of precedent-setting decisions and notable "firsts" in America's political history. Many of the buildings where these events took place are part of Independence National Historical Park. All attractions are open to the public unless noted otherwise.

Betsy Ross House
239 Arch Street
(215) 627-5343

A restored two-story Colonial home is where Betsy Ross maintained her seamstress shop — and was credited with sewing the first American flag at the request of George Washington.

Christ Church
22–26 N. 2nd Street
(215) 922-1695

Christ Church, built between 1727 and 1754, is considered an outstanding example of 18th-century American architecture. George and Martha Washington worshipped here. Their pew is marked, as is that of Benjamin Franklin.

Congress Hall
6th and Chestnut
(215) 597-8774

Meeting place of the United States Congress from 1790 to 1800.

Jacob Graff, Jr., House
Seventh and Market

The Jacob Graff, Jr., House is where Thomas Jefferson wrote the first draft of the Declaration of Independence.

Independence Hall
Chestnut Street between 5th and 6th
(215) 597-8974

Independence Hall is where the Declaration of Independence was adopted, George Washington was named Commander-in-Chief of the Continental Army and the United States Constitution was drafted.

Liberty Bell Pavilion
Market Street between 5th and 6th

The Liberty Bell, the most revered symbol of American freedom, is displayed in its own shrine.

First Bank of the United States
120 S. 3rd Street

The oldest bank building in the country — home of the government's bank from 1797 to 1811. The exterior has been restored.

Second Bank of the United States
420 Chestnut Street

The Second Bank building, an outstanding example of Greek Revival architecture, is home to Independence Park's portrait gallery.

City Tavern
2nd and Walnut
(215) 923-6059

City Tavern was the most popular gathering place and watering hole in Philadelphia for early patriots and politicians. The tavern was reconstructed in 1975 by the National Park Service to reflect its glory as America's finest dining spot. Under private concession, it remains a working restaurant allowing today's visitors to experience a taste of the past as enjoyed by our nation's founders.

Thomas Bond House
129 South 2nd Street
(800) 845-BOND

The Bond House was built across the street from City Tavern by prominent physician Thomas Bond in 1769. The center of a fashionable residential area, it is probable that Washington visited on occasion. This house was restored and opened as a bed and breakfast inn in 1988.

Old City Hall
5th and Chestnut
(215) 597-8974

Old City Hall was home to the United States Supreme Court from 1791 to 1800. The room used by the Court has been restored.

Old Saint Josephs Church
321 Willings Alley

The first Roman Catholic Church in Philadelphia. French generals Lafayette and Rochambeau were congregants.

Saint Peters Church
3rd and Pine Streets
(215) 925-5968

This Episcopal church was erected in 1761 and served four signers of the Declaration of Independence as their Philadelphia church home. George Washington belonged to Christ Church but it is known that he attended Saint Peters on occasion.

Franklin Court
Between 3rd and 4th, Chestnut and Market

Benjamin Franklin was an entrepreneur and real estate investor who owned an entire city block of commercial buildings. The present complex contains an underground theater and museum, as well as five Market Street houses. The exteriors have been restored to represent the Franklin era.

Deshler-Morris House
5442 Germantown Avenue
(215) 596-1748

A yellow fever epidemic swept Philadelphia in 1794, forcing President Washington to flee the city for the more salubrious atmosphere of Germantown where the business of government was conducted in a Georgian mansion. The setting was so pleasant that Washington returned the following year; thus the house is considered the first vacation White House. It is part of Independence Park although maintained as a house museum in association with the Deshler-Morris House Committee, Inc.

Carpenters Hall
320 Chestnut Street
(215) 925-0617

This building was lent to the government by the Carpenters Company for use by the First Continental Congress debating " taxation without representation." Today the same Carpenters Company operates the hall as a museum emphasizing early carpentry tools and the original chairs used at the Congress.

Bishop White House
309 Walnut Street
(215) 597-8974

A house built for Pennsylvania's first Protestant Episcopal bishop contains many original artifacts. It is a restoration.

New Hall Military Museum
Chestnut Street between 3rd and 4th
(215) 597-8974

The Army-Navy Museum and the Marine Corps Memorial Museum were recently combined in a single building, a replica of the 18th century home of Joseph Pemberton, successful Quaker merchant. The museum details the contribution made by the Army, Navy and Marine Corps to the emerging nation's security in the period 1775–1800.

Saint Georges Methodist Church
235 N. 4th Street
(215) 925-7788

Saint Georges Methodist Church, the oldest Methodist church in the nation in continuous use, was dedicated in 1769. The adjoining Methodist Historical Center contains many church relics.

Thaddeus Kosciuszko National Memorial
3rd and Pine
(215) 597-9618

Thaddeus Kosciuszko, a trained engineer and life-long champion of freedom, was one of the first foreign volunteers to come to the aid of the American Revolutionary army. He performed heroic duty throughout the war, especially in designing fortifications at Saratoga and West Point. After the war he returned to his native Poland, only to fail in efforts to free that country from foreign domination. He came back to America where he received a hero's welcome. The house he rented during the winter of 1797–1798 has been restored to look much as it did at that time.

Todd House
4th and Walnut
(215) 597-8974

The Todd House was the home of Dolley Payne Todd before her marriage to James Madison, fourth President of the United States.

Powel House
24 S. 3rd Street
(215) 627-0364

The residence of Samuel Powel, Philadelphia's first mayor following the revolution is an elegant Georgian townhouse, circa 1765, with a formal 18th-century garden. All early leaders were visitors. The Powel House is not part of Independence Park. Open to the public.

Elfreths Alley
2nd Street between Arch and Race Streets
(215) 574-0560

Elfreths Alley is the oldest residential street in America, with 30 houses dating from 1728 to 1836. Elfreths Alley was made famous on

August 24, 1777, as the British army moved on Philadelphia. General Washington marched the Continental Army through the Alley in an effort to boost the morale of the patriot population before engaging the enemy. House number 126 houses a Colonial museum with period furniture and changing exhibits. Open to the public.

Pennsylvania Hospital
800 Spruce Street
Philadelphia, Pennsylvania 19107
(215) 829-3000

The Pennsylvania Hospital's first building, a three-story brick known as Pine Building East, was completed in 1755 and has remained in continuous service since. George Washington's diary entry for September 26, 1774, reads *went to hospital,* presumably for inspection or to visit a patient. Pine Building East currently is utilized as an administrative complex and is not open to the public.

Wistar House
240 South 4th Street
Philadelphia, Pennsylvania 19106
(215) 627-6434

The Wistar House is a brick townhouse serving today as office headquarters for the Episcopal Diocese of Pennsylvania. In the Colonial period it was a private home where President Washington, according to his diary, *drank tea at Dr. Shippen's with Mrs. Livingston's party* on June 16, 1787. Not open to the public.

Woodlands
4000 Woodland Avenue
Philadelphia, Pennsylvania 19104
(215) 386-2181

Washington's diary for May 23, 1787, reads *in company with Mr. Madison, Mr. Rutledge and others, I crossed the Schuylkill above the falls — visited Mr. Peters and Mr. Wm. Hamilton.* Hamilton, grandson of the lawyer who successfully defended New York printer Peter Zenger, inherited the landholdings in 1747, proceeding to indulge his passions for architecture, botany and landscape design, the resulting home and gardens described by another visitor, Thomas Jefferson, as *the only rival I have known in America to what may be seen in England.* The mansion is currently (1998) under extensive renovation although its owner, The Woodlands Cemetery Company, hopes to open it to the public in the near future.

Belmont Mansion
Belmont Mansion Drive
Fairmount Park
Philadelphia, Pennsylvania 19104

Belmont, a three-story brick masterpiece, was built in the mid-18th century by William Peters, a staunch Tory forced to flee to England. His son Richard, in contrast, was a prominent patriot who entertained his friend George Washington on many occasions. A perhaps apocryphal story is that Washington once dug a hole in the ground with his walking stick into which he planted a Spanish Chestnut tree whose descendent still lives at the side of the mansion. The mansion, owned by the American Women's Heritage society, is situated in Fairmount Park, one of America's great urban open spaces. Renovations are continuous with plans (1998) to open the house for public visitation in the near future.

Solitude
The Philadelphia Zoo
3400 Girard Avenue
Philadelphia, Pennsylvania 19104
(215) 243-1100

John Penn, a grandson of Pennsylvania's founder, built Solitude, a 2½-story stucco house surrounded by acres of landscaped lawns and exquisite gardens reflecting his desire for a retreat of quiet contemplation. Somewhat of a recluse, he left for England only a few years later. The property remained in the family for many years before its acquisition by the City of Philadelphia which leases it to the Philadelphia Zoo for use as office space. The first floor parlor and library appear as original but Solitude is not open to the public though visible from the zoo grounds.

COLONIAL WILLIAMSBURG, VIRGINIA

Williamsburg was the capital of Virginia from 1699 to 1799 — the center of southern leadership in the period preceding the American Revolution. George Washington, Thomas Jefferson, Patrick Henry and others met in Williamsburg to frame our principles of liberty. Historic Williamsburg today is a 173-acre community of four hundred reconstructed or restored buildings of the Colonial era — one of America's great tourist attractions — a repository of history, tradition and the values that have made our country the envy of nations around the world.

Colonial Williamsburg Foundation
Box 1776
Williamsburg, Virginia 23187
(800) HISTORY
(All attractions are open to the public)

Richmond became the capital of Virginia during the Revolutionary War and Williamsburg began a slow decline, resurrected in 1926 when Reverend W. A. R. Goodwin of Bruton Church persuaded John D. Rockefeller to purchase the town, thus beginning the most ambitious historical restoration effort in the nation's experience. The reconstructed Colonial town is lovingly maintained and operated by the Colonial Williamsburg Foundation.

George Wythe House
Palace Green, south of Prince George Street

George Wythe was the period's most prominent and distinguished lawyer and teacher whose students included Thomas Jefferson, James Monroe, Henry Clay and John Marshall. His house was built in the mid-18th century, and was used briefly as George Washington's headquarters prior to the Siege of Yorktown.

James Geddy House
Duke of Gloucester Street

The Geddy House, circa 1750, housed a silversmith shop and foundry. George Washington was known to have been a patron.

Christiana Campbells Tavern
Waller Street

The favorite dining place for George Washington and others.

Bruton Parish Church
Duke of Gloucester Street

Bruton, the earliest Anglican church still active, was erected in 1711 when Martha Washington's great-great grandfather was its first rector. The tower bell, circa 1761, still calls worshipers to services. It is more than likely that George Washington, Thomas Jefferson, James Monroe and others who served in the capital of Williamsburg worshipped at Bruton.

The Capitol
Duke of Gloucester Street

The 1705 capitol building has been replicated on its original foundation and furnished in period. Rare portraits of George Washington, Thomas Jefferson and James Madison are on display.

Raleigh Tavern (circa 1742)
Duke of Gloucester Street

George Washington, Thomas Jefferson and Patrick Henry are but a few of the patriots who frequented the Raleigh, one of the centers of political and social life. The Raleigh was reconstructed in 1859 after a fire.

Wetherburns Tavern
Duke of Gloucester Street

Wetherburns figured prominently in the commercial life of Williamsburg and has been in continuous use for more than two centuries. George Washington was a patron.

Governors Palace
The Palace Green

The Palace was completed in 1720 under the supervision of Governor Alexander Spotswood. He and his royal successors lived here until 1775 when the last resident fled in the face of armed resistance in the Virginia Colony. It later served as the executive mansion for the Commonwealth's first two governors, Thomas Jefferson and Patrick Henry.

Carters Grove Plantation
8 Miles south of Williamsburg on SR 60E
(757) 229-1000

The mansion at Carters Grove, circa 1754, was the showpiece of a 300,000-acre estate, and a gathering place for students of the College of William and Mary, and many activists for freedom. Legend has it that it was at Carters Grove that George Washington proposed marriage to Mary Cary and Thomas Jefferson to Rebecca Burwell. Both were rejected! Carters Grove is furnished in Colonial Revival style with exhibits describing Virginia's plantation history. Open to the public.

College of William and Mary
Duke of Gloucester Street
Williamsburg, Virginia
(757) 221-4000

The College of William and Mary, founded in 1693, is the second-oldest college in America. Three presidents — Thomas Jefferson, James Monroe and John Tyler — attended William and Mary, whose campus abuts Colonial Williamsburg. Open to the public.

Colleges Attended by the Presidents

George Washington: None

John Adams: Harvard University, Cambridge, Massachusetts

Thomas Jefferson: College of William and Mary, Williamsburg, Virginia

James Madison: College of New Jersey (now Princeton), Princeton, New Jersey

James Monroe: College of William and Mary, Williamsburg, Virginia

John Quincy Adams: Harvard University, Cambridge, Massachusetts

Andrew Jackson: None

Martin Van Buren: None

William Henry Harrison: Hampden-Sydney College, Hampden-Sydney, Virginia

John Tyler: College of William and Mary, Williamsburg, Virginia

James K. Polk: University of North Carolina, Chapel Hill, North Carolina

Zachary Taylor: None

Millard Fillmore: None

Franklin Pierce: Bowdoin College, Brunswick, Maine

James Buchanan: Dickinson College, Carlisle, Pennsylvania

Abraham Lincoln: None

Andrew Johnson: None

Ulysses S. Grant: United States Military Academy, West Point, New York

Rutherford B. Hayes: Kenyon College, Gambier, Ohio; Harvard University, Cambridge, Massachusetts

James A. Garfield: Williams College, Williamstown, Massachusetts

Chester A. Arthur: Union College, Schenectady, New York

Grover Cleveland: None

Benjamin Harrison: Miami of Ohio College, Oxford, Ohio

William McKinley: Allegheny College, Meadville, Pennsylvania

Theodore Roosevelt: Harvard University, Cambridge, Massachusetts; Columbia University, New York, New York

William Howard Taft: Yale University, New Haven, Connecticut; Cincinnati Law School, Cincinnati, Ohio

Woodrow Wilson: Davidson College, Davidson, North Carolina; Princeton University, Princeton, New Jersey; University of Virginia, Charlottesville, Virginia; Johns Hopkins University (Ph.D.), Baltimore, Maryland

Warren G. Harding: Ohio Central College, Iberia, Ohio

Calvin Coolidge: Amherst College, Amherst, Massachusetts

Herbert Hoover: Stanford University, Palo Alto, California

Franklin D. Roosevelt: Harvard University, Cambridge, Massachusetts; Columbia University, New York, New York

Harry S Truman: None

Dwight D. Eisenhower: United States Military Academy, West Point, New York

John F. Kennedy: Harvard University, Cambridge, Massachusetts

Lyndon B. Johnson: South West Texas Teachers College, San Marcos, Texas

Richard M. Nixon: Whittier College, Whittier, California; Duke University, Durham, North Carolina

Gerald R. Ford: University of Michigan, Ann Arbor, Michigan; Yale University, New Haven, Connecticut

Jimmy Carter: United States Naval Academy, Annapolis, Maryland; Georgia Southwestern College, Americus, Georgia; Georgia Institute of Technology, Atlanta, Georgia

Ronald Reagan: Eureka College, Eureka, Illinois

George Bush: Yale University, New Haven, Connecticut

William J. Clinton: Georgetown University, Washington, DC; Yale University, New Haven, Connecticut

Presidential Sites, by State and Country

ALABAMA

Battle of Talledega and Fort Lashley	Jackson
Fort Strother Site	Jackson
Fort Toulouse/ Jackson Park National Historic Landmark	Jackson
Horseshoe Bend National Military Park	Jackson
Popes Tavern	Jackson
Wilson Dam	Wilson

ALASKA

Harding Railroad Car	Harding
Mount McKinley	McKinley

ARIZONA

Bucky O'Neill Monument	T. Roosevelt
Theodore Roosevelt Dam and Lake	T. Roosevelt

ARKANSAS

Arkansas Governors Mansion	Clinton
Arkansas State Capitol	Clinton
Clinton Residences	Clinton
Fort Smith National Historic Site	Taylor

Hope "Clinton Loop"	Clinton
Hot Springs "Clinton Loop"	Clinton
Immanuel Baptist Church	Clinton
Park Place Baptist Church	Clinton

CALIFORNIA

Baptist Church of Yorba Linda	Nixon
Bel Air Presbyterian Church	Reagan
Benicia Arsenal Capitol Historic Park and Barracks	Grant
California Governors Mansion	Reagan
California State Capitol	Reagan
Encina Hall	Hoover
First Baptist Church	Nixon
Ford Residences	Ford
Forest Lawn-Memorial Parks	Washington, Jefferson, Lincoln, Reagan
Fort Humboldt State Historic Park	Grant
General Grant and Redwood Mountain Groves	Grant
Great Moments with Mr. Lincoln	Lincoln
Henry Home	Hoover
Heritage of San Clemente	Nixon
Herbert Hoover Residence	Hoover
Hoover Institutions on War, Revolution and Peace	Hoover
Hoover Residence	Hoover
Jacqueline Cochran Estate	Eisenhower
La Casa Pacifica	Nixon
Lincoln Memorial Shrine	Lincoln
Little Brown Church in the Valley	Reagan
Lou Henry Hoover House	Hoover
Mission Inn	Nixon
Nixon Residences	Nixon
Nixon Rooms	Nixon
Potomac	F. Roosevelt
Rancho del Cielo	Reagan
Reagan Residences	Reagan
Reagan Sacramento Rental	Reagan
Richard M. Nixon Library and Birthplace	Nixon
Ronald Reagan Presidential Library	Reagan
Santa Ynez Valley Presbyterian Church	Reagan

Stanford University	Hoover
Wee Kirk o' the Heather	Reagan
Whittier College	Nixon
Yearling Row Ranch	Reagan

COLORADO

Doud Home	Eisenhower
Ford Residences	Ford
Tabor House	Grant
Teller House Casino	Grant

CONNECTICUT

Elton Island	Taft
Farnum College	Taft
General Jedidiah Huntington House	Washington
Henry C. Bowen House	Grant, Hayes, Arthur, Garfield, Cleveland, B. Harrison, McKinley
George Bush Boyhood Home	Bush
Governor Jonathan Trumbull House/ Wadsworth Stable/The War Office	Washington
Great Oak, The	Washington
John MacCurdy House	Washington
Leffingwell Inn	Washington
Museum of American Political Life	
Old South College	Taft
Oliver Ellsworth Homestead	Washington, J. Adams
Oliver Wolcott House	Washington
Shaw Mansion	Washington
Sun Inn	Washington
Stafford Springs	J. Adams
Taft Residences	Taft
Webb-Deane-Stevens Museum	Washington, J. Adams
Yale University	Taft, Ford, Bush, Clinton

DELAWARE
Amstel House	Washington
Brandywine Springs Park	Washington
Hale-Byrnes House	Washington
Lincoln Collection	Lincoln
Robinson House	Washington

DISTRICT OF COLUMBIA
Abraham Lincoln Statue	Lincoln
All Souls Church	J. Q. Adams, Fillmore, Taft
Anderson House	Buchanan, Lincoln, Hayes, Arthur
Anderson House Museum	Washington
Andrew Jackson Statue	Jackson
Blair House	
Blue Room,The	Cleveland
Calvary Baptist Church	Harding
Central Presbyterian Church	Wilson
Cookes Row	Grant
Church of the Epiphany	Buchanan
Daughters of the American Revolution Library	
Decatur House	Van Buren
Eisenhower Residences	Eisenhower
Emancipation Monument	Lincoln
First Baptist Church	Truman, Carter
First Congregational Church	Coolidge
Ford Residences	Ford
Fords Theatre National Historic Site	Lincoln
Forrest-Marbury House	Washington
Fort Stevens	Lincoln
Foundry United Methodist Church	Hayes
Franklin D. Roosevelt Memorial	F. Roosevelt
Friends Meeting House	Hoover
Galt House	Wilson
Georgetown University	Clinton
George Washington Statue	Washington
Grace Reformed Church	T. Roosevelt
Harding Residence	Harding
Holy Trinity Roman Catholic Church	Kennedy

308

Tudor Place	
Union Square Statuary	Grant
United States Capitol	
USS *Williamsburg*	
US Soldiers and Airmens Home	Buchanan
Wardman Park Hotel	Eisenhower
Washington Monument	Washington
Washington National Cathedral	
White House, The	
Wilson Institution	Wilson
Woodley	Van Buren, Tyler, Grant, T. Roosevelt
Woodrow Wilson House Museum	Wilson
Woodrow Wilson International Center for Scholars	Wilson
Wyoming Apartments	Eisenhower

FLORIDA

Casa Marmac Hotel	Truman
Cape Canaveral	Kennedy
Fort San Carlos de Barrancas	Jackson
Fort Zachary Taylor	Taylor
Gold Coast Railroad and Museum	F. Roosevelt, Truman, Eisenhower, Reagan
Hall of Presidents	
John F. Kennedy Space Center	Kennedy
Kennedy Residence	Kennedy
Little White House Museum	Truman
Nixon Compound	Nixon
Okeechobee Battlefield	Taylor
Plaza Ferdinand VII	Jackson
Saint Anns Catholic Church	Kennedy
Saint Edwards Catholic Church	Kennedy
San Marcos de Apalachee State Museum	Jackson
Surgeons House	Eisenhower
Tampa Bay Hotel	T. Roosevelt

GEORGIA

Boyhood Home of President Woodrow Wilson	Wilson
Carter Center	Carter
Carter Boyhood Home	Carter
Carter Residence	Carter
Chapel of the Warm Springs Institute	F. Roosevelt
Chickamauga and Chattanooga National Military Park	Grant, Garfield
First Presbyterian Church of Augusta	Wilson
FDRs Little White House	F. Roosevelt
Georgia Governors Mansion	Carter
Georgia Institute of Technology	Carter
Georgia Southwestern College	Carter
Georgia State Capitol	Carter
Haunted House	Carter
James E. Carter, Jr. Library	Carter
Jimmy Carter National Historic Site	Carter
Kennesaw Mountain National Battlefield	B. Harrison
Lachlan McIntosh House	Washington
Maranatha Baptist Church	Carter
Mamies Cabin	Eisenhower
Museum of the Jimmy Carter Library	Carter
Old Depot	Carter
Plains Baptist Church	Carter
Plains High School	Carter
Plains United Methodist Church	Carter
Presbyterian Manse	Wilson
Public Housing Unit 9A	Carter
Southeastern Railway Museum	Harding
Wise Hospital	Carter
Woodrow Wilson College of Law	Wilson

ILLINOIS

Abraham Lincoln Statues	Lincoln
Archer House Hotel	Lincoln, Cleveland
Bryant Cottage State Historic Site	Lincoln
Chicago Historical Society Museum	Lincoln
Church of Christ	Reagan
Decatur	Lincoln
Edwards Place	Lincoln
Eureka College	Reagan

First Christian Church	Reagan
First Presbyterian Church of Springfield	Lincoln
Grant Home State Historic Site	Grant
Grants House	Grant
Illinois Governors Mansion	Lincoln
Illinois State Historical Society Library	Lincoln
J. R. Grant Leather Store	Grant
Lincoln College Museum	Lincoln
Lincoln Depot Museum	Lincoln
Lincoln-Douglas Debates	Lincoln
Lincoln Family Pew	Lincoln
Lincoln-Herndon Law Offices	Lincoln
Lincoln Home National Historic Site	Lincoln
Lincoln Ledger	Lincoln
Lincoln Log Cabin State Historic Site	Lincoln
Lincoln Monument State Memorial	Lincoln
Lincolns New Salem	Lincoln
Lincolns Tomb National Historic Site	Lincoln
Lincoln Trail State Memorial	Lincoln
Little Brick House, The	Lincoln
Macon County Historical Society Museum	Lincoln
Magnolia Mansion	Grant
Meldrick Library	Reagan
Metamora Courthouse State Historic Site	Lincoln
Moore Home State Historic Site	Lincoln
Mount Pulaski Courthouse State Historic Site	Lincoln
Ninian W. Edwards House	Lincoln
Oak Hill Cemetery	Lincoln
Old State Capitol	Lincoln
Postville Courthouse State Historic Site	Lincoln
Reagan Residences	Reagan
Ronald Reagan Birthplace	Reagan
Ronald Reagan Boyhood Home	Reagan
Tau Kappa Epsilon House	Reagan
Vermilion County Museum	Lincoln

INDIANA

Abraham Lincoln Statue	Lincoln
Corydon Historic District	W. Harrison
Crown Hill Cemetery	B. Harrison
Fort Knox II	W. Harrison

Grouseland	W. Harrison
Hazelden	Taft, Harding, Coolidge
Indiana Territory Capitol State Historic Site	W. Harrison
Jeffersonville	W. Harrison
Lincoln Boyhood National Memorial	Lincoln
Lincoln Museum	Lincoln
President Benjamin Harrison Home	B. Harrison
Studebaker National Museum	Lincoln, Grant, McKinley
Tippecanoe Battlefield	W. Harrison
Vincennes University	W. Harrison

IOWA
Harlan House	Lincoln
Herbert Hoover National Historic Site	Hoover
Herbert Hoover Presidential Library and Museum	Hoover
Mamie Doud Eisenhowers Birthplace	Eisenhower
Quaker Meeting House	Hoover
Reagan Residences	Reagan
Ryan House	Grant

KANSAS
Abraham Lincoln Statue	Lincoln
Dwight D. Eisenhower Boyhood Home #1	Eisenhower
Dwight D. Eisenhower Boyhood Home #2	Eisenhower
Eisenhower Center	Eisenhower
Eisenhower Library	Eisenhower
Eisenhower Museum	Eisenhower
Midland Railway	T. Roosevelt, Taft
Place of Meditation	Eisenhower

KENTUCKY
Abraham Lincoln Statue	Lincoln
Columbus-Belmont Civil War State Park	Grant
Corner of Celebrities	
Farmington	Lincoln
Garfield Place	Garfield
Genealogical Research Library	
Gower House	Taylor, Polk

Jefferson County Courthouse	Jefferson
Knob Creek Farm	Lincoln
Liberty Hall	Monroe, Jackson, Tyler
Lincoln Birthplace National Historic Site	Lincoln
Lincoln Heritage House	Lincoln
Lincoln Museum	Lincoln
Locust Grove	Monroe, Jackson, Taylor
Mary Todd Lincolns Home	Lincoln
Old Fort Harrod State Park	Lincoln
Old Governors Mansion	
Old Talbott Tavern	Jackson, W. Harrison, Lincoln
SAR Genealogical Research Library	
Springfield	Taylor
Thomas Jefferson Statue	Jefferson
Zachary Taylor National Cemetery	Taylor

LOUISIANA

Andrew Jackson Statue	Jackson
Chalmette National Historic Park	Jackson
Cottage, The	Jackson
Fort Jesup State Monument	Taylor
Fort Selden	Taylor
Jackson House	Jackson
Jackson Square National Historic Landmark	Jackson
Old Absinthe House Restaurant	Jackson
Pentagon Barracks	Taylor

MAINE

Blaine House	Grant
Bowdoin College	Pierce
Bush Summer Home	Bush
Jed Prouty Tavern	Van Buren, Tyler, W. Harrison
Pownalborough Courthouse	J. Adams
Roosevelt Campobello International Park	F. Roosevelt
Saint Annes Episcopal Church	Bush

Walkers Point	Bush

MARYLAND

Annapolis City Hall	Washington
Baltimore Washington Monument	Washington
Antietam National Battlefield	McKinley
Brice House, The	Washington, J. Adams, Madison
Caleb Bentley House	Madison
Camp David	
Chesapeake and Ohio Canal National Historical Park	J. Q. Adams
Christ Church, Durham Parish	Washington
Cleveland Honeymoon Cottage	Cleveland
Deer Park	Grant, Cleveland, B. Harrison
Frederick Presbyterian Church	Lincoln
Hampton National Historic Site	Washington
Johns Hopkins University	Wilson
La Grange	Washington
Maryland State House	Washington
Michael Cresap Museum	Washington
Middletons Tavern	Washington
Montpelier Mansion	Washington
Mount Airy	Washington
Rectory of Saint Annes Parish	Washington
Rising Sun Inn	Washington
Rodgers Tavern	Washington, Jefferson, Madison
Smallwoods Retreat	Washington
Saint Johns College	Washington
South Mountain	Hayes
United States Naval Academy	Carter
Washington College	Washington
Washingtons Headquarters	Washington
Washington Monument State Park	Washington

MASSACHUSETTS

Abigail Adams Cairn	J. Q. Adams

Abigail Adams House	J. Adams
Adams National Historic Site	J. Adams, J. Q. Adams
Amherst College	Coolidge
Beeches, The	Coolidge
Brookline Neighborhood	Kennedy
Brookline Unitarian Church	T. Roosevelt
Calvin Coolidge Memorial Room	Coolidge
Christ Church	Washington
Christopher Gores Country Home	J. Adams, Monroe
Coolidge Residence	Coolidge
Dexter School	Kennedy
Edward Congregational Church	Coolidge
Edward Devotion School	Kennedy
George Bush Birthplace	Bush
George Washington Statue	Washington
Harvard University	J. Adams, J. Q. Adams, Hayes, T. Roosevelt, F. Roosevelt, Kennedy
Heritage Plantation	Taft
JFK Memorial	Kennedy
John F. Kennedy Hyannis Museum	Kennedy
John F. Kennedy National Historic Site	Kennedy
John F. Kennedy Library and Museum	Kennedy
Kennedy Apartment	Kennedy
Kennedy Compound	Kennedy
Kennedy Residence	Kennedy
Kings Chapel	Washington
Lee House National Historic Landmark	Washington
Longfellow National Historic Site	Washington
Masonic Building	Coolidge
Massachusetts State House	Coolidge
Morton Downey Home	Kennedy
Munroe Tavern	Washington
Old State House	Washington
Parramatta Estate	Taft
Quincy Historical Society Museum	J. Adams
Saint Aidans Catholic Church	Kennedy

316

Saint Francis Xavier Church	Kennedy
Soldiers Monument	Washington
Springfield Armory National Historic Site	Wilson,
	F. Roosevelt,
	Eisenhower,
	Kennedy
Stetson Cottage	Taft
United First Parish Church	J. Adams,
	J. Q. Adams
Wadsworth House	Washington
Warren Tavern	Washington
White Court Estate	Coolidge
Williams College	Garfield

MICHIGAN

Gerald R. Ford Residences	Ford
Gerald R. Ford Presidential Library	Ford
Gerald R. Ford Museum	Ford
Grace Episcopal Church	Ford
Henry Ford Museum and Greenfield Village	Washington,
	Lincoln,
	T. Roosevelt,
	F. Roosevelt,
	Eisenhower,
	Kennedy,
	Reagan
U. S. Grant House	Grant
University of Michigan	Ford

MINNESOTA

Historic Fort Snelling	Taylor

MISSISSIPPI

Battle of Big Black River Bridge	Grant
Battle of Champion Hill	Grant
Civil War Earthworks at Tallahatchie Crossing	Grant
Dixie White House	Wilson
Governors Mansion	Grant
Grand Gulf Military Monument Park	Grant
Old Capitol	Grant
Old Court House Museum	Grant

Old Natchez Trace Parkway	Jackson
Port Gibson	Grant
Raymond Battlefield	Grant
Rosalie	Grant
Springfield Plantation	Jackson
Vicksburg National Military Park and Cemetery	Grant
Walter Place	Grant

MISSOURI

Audrain County Historical Society and American Saddle Horse Museum	Grant
Belton Museum	Truman
Campbell House Museum	Grant
C. K. Frank Farm	Truman
Clinton Pharmacy	Truman
Dent Townhouse	Grant
First Baptist Church of Grandview	Truman
Grants Farm	Grant
Harry S Truman Birthplace State Historic Site	Truman
Harry S. Truman Library and Museum	Truman
Harry S. Truman National Historic Site	Truman
Harry S. Truman State Park	Truman
Jackson County Courthouse	Truman
Jefferson Barracks Historic Park	Taylor, Grant
Jefferson National Expansion Memorial	Jefferson
Lincoln University	Lincoln
Missouri Pacific Depot	Truman
Presidential Suite	Truman
Ross House	Grant
Trinity Episcopal Church	Truman
Truman Farm Home	Truman
Truman Home	Truman
Truman Residences	Truman
Ulysses S. Grant National Historic Site	Grant

MONTANA

Roosevelt Arch	T. Roosevelt
Theodore Roosevelt Memorial Obelisk	T. Roosevelt

NEBRASKA

Abraham Lincoln Statue	Lincoln

Arbor Lodge State Historical Park	Cleveland
General Crook House Museum	Grant, Hayes
President Fords Birthplace Garden	Ford
Union Pacific Historical Museum	Lincoln

NEVADA

Hoover Dam	Hoover

NEW HAMPSHIRE

Acorn Lodge	Cleveland
Cleveland House	Cleveland
Eagle Hotel	Pierce, B. Harrison
Franklin Pierce Statue	Pierce
Governor John Langdon House	Washington
Lafayette House	Monroe
McNeil Residence	Pierce
Means Mansion	Pierce
Merrimack County Courthouse	Pierce
Old North Cemetery	Pierce
Phenix Hall	Lincoln, Pierce
Pierce Homestead	Pierce
Pierce Manse	Pierce
Saint Pauls Episcopal Church	Pierce
Saint Thomas Episcopal Church	Monroe
South Congregational Church	Pierce

NEW JERSEY

Boxwood Hall State Historic Site	Washington
Buccleuch Mansion and Park	Washington
Buchanan Vacation Home	Buchanan
Church of the Presidents	Grant, Garfield, Arthur, B. Harrison, McKinley, Hayes, Wilson
Cleveland Memorial Tower	Cleveland
Congress Hall Hotel	B. Harrison
Dey Mansion/ Washingtons Headquarters Museum	Washington
Drake House Museum	Washington

Ferry House State Historic Site	Washington
Fort Lee Historic Site	Washington
General Grant House	Grant
Grover Cleveland Birthplace State Historic Site	Cleveland
Hermitage, The	Monroe
Holcombe-Jimison Farmstead Museum	Washington
James A. Garfield Statue	Garfield
Joseph Stout House	Washington
Lambert Castle	McKinley
Military Park	Kennedy
Monmouth Battlefield State Park	Washington, Monroe
Morristown National Historic Park	Washington
Nassau Hall	Washington, Madison
New Jersey State House	Wilson
Nixon Residences	Nixon
Old Barracks Museum	Washington
Old Dutch Parsonage State Historic Site	Washington
Princeton Battlefield State Park	Washington
Princeton Cemetery	Cleveland
Princeton Inn	Wilson
Princeton University	Madison, Wilson
Prospect	Wilson
Richard Holcombe House	Washington
Ringwood State Park	Washington
Rockingham State Historic Site	Washington
Steuben House	Washington
Van Allen House	Washington
Village Inn, The	Washington
Wallace House State Historic Site	Washington
Washington Crossing State Park	Washington
Washington Rock State Park	Washington
Westland	Cleveland
Wilson Residences	Wilson
Witherspoon Hall	Wilson
Woodrow Wilson Hall	Wilson

NEW MEXICO

Rough Riders Memorial and City Museum	T. Roosevelt

NEW YORK

Abigail Adams Smith Museum	J. Adams
Antique Boat Museum	Grant, Garfield
Arcade and Attica Railroad	Cleveland
Arthur Residence	Arthur
Baptist Church of Perry, The	Arthur
Beekman Arms Hotel	Washington
	Van Buren,
	F. Roosevelt
Berkeley Lodge	B. Harrison
Calvary Church	Arthur
Chester A. Arthur Residences	Arthur
Christ Episcopal Church	T. Roosevelt
Church of the Ascension	Tyler
City Hall Park	Washington
Columbia University	T. Roosevelt,
	F. Roosevelt,
	Eisenhower
Conference House	J. Adams
Cooper Union	Lincoln
David Conklin Farmhouse	Washington
Denning House	Washington
Derick Brinckerhoff House	Washington
DeWint House	Washington
Eleanor Roosevelt National Historic Site	F. Roosevelt
Federal Hall National Historic Site	Washington
Fillmore Home	Fillmore
Fillmore House Museum	Fillmore
First Baptist Church of Troy	Arthur
First Presbyterian Church of Buffalo	Cleveland
First Presbyterian Church of Holland Patent	Cleveland
First Presbyterian Church of Rye	Bush
Forest Lawn Cemetery	Fillmore
Fort Ticonderoga	Washington
Fowler House	Washington
Franklin D. Roosevelt Library and Museum	F. Roosevelt
Franklin D. Roosevelt National Historic Site	F. Roosevelt
Fraunces Tavern	Washington
George Washington Masonic Shrine	Washington
George Washington Statues	Washington
General Philip Schuyler House	Washington

Grant Cottage State Historic Site	Grant
Grants Tomb	Grant
Griffins Tavern	Washington
Grover Cleveland Boyhood Homes	Cleveland
Hall of Fame for Great Americans	
Hendrick Kip House	Washington
Herbert Hoover Building	Hoover
Hoover Apartment	Hoover
John Brinckerhoff House	Washington
John F. Kennedy International Airport	Kennedy
John Kane House	Washington
Judge Powers House	Fillmore
Judge Woods House	Fillmore
Kinderhook Cemetery	Van Buren
Knoxs Headquarters State Historic Site	Washington
Kortright House	Monroe
Lincoln Center for the Performing Arts	Lincoln
Madam Brett Homestead	Washington
Madison Barracks	Grant
Mandeville House	Washington
Martin Van Buren Birthplace	Van Buren
Martin Van Buren National Historic Site	Van Buren
Millard Fillmore Birthplace	Fillmore
Millard Fillmore Log Cabin	Fillmore
Millard Fillmore Statue	Fillmore
Morris-Jumel Mansion	Washington
Moses and Christine Cantine House	Van Buren
Mount Gulian Historic Site	Washington
New Windsor Cantonment State Historic Site	Washington
New York Executive Mansion	Cleveland, T. Roosevelt, F. Roosevelt
New York State Capitol	Cleveland, T. Roosevelt, F. Roosevelt
Nixon Residences	Nixon
North Creek Railroad Station	T. Roosevelt
Old Fort House Museum	Washington
Parish-Ludlow Houses	F. Roosevelt
Presidents House	Eisenhower
Prospect Park	Kennedy
Purdy House, The	Washington

Roosevelt Residences	T. Roosevelt, F. Roosevelt
Rose Garden, The	F. Roosevelt
Rural Cemetery	Arthur
Sagamore Hill National Historic Site	T. Roosevelt
Saint Bartholomews Church	Hoover
Saint James Episcopal Church	F. Roosevelt
Saint Josephs Roman Catholic Church	Kennedy
Saint Pauls Chapel	Washington
Saint Thomas Episcopal Church	B. Harrison
Saratoga National Historical Park	Washington
Schuyler Mansion	Fillmore
Square House, The	Washington, J. Adams, Van Buren
Stony Point Battlefield State Historic Site	Washington
Storm-Adriance-Brinckerhoff House	Washington
Theodore Roosevelt Bird Sanctuary and Trailside Museum	T. Roosevelt
Theodore Roosevelt Birthplace National Historic Site	T. Roosevelt
Theodore Roosevelt Inaugural National Historic Site	T. Roosevelt
Theodore Roosevelt Memorial Building	T. Roosevelt
Top Cottage	F. Roosevelt
Tyler Mansion	Tyler
Union College	Arthur
Union Square Statue	Washington
Unitarian Universal Church	Fillmore
United States Military Academy	Grant, Eisenhower
U. S. Grant House	Grant
Van Cortlandt House Museum	Washington
Van Wyck Homestead Museum	Washington
Washington Arch	Washington
Washingtons Headquarters Museum	Washington
Washingtons Headquarters State Historic Site	Washington
Wave Hill House	T. Roosevelt
West Point	Washington
White Pine Camp	Coolidge
White Plains National Battlefield Site	Washington
William H. Seward House	J. Q. Adams, Grant, Van Buren

Youngs House	T. Roosevelt
Youngs Memorial Cemetery	T. Roosevelt

NORTH CAROLINA

Andrew Jacksons Birthplace	Jackson
Andrew Johnson Birthplace	A. Johnson
Davidson College	Wilson
Duke University	Nixon
Francis McNairy House	Jackson
Guilford Courthouse National Military Park	Washington
James K. Polk Memorial	Polk
John Wright Stanly House	Washington
Presidential Memorial	Jackson, Polk, A. Johnson
Rowan House Hotel	Jackson
Salem Tavern	Washington
South Building	Polk
Tryon Palace Restorations and Gardens	Washington
University of North Carolina	Polk

NORTH DAKOTA

Fort Abraham Lincoln State Park	Lincoln
Maltese Cross Cabin	T. Roosevelt
Theodore Roosevelt National Park	T. Roosevelt

OHIO

Abraham Lincoln Statue	Lincoln
Benjamin Harrison Birthplace	B. Harrison
Blooming Grove Baptist Church	Harding
Buffington Island State Park Monument	McKinley
Camp Jackson	Hayes
Church of the Savior	McKinley
Cincinnati Law School	Taft
Columbine II	Eisenhower
Dr. John W. Scott House	Garfield
First Brethren Church	Hayes
First Presbyterian Church of Canton	McKinley
First Unitarian Church of Cincinnati	Taft
Fort Amanda State Memorial	W. Harrison
Fort Meigs State Memorial	W. Harrison
Garfield House	Garfield

Grant Memorial Building	Grant
Grants Birthplace	Grant
Grants Boyhood Home	Grant
Harding Birthplace	Harding
Harding Memorial	Harding
Harrison Headquarters	W. Harrison
Harrison Tomb State Memorial	W. Harrison
Hayes Presidential Center	Hayes
Herron Home	Taft
Independence	Truman
James A. Garfield Birthplace	Garfield
James A. Garfield Monument	Garfield
John Cleve Symmes House	W. Harrison
Kenyon Building	Hayes
Lawnfield	Garfield
Lincoln Statue	Lincoln
McKinley Memorial Library	McKinley
McKinley National Memorial and Museum	McKinley
Miami of Ohio College	B. Harrison
Montgomery County Historical Society Courthouse Museum	Lincoln
Mrs. Maria Webb Residence	Hayes
Ohio Central College	Harding
Ohio State Capitol	Hayes, McKinley
President Hardings Home	Harding
Quarry, The	Taft
Rudulph Home	Garfield
Rutherford B. Hayes Birthplace	Hayes
Second Harding Home	Harding
Saxton-Barber House	McKinley
Spiegel Grove	Hayes
Taft Museum	Taft
Third Harding Home	Harding
Treber Inn	Jackson
Trinity Baptist Church of Marion	Harding
Warren G. Harding Birthplace	Harding
Warren G. Harding Homes	Harding
William Henry Harrison Statue	W. Harrison
William Howard Taft National Historic Site	Taft
William McKinley Birthplace	McKinley
William McKinley Statue	McKinley

325

Ulysses S. Grant Birthplace	Grant
Ulysses S. Grant Boyhood Home	Grant
OKLAHOMA	
Fort Gibson Military Park	Taylor
Fort Washita	Taylor
Osage Agency House	Hoover
OREGON	
George Fox College	Hoover
Hoover-Minthorn House	Hoover
Minthorn House	Hoover
PENNSYLVANIA	
Alleghany College	McKinley
Bartrams Garden	Washington
Bedford Springs Hotel	Buchanan,
	W. Harrison,
	Polk, Taylor,
	Garfield,
	Eisenhower
Belmont Mansion	Washington
Betsy Ross House	Washington
Bishop White House	Washington
Blue Bell Inn	Washington
Brandywine Battlefield Park	Washington
Buchanan Historic Site	Buchanan
Carpenters Hall	
Castleberry House	Washington
Christ Church	Washington
City Tavern	
Civil War Library and Museum	Lincoln
Cliveden	Washington
Congress Hall	
Dawesfield	Washington
Deshler-Morris House	Washington
Dickinson College	Buchanan
East Broadtop Railroad	Cleveland
Elfreths Alley	Washington
Eisenhower Residences	Eisenhower
Eisenhower National Historic Site	Eisenhower

Emlen House	Washington
Espy House	Washington
Fatlands	Washington
Fell House	Washington
First Bank of the United States	
First Presbyterian Church of Lancaster	Buchanan
Fort Bedford Museum	Washington
Fort Ligonier	Washington
Fort Necessity National Battlefield	Washington
Fort Prince George	Washington
Fort Washington State Park	Washington
Franklin Court	
General Wayne Inn	Washington
Gettysburg National Cemetery	Lincoln
Gettysburg Presbyterian Church	Eisenhower
Gettysburg Railroad Steam Train	Lincoln
Hall of Presidents and First Ladies	
Historic Antes House	Washington
Historic Old Saint Augustines Catholic Church	Washington
Historic Summerseat	Washington
Historic Yellow Springs	Washington
Hope Lodge	Washington
Independence Hall	
Independence National Historical Park	
Jacob Graff, Jr. House	Jefferson
Liberty Bell Pavilion	
Lincoln Gettysburg Address Exhibit	Lincoln
Lincoln Room Museum	Lincoln
Lincoln Train Museum	Lincoln
Malin Hall	Washington
Moland House	Washington
New Hall Military Museum	
Old Baptist Parsonage	Wilson
Old City Hall	
Old Pine Street Presbyterian Church	J. Adams
Old Saint Georges Church	
Old Saint Josephs Church	
Pennsylvania Hospital	Washington
Pennypacker Mills and Mansion	Washington
Peter Wentz Farmstead	Washington
Philadelphia	
Point State Park	Washington

Powel House	Washington
Pottsgrove Mansion	Washington
Red Lion Inn	Washington
Redding Furnace Farm	Washington
Saint Georges Methodist Church	
Saint Peters Church	
Second Bank of the United States	
Solitude	Washington
Stenton	Washington
Stride-Madison Residence	Madison
Sun Inn	Washington
Thaddeus Kosciuszko National Memorial	
Thomas Bond House	Washington
Todd House	Madison
Valley Forge National Historical Park	Washington, Monroe
Washington Crossing Historic Park	Washington
Wheatland	Buchanan
Wistar House	Washington
Woodlands	Washington, Jefferson
Woodward Hill Cemetery	Buchanan

RHODE ISLAND

Fort Adams	Eisenhower
General James Mitchell Varnum Museum	Washington
Governor Stephen Hopkins House	Washington
Hammersmith Farm	Kennedy
John Brown House	Washington
Kingston Free Library	Washington
Mohegan Bluffs and Southeast Lighthouse	Grant
Old Colony House	Washington
Old Mansion, The	Hayes
Saint Marys Church	Kennedy
Touro Synagogue National Historic Site	Washington
Trinity Church	Washington
Vernon House	Washington
Woonsocket City Hall	Lincoln

SOUTH CAROLINA

Andrew Jacksons Birthplace	Jackson

Andrew Jackson State Park	Jackson
Benjamin Allston House	Washington
Edward McCradys Tavern	Washington
Fort Jackson Museum	Jackson
Fort Johnson	Washington
Fort Moultrie	Washington
First Presbyterian Church of Columbia	Wilson
George Washington Statue	Washington
Hampton Plantation State Park	Washington
Heyward-Washington House	Washington
John Rutledge House Inn	Washington
Old Exchange Building and Provost Dungeon	Washington
Saint Michaels Episcopal Church	Washington
Snee Farm	Washington
Washington House	Washington
Woodrow Wilson Boyhood Home	Wilson

SOUTH DAKOTA

Lincoln Prairie Shrine	Lincoln
Mentor Graham House	Lincoln
Mount Rushmore National Memorial	Washington, Lincoln, Jefferson, T. Roosevelt
Parade of Presidents Wax Museum	
State Game Lodge	Coolidge
Theodore Roosevelt Monument	T. Roosevelt

TENNESSEE

Abraham Lincoln Museum	Lincoln
American Historical Wax Museum	
Andrew Jackson Statue	Jackson
Andrew Johnson Library and Museum	A. Johnson
Andrew Johnson Marriage Site	A. Johnson
Andrew Johnson National Cemetery	A. Johnson
Andrew Johnson National Historic Site	A. Johnson
Andrew Johnson Statue	A. Johnson
Belle Meade Plantation	Cleveland
Carnton Mansion	Jackson, Polk
Cherry House	Grant
Chester Inn	Jackson, Polk,

	A. Johnson
Childress Home	Polk
Christopher Taylor House	Jackson
Cragfront	Jackson
Dickson-Williams Mansion	Jackson, Polk
First Presbyterian Church of Nashville	Polk
Fort Donelson National Military Park	Grant
Hale Springs Inn	Jackson, Polk,
	A. Johnson
Hermitage, The	Jackson
Historic Fontaine House	Cleveland
Hunt-Phelan House	Grant
Netherland Inn	Jackson, Polk,
	A. Johnson,
Old Hermitage Church	Jackson
Pillars, The	Jackson, Polk
Polk Ancestral Home	Polk
Rally Hill	Polk
Rocky Mount	Jackson
Rowan House Hotel	Jackson
Shepards Inn	Jackson, Polk
Shiloh Battlefield National Military Park	Grant
Tennessee State Capitol Grounds	Polk
Tennessee State Museum	
Travellers Rest	Jackson
Tulip Grove	Jackson
Wynnewood	Jackson
TEXAS	
Alumni House	L. Johnson
Bush Residence	Bush
Eisenhower Birthplace State Historic Site	Eisenhower
Excelsior Hotel	Grant, Hayes
Fort Brown	Taylor
Fort Sam Houston	Eisenhower
George Bush Presidential Library	Bush
John F. Kennedy Memorial Plaza	Kennedy
Johnson Austin Residences	Johnson
Lyndon B. Johnson Library and Museum	L. Johnson
Lyndon B. Johnson National Historical Parks	L. Johnson
Lyndon B. Johnson Residences	L. Johnson

Lyndon B. Johnson Space Center	L. Johnson
LBJ Ranch	L. Johnson
LBJ School of Public Affairs	L. Johnson
Menger Hotel	T. Roosevelt
Nimitz Hotel	Bush
Palo Alto Battlefield National Historic Site	Taylor, Grant
Presidential Museum	
Resaca de la Palma Battlefield	Taylor
Roosevelt Park	T. Roosevelt
Saint Marks Episcopal Church	L. Johnson
Saint Martins Episcopal Church	Bush
Sixth Floor Museum	Kennedy
South West Texas Teachers College	L. Johnson
Trinity Lutheran Church	L. Johnson
Welhausen School	L. Johnson

UTAH
Beehive House	Grant

VERMONT
American Museum of Fly Fishing	Cleveland, Hoover, Eisenhower, Carter
Black River Academy Museum	Coolidge
Chester A. Arthur State Historic Site	Arthur
Equinox House Historic District	T. Roosevelt, Taft
Fairfield Baptist Church	Arthur
Goodhue Home	Coolidge
Hildene	Lincoln
Moore-Woodbury House	McKinley, T. Roosevelt, Taft
Old Tavern, The	Grant, T. Roosevelt, Wilson
Plymouth Cemetery	Coolidge
Plymouth Notch Historic District	Coolidge
Union Christian Church	Coolidge

VIRGINIA
Albemarle County Courthouse   Jefferson,
                                                           Madison,
                                                           Monroe
Alexandria Canal Tidal Lock   Washington
Alexandria Historical District   Washington
Ampthill   Washington
Appomattox Court House National Historic Park   Grant
Arlington National Cemetery   Taft, Kennedy
Ash Lawn-Highland   Monroe
Bank of Alexandria   Washington
Barboursville Ruins   Jefferson
Bel Air   Washington
Belle Air   Washington,
                                                           Jefferson,
                                                           Monroe,
                                                           W. Harrison

Belle Grove   Jefferson
Belvoir   Washington
Berkeley Plantation   W. Harrison
Botetourt County Courthouse   Jefferson
Boyhood Home of Robert E. Lee   Washington
Brandon Plantation   Jefferson
Bruton Parish Church
Buckingham Courthouse Historic District   Jefferson
Camp Hoover   Hoover
Capitol, The
Carlyle House   Washington
Carr-Brooks House   Jefferson
Carters Grove Plantation   Washington,
                                                           Jefferson
Cedar Creek Battlefield   Hayes
Cedar Grove   Tyler
Centre Hill Mansion Museum   Tyler, Lincoln,
                                                           Taft
Charles Dick House   Washington
Charlotte County Courthouse
Chatham Manor   Washington
Christ Church   Washington
Christ Church, Glendower   T. Roosevelt
Christiana Campbell's Tavern   Washington

332

Cocks Residence	Washington
Colonial National Historical Park	Washington
Colonial Williamsburg	
College of William and Mary	Jefferson, Monroe, Tyler
Conway House	Madison
Edgemont	Jefferson
Eppington	Jefferson
Falls Church	Washington
Farmington	Jefferson
Federal Hill	Jefferson
Finnie House	Monroe
Fishers Hill	McKinley
Ford Residences	Ford
Forest, The	Jefferson
Fort Monroe	Lincoln
Fort Young	Washington
Fredericksburg Historic District	Washington, Monroe
Fredericksburg and Spotsylvania National Historic Site	Grant
Friendship Firehouse Museum	Washington
Gadsbys Tavern	Washington
Generals Row	Eisenhower
George Washington Birthplace National Monument	Washington
George Washington Masonic National Memorial	Washington
George Washington Office Museum	Washington
George Washington Memorial Highway	Washington
George Washington Statuary	Washington
George Washington Townhouse	Washington
George Washington's Grist Mill Historical State Park	Washington
George Wythe House	Washington, Jefferson, Monroe
Giles County Courthouse	Hayes
Glen Ora	Kennedy
Governors Mansion	
Governors Palace	Jefferson
Grace Episcopal Church	Washington
Great Dismal Swamp National Wildlife Refuge	Washington
Great Falls Park	Washington
Greenway	Tyler
Gunston Hall	Washington,

333

	Jefferson, Madison, Monroe
Hampden-Sydney College	W. Harrison
Harewood	Madison
Hickory Hill	Kennedy, Reagan
Historic Michie Tavern	Washington, Jefferson
Historic Sully	Madison
Hollywood Cemetery	Monroe, Tyler
Homestead, The	Jefferson, Wilson
Hopewell and City Point	Grant
Hugh Mercer Apothecary Shop	Washington
Immanuel on-the-Hill Church	Ford
James Geddy House	Washington
James Madison Museum	Madison
James Monroe Family Home Site	Monroe
James Monroe Museum	Monroe
James Semple House	Tyler
Jones House	Monroe
Kenmore	Washington
Kennedy Residences	Kennedy
Kenwood	F. Roosevelt
Lancaster Historic District	Washington
Lee-Fendall House	Washington
Loudoun Museum	Washington
Lyndon B. Johnson Memorial Grove on the Potomac	L. Johnson
Mary Washington House	Washington
Mary Washington Monument and Grave	Washington
Mary Washington Museum and Library	Washington
Masonic Lodge No. 4 A. F. and A. M.	Washington
"Middle Church"	Madison
Monroe Hall	Monroe
Montebello	Taylor
Monticello	Jefferson
Montpelier (Sperryville)	Washington
Montpelier (Montpelier Station)	Madison
Moore House	Washington
Moses Myers House	Monroe
Mount Athos	Jefferson

Mount Vernon	Washington
Mrs. Coxes Tavern	Washington
Museum of American Presidents	
Nixon Homes	Nixon
Natural Bridge Village	Washington, Jefferson
Nelson House	Washington
North Bend Plantation	W. Harrison
Oak Hill	Monroe
Old Presbyterian Meeting House	Washington
Peaks of Otter	Jefferson
Petersburg National Battlefield	Grant
Pine Knot	T. Roosevelt
Pohick Episcopal Church	Washington
Popes Creek Plantation	Washington
Poplar Forest	Jefferson
Quarters #1, Fort Monroe	Lincoln
Raleigh Tavern	Washington
Ramsay House	Washington
Red Fox Inn	Washington
Residence, The	Jefferson
Richmond National Battlefield Park	Grant
Rippon Lodge	Washington
Rising Sun Tavern	Washington
River Farm	Washington
Room 31, West Range Hotel, University of Virginia	Wilson
Rosewell Ruins	Jefferson
Saint James House	Washington
Saint Georges Episcopal Church	Monroe
Saint Johns Church	
Saint Pauls Episcopal Church	Washington
Saint Peters Parish Church	Washington
Saint Thomas Episcopal Church	Madison
Salona	Madison
Sandusky	Hayes, McKinley, Garfield
Sequoia	
Shadwell	Jefferson
Sherwood Forest	Tyler, W. Harrison
Shirley Plantation	

Site of Washingtons Headquarters at Yorktown	Washington
Stabler-Leadbeater Apothecary Shop and Museum	Washington
Stagecoach Inn	Washington
Stratford Plantation	Washington
Tallwood	Eisenhower
Tavern, The	Jackson
Theodore Roosevelt Island	T. Roosevelt
Thomas Jefferson Religious Freedom Monument	Jefferson
Thomas Jefferson Statue	Jefferson
Thomas Wallace House	Lincoln, Grant
Thornton Hill	Washington
21 A. Loudoun Street	Washington
Toliver House Restaurant	Washington, Madison, Monroe
Tuckahoe Plantation	Jefferson
United States Army Quartermaster Museum	Pierce, Grant, Eisenhower
University of Virginia	Jefferson, Madison, Monroe
Upper Valley Regional Park	Washington, Jefferson, Madison
Virginia Governor's Mansion	Jefferson, Monroe, Tyler, W. Harrison
Virginia State Capitol	Jefferson, Monroe, Tyler
Washington Historic District	Washington
Washington and Lee University	Washington
Washingtons Boyhood Home	Washington
Washingtons Horse-Chestnut Tree	Washington
Wax Museum at Natural Bridge	
Weems-Botts Museum	Washington
Weston Manor Plantation	Jefferson
Westover Plantation	
Westover Church	W. Harrison, Tyler
Wetherburns Tavern	Washington
Wexford	Kennedy, Reagan

Williams Ordinary	Washington
Wilton House Museum	Washington, Jefferson
Woodbourne	Jefferson
Woodburn	Tyler
Woodlawn Plantation	Washington
Woodrow Wilson Birthplace and Museum	Wilson
Wren Building	Monroe
Yew Hill	Washington
Yorktown Battlefield	Washington
Yorktown Victory Center	Washington

WASHINGTON

Grant House	Grant
Officers Row	Grant, Hayes, F. Roosevelt

WEST VIRGINIA

Berkeley Springs	Washington, Madison, Van Buren, Taylor, Fillmore
Campbell Mansion	Garfield
Carnifex Ferry Battlefield State Park	Hayes
Carriage Inn	Grant
Fort Ashby	Washington
Fort Scammon	Hayes
Greenbrier River Inn	Van Buren
Harewood	Madison
Harpers Ferry National Historical Park	Washington, Jefferson
Jefferson Rock	Jefferson
Mansion House	Washington
Point Pleasant Monument State Park	Washington
Presidents Cottage Museum	Van Buren, Fillmore, Pierce, Buchanan, Tyler

WISCONSIN	
Cedar Island Lodge	Coolidge
Fort Howard	Taylor
Lincoln-Tallman Restorations	Lincoln
National Railroad Museum	Eisenhower
Second Fort Crawford	Taylor
WYOMING	
Lincoln Monument	Lincoln
Roosevelt Arch	T. Roosevelt
CANADA	
Campobello Island	F. Roosevelt
Saint Annes Anglican Church	F. Roosevelt
ENGLAND	
Saint Georges Church	T. Roosevelt
Church of All-Hallows by the Towers	J. Q. Adams
ITALY	
USS *Williamsburg*	Truman

Bibliography

Listed below are several publications that deal with presidential sites in general. The reader might wish to consult these books for additional information about presidential sites or to obtain differing perspectives on those sites.

American Heritage. 1971. *Historic Houses of America*. New York: American Heritage Publishing Company.

Benbow, Nancy D. Meyers, and Christopher H. Benbow. 1995. *Cabins, Cottages and Mansions: Homes of the Presidents of the United States*. Gettysburg: Thomas Publications.

Bowling, Kenneth R. 1988. *Creating the Federal City. 1774-1800: Potomac Fever*. Washington, DC: AIA Press.

Brooks, Chester L., and Ray H. Mattison. 1983. *Theodore Roosevelt and the Dakota Badlands*. Medora: Theodore Roosevelt Nature and History Association.

Clotworthy, William G. 1995. *Homes and Libraries of the Presidents*. Blacksburg: The McDonald & Woodward Publishing Company.

Daniels, Jonathan. 1950. *The Man of Independence*. Philadelphia: J. B. Lippincott Company.

Davenport, Don. 1991. *In Lincoln's Footsteps: A Historic Guide to the Lincoln Sites in Illinois, Indiana and Kentucky.* Madison: Prairie Oak Press.

Dennis, Ruth. 1986. *The Homes of the Hoovers.* West Branch: Herbert Hoover Library Association, Inc.

Felder, Paula S. 1993. *Handbook of Historic Fredericksburg, Virginia.* Fredericksburg: Historic Fredericksburg Foundation, Inc.

Flexner, James Thomas. 1967, 1968. *George Washington in the American Revolution (1775-1783).* Boston: Little, Brown and Company.

Haas, Irvin. *America's Historic Battlefields.* 1987. New York: Hippocrene Books.

Jones, Cranston. 1962. *Homes of the American Presidents.* New York: McGraw Hill.

Kern, Ellyn R. 1982. *Where the American Presidents Lived.* Indianapolis: Cottontail Publications.

Ketchum, Richard M., editor. 1957. *The American Heritage Book of Great Historic Places.* New York: American Heritage Publishing Company.

Ketchum, Richard M. 1974. *The World of George Washington.* New York: American Heritage Publishing Company.

Kochman, Rachel 1991. *Presidents' Birthplaces, Homes and Burial Places.* Revised edition. Osage: Osage Publications.

Kruh, David, and Louis Kruh. 1992. *Presidential Landmarks.* New York: Hippocrene Books.

Ladies' Hermitage Association, The. 1987. *Andrew Jackson's Hermitage.* Hermitage: The Ladies' Hermitage Association.

Lipscomb, Terry W. 1993. *South Carolina in 1791. George Washington's Southern Tour.* Columbia: South Carolina Department of Archives and History.

McLaughlin, Jack. 1988. *Jefferson and Monticello: The Biography of a Builder.* New York: Henry Holt, Inc.

Mount Vernon Ladies' Association. 1985. *Mount Vernon: A Handbook.* Mount Vernon: Mount Vernon Ladies' Association.

National Park Service. 1977. *The Presidents. National Survey of Historic Sites and Buildings.* Volume XX, revised edition. Robert G. Ferris, series editor. Washington, DC: US Department of the Interior, National Park Service.

National Park Service. 1985. *The Complete Guide to America's National Parks (1884-1985)*. New York: Viking Press.

National Register of Historic Places. 1976. [title]. US Department of the Interior: Heritage Conservation and Recreation Service. Washington, DC.

Pennsylvania Historical Commission. 1937. *Philadelphia. A Guide to the Nation's Birthplace*. Compiled by the Federal Writer's Project. Philadelphia: The Telegraph Press.

Roberts, Bruce. 1990. *Plantation Homes of the James River*. Chapel Hill: University of North Carolina Press.

Rouse, Park, Jr., and Susan T. Burtch. 1980. *Berkeley Plantation and Hundred*. Williamsburg: Williamsburg Publishing Company.

Smithsonian Institution. 1989. *Smithsonian Guides to Historic America:* 12 vols. Roger G. Kennedy, editorial director. New York: Stewart, Tabori and Chang, Inc.

Vila, Bob. 1993. *Bob Vila's Guides to Historic Homes:* 3 vols. New York: Lintel Press, William Morrow.

White House Historical Association. 1991. *The White House: An Historic Guide*. Washington, DC: The White House Historical Association.

Williams, Henry Lionel, and Ottalie K. Williams. 1969. *Great Houses of America*. New York: G. P. Putnam's Sons.

Wilson, Susan. 1994. *Boston Sights and Insights*. Boston: Beacon Press.

Yetter, George Humphrey. 1988. *Williamsburg Before and After: The Rebirth of Virginia's Colonial Capital*. Williamsburg: Colonial Williamsburg Foundation.

Index

343

345

349

351

356

357